Praise for *Software Engineering for Data Scientists*

This book is the missing link data scientists have long sought, masterfully bridging the gap between data science and software engineering. It offers a clear, actionable guide that fills the crucial skill gap many data scientists face in software engineering, elevating their coding practices to new heights. Truly, this is the book we've been waiting for.

—*Gabriela de Queiroz,*
Director of AI, Microsoft; Startup Advisor and Angel Investor

Catherine's book demystifies how to scale your individual work to production capacity. Whether you are a data scientist, developer, or executive, she makes data services at scale accessible. From startup to massive corporate data, following her best practices will set your data projects up for success.

—*Carol Willing,*
Core Developer of Python;
2017 ACM Software System Award recipient for Jupyter's lasting influence

I love this book! It's the missing piece on every data scientist's shelf. For years, bootcamps, universities, and industry managers have been trying to get skilled scientists to function more like software engineers. No book bridges that gap, until this one.

—*Shawn Ling Ramirez,*
CEO, eloraHQ

Software Engineering for Data Scientists is a must read if you want to take your data science skills from ideas to fully implemented systems. It's a terrific guide to help you through the most important *engineering* aspects of coding. I wish I'd had this book years ago, it would have saved me countless hours! I thoroughly recommend it.

—*Laurence Moroney,*
AI Advocacy Lead, Google

Since its beginnings, data scientists have come from a wide variety of backgrounds in education and experience. While in many ways this has been a strength of the field, often data scientists lack the software engineering skills to work closely with peers from more traditional software development backgrounds. In this book, Catherine Nelson provides a much-needed bridge between the two disciplines, giving data scientists the knowledge to level up their own work and impact.

—*Chris Albon,*
Director of Machine Learning, The Wikimedia Foundation

Software Engineering for Data Scientists

From Notebooks to Scalable Systems

Catherine Nelson

Beijing · Boston · Farnham · Sebastopol · Tokyo

Software Engineering for Data Scientists

by Catherine Nelson

Published by O'Reilly Media, Inc., 1005 Gravenstein Highway North, Sebastopol, CA 95472.

O'Reilly books may be purchased for educational, business, or sales promotional use. Online editions are also available for most titles (*http://oreilly.com*). For more information, contact our corporate/institutional sales department: 800-998-9938 or *corporate@oreilly.com*.

Acquisitions Editor: Nicole Butterfield	**Indexer:** WordCo Indexing Services, Inc.
Development Editor: Virginia Wilson	**Interior Designer:** David Futato
Production Editor: Christopher Faucher	**Cover Designer:** Karen Montgomery
Copyeditor: Piper Editorial Consulting, LLC	**Illustrator:** Kate Dullea
Proofreader: Krsta Technology Solutions	

April 2024:   First Edition

Revision History for the First Edition
2024-04-16:   First Release

See *http://oreilly.com/catalog/errata.csp?isbn=9781098136208* for release details.

978-1-098-13620-8

[LSI]

Table of Contents

Preface

Data science happens in code. Whether you're building a machine learning system, exploring your data for the first time, visualizing the distribution of your data, or running a statistical analysis, your coding and computation skills are what make it happen. If you are working on production code, these skills are essential for writing successful, maintainable code. Even if you aren't working in a production software team, you'll find it beneficial to write more robust, reproducible code that other data scientists can use easily. And if you're working alone, good practices will accelerate your coding and help you pick up your code after a break.

I didn't always see the value of good engineering. Earlier in my data science career, I joined a team where I was the only data scientist. My teammates were software engineers and designers, and I was concerned that it would be hard to increase my skills with no other data scientists to learn from. I expressed my concern to my coworker, a developer. He said, "But learning to write better code will let you do more data science." This comment stuck with me, and I've found since then that improving my software engineering skills has been incredibly beneficial in doing data science. It's helped me write code that is easier for my coworkers to use and that is still easy to change when I go back to it many months later.

My aim with this book is to guide you on your journey to writing better data science code. I'll describe best practices for common tasks including testing, error handling, and logging. I'll explain how to write code that is easier to maintain and that will remain robust as your projects grow. I'll show you how to make your code easy for other people to use, and by the end of this book you'll be able to integrate your data science code with a larger codebase.

You might think that software engineering skills are less useful in the age of generative AI. Can't ChatGPT just write your code for you? I'd argue that the content in this book is still just as useful even when you can speed up your coding with an AI assistant. As I'll show throughout this book, there are many choices available for every function you write, and it's incredibly helpful to understand the principles for why you might pick one line of code over another. You'll need to evaluate the output of any AI assistant and check that it has made a good choice for the problem you're working on. This book will help you do that.

Who Is This Book For?

This book is aimed at data scientists, but people working in closely related fields such as data analysts, machine learning (ML) engineers, and data engineers will also find it useful. I'll explain well-established software engineering principles that will be useful to anyone who writes code, but the examples I'll use to illustrate these principles will be most familiar to data scientists.

I've aimed to make this book accessible to data scientists who are relatively new to the field. Maybe you've just finished a degree in data science or you're starting your first job in industry. This book will cover the practical software engineering skills that are not always included in introductory data science courses. Or maybe you didn't take a formal data science course. Maybe you're self-taught or you're moving into data science from math or another science. No matter which route you're taking into data science, this book is for you.

More experienced data scientists will also learn a great deal, and you'll find this book especially useful if you're in a job where you'll often interact with software developers. You'll learn the skills that will help you work effectively on a larger codebase and how to write Python code that will work efficiently in production.

I'm assuming that you already know the fundamentals of data science, including data exploration, data visualization, data wrangling, basic ML, and the math skills that go along with these. I'm also assuming that you already know the basics of how to code in Python: how to write functions and control flow statements, and the basics of how to use modules including NumPy, Matplotlib, pandas, and scikit-learn. If these are new to you, I recommend the following books:

- *Python Data Science Handbook* by Jake VanderPlas (O'Reilly, 2023)
- *Data Science From Scratch* by Joel Grus (O'Reilly, 2019)
- *Learning Data Science* by Sam Lau, Joseph Gonzalez, and Deborah Nolan (O'Reilly, 2023)

This is not a book for software developers who are looking to learn data science and machine learning skills. If this is your situation, I recommend *AI and Machine Learning for Coders* by Laurence Moroney (O'Reilly, 2020).

> ## Software Engineering Versus Data Science
>
> It's useful at this point to define what I see as the distinction between data science and software engineering mindsets. Data scientists generally come from a background that emphasizes the scientific processes of exploration, discovery, and hypothesis testing. The end result of a project is not known at the beginning. Software engineering, in contrast, is a process that focuses on planning what to build, designing the best way to build, then writing the code to build what was planned. The expected outcome of the project is known at the start of the project. Software engineering practices emphasize standardization and automation. Data scientists can use aspects of the engineering mindset to improve the quality of their code, a subject I will discuss in detail in Chapter 1.

Why Python?

All the code examples in this book are written in Python, and many of the chapters describe Python-specific tools. In recent years, Python has become the most popular programming language for data science. The following quote is from a 2021 survey (*https://oreil.ly/kmmBp*) of over 3,000 data scientists carried out by Anaconda:

> "63% of respondents said they always or frequently use Python, making it the most popular language included in this year's survey. In addition, 71% of educators are teaching Python, and 88% of students reported being taught Python in preparation to enter the data science/ML field."

Python has an extremely solid set of open source libraries for data science, with good backing and a healthy community of maintainers. Large trend-setting companies have chosen Python for their main ML frameworks, including TensorFlow (Google) and PyTorch (Meta). Because of this, Python appears to be especially popular among data scientists working on production machine learning code, where good coding skills are particularly important.

In my experience, the Python community has been friendly and welcoming, with many excellent events that have helped me improve my skills. It's my preferred programming language, so it was an easy choice for this book.

What Is Not in This Book

As I mentioned in "Who Is This Book For?" on page xii, this is not an introduction to data science or an introduction to programming. Additionally, none of the following topics appears in this book:

Installing Python: I assume that you have already installed a recent version of Python (3.9 or later) and you have some form of IDE (integrated development environment) where you can write code, such as VS Code or PyCharm. I won't describe how to install Python, but I will explain how to set up a virtual environment in Chapter 10.

Other programming languages: This book covers only Python, for the reasons given in "Why Python?" on page xiii. I haven't included any examples in R, Julia, SQL, MAT-LAB or any other language.

Command line scripting: Command line or shell scripting is a powerful way to work with files and text. I don't include it here because other sources cover it in great detail, including *Data Science at the Command Line* by Jeroen Janssens (O'Reilly, 2021).

Advanced Python: The examples in this book contain relatively simple code. For coverage of more advanced Python coding, I recommend *Robust Python* by Patrick Viafore (O'Reilly, 2021).

Guide to This Book

In this book, I start by walking through good practices at the level of writing individual functions and go into detail about how you can improve your coding. In later chapters, I'll describe how you can take that code and make it easy for someone else to use, and I'll explain some common techniques for deployment and best practices for working in software.

This book is divided into 14 chapters. Here is an overview of their contents:

Chapter 1, "What Is Good Code?", introduces the basics of how to write code that is simple, modular, readable, efficient, and robust.

Chapter 2, "Analyzing Code Performance", describes how to measure the performance of your code and discusses some options for making your data science code run more efficiently.

Chapter 3, "Using Data Structures Effectively", discusses the trade-offs involved in choosing the data structures you work with. The data structure you choose can make a huge difference to the efficiency of your code.

Chapter 4, "Object-Oriented Programming and Functional Programming", describes the basics of these styles of programming. Used correctly, they can help you write code that is well structured and efficient.

Chapter 5, "Errors, Logging, and Debugging", walks you through what to do when your code breaks, how to raise useful errors, and strategies to identify where those errors are coming from.

Chapter 6, "Code Formatting, Linting, and Type Checking", describes how to standardize your code using tools that can automate this process.

Chapter 7, "Testing Your Code", covers how to make your code robust to changes in inputs through testing. This is a vital step in writing code that is easy to maintain.

Chapter 8, "Design and Refactoring", discusses how to structure your projects in a standardized, consistent way and how to go from a notebook to a script.

Chapter 9, "Documentation", shows you how to make your code readable for other people, including best practices for naming and commenting on your code.

Chapter 10, "Sharing Your Code: Version Control, Dependencies, and Packaging", covers the basics of version control using Git and how to manage your project's dependencies in virtual environments. It also shows the steps involved in turning a script into a Python package.

Chapter 11, "APIs", introduces the concept of APIs, shows how you can use them, and includes a basic example using FastAPI.

Chapter 12, "Automation and Deployment", describes the basics of deploying code, how to automate your code deployments using CI/CD (Continuous Integration/ Continuous Deployment or Delivery) and GitHub Actions, and how to deploy your code to a cloud environment in a Docker container.

Chapter 13, "Security", discusses common security risks, how these risks can be mitigated, and some of the security threats unique to machine learning.

Chapter 14, "Working in Software", introduces you to common practices in software development teams including Agile ways of working, describes common roles in software teams, and introduces the wider community.

Chapter 15, "Next Steps", wraps up with some thoughts on how coding might change in the future and some suggestions for what you can do next.

Reading Order

You don't necessarily need to read the chapters in this book in order, but I recommend that you start by reading Chapter 1. In this chapter, I'll explain the fundamentals of how to write good code, and I'll introduce topics that I'll cover in greater detail in the rest of the book. I'll also introduce several of the code examples that I'll use throughout the book.

Following Chapter 1, many of the chapters can be read on their own, with these exceptions:

- You should read Chapter 2 before reading Chapter 3.
- You should read Chapters 6, 7, 10, and 11 before you read Chapter 12.

Some chapters include a section that goes deeper into a machine learning topic. These sections always include ML in the section name, and if your job doesn't involve ML you can skip these sections without missing anything that you would need to understand the rest of the chapter.

Conventions Used in This Book

The following typographical conventions are used in this book:

Italic
> Indicates new terms, URLs, email addresses, filenames, and file extensions.

`Constant width`
> Used for program listings, as well as within paragraphs to refer to program elements such as variable or function names, databases, data types, environment variables, statements, and keywords.

`Constant width bold`
> Shows commands or other text that should be typed literally by the user.

`Constant width italic`
> Shows text that should be replaced with user-supplied values or by values determined by context.

 This element signifies a tip or suggestion.

 This element signifies a general note.

 This element indicates a warning or caution.

Using Code Examples

Supplemental material (code examples, exercises, etc.) is available for download at *https://github.com/catherinenelson1/SEforDS*.

This book is here to help you get your job done. In general, if example code is offered with this book, you may use it in your programs and documentation. You do not need to contact us for permission unless you're reproducing a significant portion of the code. For example, writing a program that uses several chunks of code from this book does not require permission. Selling or distributing examples from O'Reilly books does require permission. Answering a question by citing this book and quoting example code does not require permission. Incorporating a significant amount of example code from this book into your product's documentation does require permission.

We appreciate, but generally do not require, attribution. An attribution usually includes the title, author, publisher, and ISBN. For example: "*Software Engineering for Data Scientists* by Catherine Nelson (O'Reilly). Copyright 2024 Catherine Nelson, 978-1-098-13620-8."

If you feel your use of code examples falls outside fair use or the permission given above, feel free to contact us at *permissions@oreilly.com*.

O'Reilly Online Learning

 For more than 40 years, *O'Reilly Media* has provided technology and business training, knowledge, and insight to help companies succeed.

Our unique network of experts and innovators share their knowledge and expertise through books, articles, and our online learning platform. O'Reilly's online learning platform gives you on-demand access to live training courses, in-depth learning paths, interactive coding environments, and a vast collection of text and video from O'Reilly and 200+ other publishers. For more information, visit *https://oreilly.com*.

How to Contact Us

Please address comments and questions to *sefordatascientists@gmail.com* or to the publisher:

> O'Reilly Media, Inc.
> 1005 Gravenstein Highway North
> Sebastopol, CA 95472

800-889-8969 (in the United States or Canada)
707-827-7019 (international or local)
707-829-0104 (fax)
support@oreilly.com
https://www.oreilly.com/about/contact.html

We have a web page for this book, where we list errata, examples, and any additional information. You can access this page at *https://oreil.ly/software-engineering-data-scientists*.

For news and information about our books and courses, visit *https://oreilly.com.*

Find us on LinkedIn: *https://linkedin.com/company/oreilly-media*

Watch us on YouTube: *https://youtube.com/oreillymedia*

Acknowledgments

Sending a huge thank you to everyone who has helped me with this book! Your comments, feedback, discussions, and support have been so valuable.

It's been an absolute pleasure working with the team at O'Reilly. Thank you to Virginia Wilson for being a superb, supportive editor. I really enjoyed working with you. Thank you to Nicole Butterfield for valuable overall direction and your help with the book proposal process. Thank you to Jeff Bleiel for thorough reviews of several of the chapters and Chris Faucher for making the production process go smoothly.

Thank you so much to my technical reviewers William Jamir Silva, Ganesh Harke, Jo Stichbury, Antony Milne, Jess Males, and Swetha Kommuri. Your feedback was super constructive, and it's made the final book so much better. I really appreciated your attention to detail and your helpful suggestions. Thank you to Rob Masson for great feedback on the final draft and thoughtful discussions throughout the writing process.

Thank you to Carol Willing, Ricardo Martín Brualla, Chris Trudeau, Michelle Liu, Maryam Ehsani, Shivani Patel, John Sweet, Andy Ross, and Abigail Mesrenyame Dogbe for valuable technical discussions and insightful conversations. I've also benefited hugely from being part of the wider Python and PyLadies community; thank you to all the volunteers who give their time to it.

Finally, thank you to my amazing friends and family for all your support. Rob, Mum, Richard, Lina, Salomé, Ricardo, Chris, Kiana, and Katie—I appreciate you all so much.

## CHAPTER 1

What Is Good Code?

This book aims to help you write better code. But first, what makes code "good"? There are a number of ways to think about this: the best code could be the code that runs fastest. Or it could be easiest to read. Another possible definition is that good code is easy to maintain. That is, if the project changes, it should be easy to go back to the code and change it to reflect the new requirements. The requirements for your code will change frequently because of updates to the business problem you're solving, new research directions, or updates elsewhere in the codebase.

In addition, your code shouldn't be complex, and it shouldn't break if it gets an unexpected input. It should be easy to add a simple new feature to your code; if this is hard it suggests your code is not well written. In this chapter, I'll introduce aspects of good code and show examples for each. I'll divide these into five categories: simplicity, modularity, readability, performance, and robustness.

Why Good Code Matters

Good code is especially important when your data science code integrates with a larger system. This could be putting a machine learning model into production, writing packages for wider distribution, or building tools for other data scientists. It's most useful for larger codebases that will be run repeatedly. As your project grows in size and complexity, the value of good code will increase.

Sometimes, the code you write will be a one-off, a prototype that needs to be hacked together today for a demo tomorrow. And if you truly will run the code only once, then don't spend the time making it beautiful: just write code to do the job it's needed for. But in my experience, even the code you write for a one-off demo is almost always run again or reused for another purpose. I encourage you to take the time to go back to your code after the urgency has passed and tidy it up for future use.

Code as Craft

Many software engineers see code as something worth doing well for its own sake. There is inherent value in an efficient, elegant piece of code. They take pride in something well done in the same way that a carpenter takes pride in a beautiful wooden cabinet, where the doors open smoothly and the drawers fit exactly. They derive job satisfaction from building something that will last.

This doesn't mean you should spend endless hours polishing the details of your code, but there are a great many small decisions you will make every time you sit in front of a keyboard. Once you know what to look for, you can choose to write better code. It's a good feeling to practice the craft of writing software and to make something you are proud of.

Good code is also easier to maintain. There's a phenomenon known as "bit-rot": the need to update code that hasn't been used in some time. This happens because things your code depends on also change (for example, third-party libraries or even the operating system you're using). If you come back to code you haven't used for a while, you'll probably need to do some work to modernize it. This is much easier if your code is well structured and well documented.

 Technical debt (often abbreviated as tech debt) is a commonly used term for deferred work resulting from when code is written quickly instead of correctly. Tech debt can take the form of missing documentation, poorly structured code, poorly named variables, or any other cut corners. These make the code harder to maintain or refactor, and it's likely that you will spend more time in the future fixing bugs than you would have spent writing the code well in the first place. That said, tech debt is often necessary because of business deadlines and budgets. You don't always have time to polish your code.

Adapting to Changing Requirements

Writing code is not like building a bridge, where the design is thoroughly worked out, the plans are fixed, and then construction happens. The one constant in writing code, for a data science project or anything else, is that you should expect things to change as you work on a project. These changes may be the result of your discoveries through your research process, changing business requirements, or innovations that you want to include in the project. Good code can be easily adapted to work well with these changes.

This adaptability becomes more important as your codebase grows. With a single small script, making changes is simple. But as the project grows and gets broken out into multiple scripts or notebooks that depend on each other, it can become more complex and harder to make changes. Good practices from the start will make it easier to modify the code in a larger project.

Data science is still a relatively new field, but data science teams are starting to encounter situations where they have been working on the same codebase for multiple years, and the code has been worked on by many people, some of whom may have left the company. In this situation, where a project is handed over from one person to another, code quality becomes even more important. It is much easier to pick up on someone else's work if it is well documented and easy to read.

Software engineering as a discipline has been dealing with changing requirements and increasing complexity for decades. It has developed a number of useful strategies that you, as a data scientist, can borrow and take advantage of. If you start to look into this, you may see references to "clean code," from the book of the same name by Robert C. Martin, or acronyms such as SOLID (*https://oreil.ly/16t90*).

As I mentioned, in this chapter, I've chosen to divide these principles into five features of good code: simplicity, modularity, readability, performance, and robustness. I'll describe each of these in detail in the rest of this chapter.

Simplicity

> *Simple is better than complex.*
>   —Tim Peters, *The Zen of Python*

If you are working on a small project, maybe a data visualization notebook or a short data wrangling script, you can keep all the details in your mind at one time. But as your project grows and gets more complex, this stops being feasible. You can keep the training steps of your machine learning model in your head but not the input data pipeline, or the model deployment process.

Complexity makes it hard to modify code when your requirements change, and it can be defined as follows:

> *Complexity is anything related to the structure of a system that makes it hard to understand and modify a system.*
>   —John K. Ousterhout, *A Philosophy of Software Design*

This isn't a precise definition, but with experience you'll get a sense of when a system becomes more complex. One way of thinking about it is that when you make a change, it breaks something unrelated in an unexpected way. For example, you might train a machine learning model on customer review data to extract the item that the customer bought using natural language processing (NLP) techniques. You have a separate preprocessing step that truncates the review to 512 characters. But when you deploy the model, you forget to add the preprocessing step to the inference code. Suddenly, your model throws errors because the input data is larger than 512 characters. This system is starting to get hard to reason about and is becoming complex.

When I'm talking about complexity in code, this is generally accidental and different from the essential complexity of a project. Your machine learning project may be complex because you want to try many different types of models and many different combinations of features to see which one works best. Your analysis may be complex because the data you're using has many different interdependent parameters. Neither of these can be made simpler; the complexity is just part of the project. In contrast, accidental complexity is when you're not sure which function within your code you need to change to achieve some action.

However, there are tools you can use to help decrease complexity in your code. Making everything a little bit simpler as you go along has huge benefits when the project becomes large. In the next section, I'll describe how to keep your code simple by avoiding repetition. Then I'll discuss how to keep your code concise. You can also keep your code from becoming complex by dividing it into reusable pieces, as I'll describe in "Modularity" on page 6.

Don't Repeat Yourself (DRY)

One of the most important principles in writing good code is that information should not be repeated. All knowledge should have one single representation in code. If information is repeated in multiple places, and that information needs updating because of changing requirements, then one change means many updates. You would need to remember all the places where this information needs to be updated. This is hard to do and increases code complexity. Additionally, duplication increases opportunities for bugs, and longer code requires more time to read and understand.

There's also an increase in mental effort when you see two pieces of code that are very similar but not exact duplicates. It's hard to tell if the two pieces of code are doing the same thing or something different.

Here's a simple example: you want to open three CSV files, read them into a pandas DataFrame, do some processing, and return each DataFrame. The data in this example is from the UN Sustainable Development Goals (*https://oreil.ly/2MeuI*) (SDGs), and I'll be using data from this site throughout the book. You can find more details on this data in "Data in This Book" on page 11. The code and the CSV files are available in the GitHub repository for this book (*https://oreil.ly/SEforDS*).

For a first pass, you could do something like this:

```python
import pandas as pd

df = pd.read_csv("sdg_literacy_rate.csv")
df = df.drop(["Series Name", "Series Code", "Country Code"], axis=1)
df = df.set_index("Country Name").transpose()

df2 = pd.read_csv("sdg_electricity_data.csv")
df2 = df2.drop(["Series Name", "Series Code", "Country Code"], axis=1)
df2 = df2.set_index("Country Name").transpose()

df3 = pd.read_csv("sdg_urban_population.csv")
df3 = df3.drop(["Series Name", "Series Code", "Country Code"], axis=1)
df3 = df3.set_index("Country Name").transpose()
```

But this is unnecessarily long-winded and repetitive. A better way to achieve the same result would be to put the repeated code inside a for loop. If this is something you'll be using repeatedly, you can put the code inside a function, like this:

```python
def process_sdg_data(csv_file, columns_to_drop):
    df = pd.read_csv(csv_file)
    df = df.drop(columns_to_drop, axis=1)
    df = df.set_index("Country Name").transpose()
    return df
```

Other, more subtle cases can give rise to code duplication. Here are a few examples:

- You might find yourself using very similar code in multiple projects without realizing it, for example, data processing code. Breaking out the processing code so that it can take slightly varying data rather than rigidly accepting only one exact type of data, could help you avoid this duplication.

- Multiple people working on similar projects might write similar code, particularly if they don't communicate about what they're working on. Making code easy for other people to use and providing good documentation will help to reduce this type of duplication.

- Comments and documentation can also be a form of duplication. The same knowledge is represented in the code and the documentation that describes it. Don't write comments that describe exactly what the code is doing; instead, use them to add knowledge. I'll describe this in more detail in Chapter 9.

The DRY principle is extremely important to consider when writing good code. It sounds trivial, but avoiding repetition means that your code needs to be modular and readable. I'll discuss these concepts later in this chapter.

Avoid Verbose Code

Sometimes, you can make your code simpler by having fewer lines of code. This means fewer opportunities for bugs and less code for someone else to read and understand. However, there's often a trade-off between making your code shorter and making it less readable. I'll talk about how to ensure your code is readable in "Readability" on page 7.

I recommend that you aim to make your code concise but still readable. To do this, avoid doing things that make your code unnecessarily long-winded, such as writing your own functions instead of using built-in functions or using unnecessary temporary variables. You should also avoid repetition, as described in the previous section.

Here's an example of an unnecessary temporary variable:

```
i = float(i)
image_vector.append(i/255.0)
```

This can be simplified to the following:

```
image_vector.append(float(i)/255)
```

Of course, there are downsides to squeezing your code into fewer lines. If a lot is happening on one line, it can be extremely hard for anyone else to understand what is going on. This means it is harder for someone else to work on your code, and this could lead to more bugs. If in doubt, I recommend that you keep your code readable even if it means you use a few extra lines.

Modularity

Writing modular code is the art of breaking a big system into smaller components. Modular code has several important advantages: it makes the code easier to read, it's easier to locate where a problem comes from, and it's easier to reuse code in your next project. It's also easier to test code that is broken into smaller components, which I discuss in Chapter 7.

But how do you tackle a large task? You could just write one big script to do the whole thing, and this might be fine at the start of a small project. But larger projects need to be broken into smaller pieces. To do this, you'll need to think as far ahead into the future of the project as possible and try to anticipate what the overall system will do and what might be sensible places to divide it up. I'll discuss this planning process in much more detail in Chapter 8.

Writing modular code is an ongoing process, and it's not something you'll get completely correct from the beginning, even if you have the best intentions. You should expect to change your code as your project evolves. I'll cover techniques that will help you improve your code in "Refactoring" on page 126.

You might break a large data science project into a series of steps by thinking about it as a flowchart, as shown in Figure 1-1. First you extract some data, then explore it, then clean it, and then visualize it.

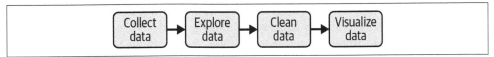

Figure 1-1. Breaking down a large data science project into discrete steps

At first, this could be a series of Jupyter notebooks. At the end of each one, you could save the data to a file, then load it again into the next notebook. As your project matures, you might find that you want to run a similar analysis repeatedly. Then, you can decide what the skeleton of the system should be: maybe there's one function that extracts the data, then passes it to the function that cleans the data. The example below uses the `pass` statement to create an empty function. This ensures that when you call this function, it won't cause an error before it is written.

For example, this could be the skeleton of a system that loads some data, cleans it by cropping it to some maximum length, and plots it with some plotting parameters:

```
def load_data(csv_file):
    pass

def clean_data(input_data, max_length):
    pass

def plot_data(clean_data, x_axis_limit, line_width):
    pass
```

By creating this framework, you have broken down the system into individual components, and you know what each of those components should accept as an input. You can do the same thing at the level of a Python file. Using a programming paradigm such as object-oriented programming or functional programming can help you figure out how to break your code down into functions and classes (more on this in Chapter 4). However you divide up your system, each of the components should be as independent and self-contained as possible so that changing one component doesn't change another. I'll discuss modular code in more detail in Chapter 8.

Readability

> ...code is read much more often than it is written...
>
> —PEP8

When you write code, it's important that other people are also able to use it. You might move on to a different project, or even a different job. If you leave a project for a while and come back to it in a month, six months, or even six years, can you still understand what you were doing at the time you wrote it? You wrote that code for a reason, for a task that was important, and making your code readable gives it longevity.

Methods to make your code more readable include adhering to standards and conventions for your programming language, choosing good names, removing unused code, and writing documentation for your code. It's tempting to treat these as an afterthought and concentrate more on the functionality of the code, but if you pay attention to making your code readable at the time of writing it, you will write code that is less complex and easier to maintain. I'll introduce these methods in this section, and I'll cover them in much more detail in Chapters 6 and 9.

Standards and Conventions

Coding standards and formatting may seem like the least exciting topics I'll cover in this book, but they are surprisingly important. There are many ways to express the same code, even down to small details such as the spacing around the + sign when adding two integers. Coding standards have been developed to encourage consistency across everyone writing Python code, and the aim is to make code feel familiar even when someone else has written it. This helps reduce the amount of effort it takes to read and edit code that you haven't written yourself. I'll cover this topic in more detail in Chapter 6.

Python is inherently very readable compared to many programming languages; sticking to a coding standard will make it even easier to read. The main coding standard for Python is PEP8 (*https://oreil.ly/UwHsO*) (Python Enhancement Proposal 8), established in 2001. The example below shows an extract from PEP8, and you can see that there are conventions for even the smallest details of your code. Style guides such as Google's Python Style Guide (*https://oreil.ly/Q3eZL*) complement PEP8 with additional guidance and information.

Here's an example of the details that PEP8 specifies, showing the correct and incorrect ways of formatting spaces within brackets:

```
# Correct:
spam(ham[1], {eggs: 2})

# Wrong:
spam( ham[ 1 ], { eggs: 2 } )
```

Fortunately, there are many automated ways to check that your code conforms with coding standards, which saves you from the boring work of going through and checking that every + sign has one single space around it. Linters such as Flake8 and Pylint highlight places where your code doesn't conform with PEP8. Automatic formatters such as Black will update your code automatically to conform with coding standards. I'll cover how to use these in Chapter 6.

Names

When writing code for data science, you'll need to choose names at many points: names of functions, variables, projects and even whole tools. Your choice of names affects how easy it is to work on your code. If you choose names that are not descriptive or precise, you'll need to keep their true meaning in your head, which will increase your code's cognitive load. For example, you could import the pandas library as p and name your variables x and f, as shown here:

```
import pandas as p

x = p.read_csv(f, index_col=0)
```

This code runs correctly, with no errors. But here's an example code that's easier to read because the variable names are more informative and follow standard conventions:

```
import pandas as pd

df = pd.read_csv(input_file, index_col=0)
```

There's more detail about writing good names in Chapter 9.

Cleaning up

Another way to make your code more readable is to clean it up after you have finished creating a function. Once you've tested it and you are confident it is working, you should remove code that has been commented out and remove unnecessary calls to the print() function that you may have used as a simple form of debugging. It's very confusing to see commented out sections in someone else's code.

When you see untidy sections of code, it sends a message that poor code quality is acceptable in a project. This means there's less incentive for other contributors to write good code. The untidy code may also be copied and adapted in other parts of the project. This is known as the Broken Window Theory (*https://oreil.ly/3sa7c*). Setting high standards in a project encourages everyone working on it to write good code.

If you want to improve your code quality, you may decide to refactor it. Refactoring means changing the code without changing its overall behavior. You may have thought of ways that your code could be more efficient, or you have thought of a better way to structure it that would let your teammate use pieces of the code in another project. Tests are essential in this process, because they will check that your new code still has the same overall behavior. I'll cover refactoring in "Refactoring" on page 126.

Documentation

Documentation also helps other people read your code. Code can be documented at multiple levels of detail, starting with simple inline comments, moving up to docstrings that explain a whole function, going on to the README page displayed in a GitHub repository and even tutorials to teach users how to use a package. All of these aspects of documentation help explain to other people how to use your code. They might even explain your code to you in the future (a very important audience!). If you want other people to use your code, you should make it easy for them by writing good documentation.

Writing great documentation is one thing, but you also need to maintain and keep it updated. Documentation that refers to an outdated version of the code is worse than no documentation at all. It will cause confusion that will take extra time to resolve. I'll discuss all forms of documentation in much more detail in Chapter 9.

Performance

Good code needs to be performant. This is measured in both the running time of the code and in the memory usage. When you're making decisions about how to write your code, it's useful to know what data structures and algorithms are more efficient. It's really good to know when you are doing things that will slow your code significantly, especially when there's a readily available alternative. You should also be aware of which parts of your code are taking a long time.

Performance is particularly important when you are writing production code that is going to be called every time a user takes a particular action. If your user base grows, or your project is successful, your code could be called millions of times every day. In this case, even small improvements in your code can save many hours for your users. You don't want your code to be the slow point in a large application. I'll explain how to measure the performance of your code in Chapter 2, and I'll show you how to choose the best data structures to optimize your code's performance in Chapter 3.

Robustness

Good code also should be robust. By this, I mean it should be reproducible: you should be able to run your code from start to end without it failing. Your code also should be able to respond gracefully if system inputs change unexpectedly. Instead of throwing an unexpected error that could cause a larger system to fail, your code should be designed to respond to changes. Your code can be made more robust by properly handling errors, logging what has happened, and writing good tests.

Errors and Logging

Robust code shouldn't behave unexpectedly when it gets an incorrect input. You should choose if you want your code to crash on an unexpected input, or handle that error and do something about it. For example, if your CSV file is missing half the rows of data you expect, do you want your code to return an error or continue to evaluate only half the data? You should make an explicit choice to give an alert that something is not as it should be, handle the error, or fail silently. I'll cover errors in more detail in Chapter 5.

If the error is handled, it can still be important to record that it has happened so that it doesn't fail silently, if that's not what you want to happen. This is one use case for logging; I'll explore other uses for logging in Chapter 5.

Testing

Testing is key to writing robust code. Software engineering uses two main types: user testing, where a person uses a piece of software to confirm that it works correctly, and automated testing. A common method for automated testing is sending an example input into a piece of code and confirming that the output is what you expected. I'll cover only automated tests in this book.

Tests are necessary because even if your code runs perfectly on your machine, this doesn't mean it will work on anyone else's machine, or even on your own machine in the future. Data changes, libraries are updated, and different machines run different versions of Python. If someone else wants to use your code on their machine, they can run your tests to confirm it works.

There are several different types of tests. Unit tests test a single function, end-to-end tests test a whole project, and integration tests test a chunk of code that contains many functions but is still smaller than a whole project. I'll describe testing strategies and libraries in detail in Chapter 7. But a good strategy for getting started, if you have a large codebase with no tests, is to write a test when something breaks to ensure that the same thing doesn't happen again.

Data in This Book

Throughout this book, I'll use data from the United Nations Sustainable Development Goals (*https://sdgs.un.org/goals*) (SDGs). The SDGs are a set of 17 goals that are part of the 2030 Agenda for Sustainable Development adopted by UN member nations in 2015. The goals include ending poverty, ending hunger, access to education, gender equality, and many more. The SDGs are divided into subsidiary targets and tracked using a set of more than 200 statistical indicators. The indicators measure progress toward these goals quantitatively.

For example, Goal 1 is "End poverty in all its forms everywhere." Target 1.1 is "By 2030, eradicate extreme poverty for all people everywhere, currently measured as people living on less than $1.25 a day." Indicator 1.1.1 is "Proportion of the population living below the international poverty line by sex, age, employment status and geographic location (urban/rural)."

The data for these indicators is available in an online database (*https://oreil.ly/X3rDE*) and via an API (*https://oreil.ly/rBEv-*). I'll use the data from the indicators in the sample code in this book.

Key Takeaways

Writing good code will help you in many ways: it will be easier for other people to use your code; it will help you understand what you were doing when you come back to your work six months after you last touched it; and it will help your code scale up and interface with a larger system. Good code also will make your life much easier if you need to add features to your code that weren't in the original project plan.

If you'd like to read more about the principles for writing good code, I recommend these books:

- *The Pragmatic Programmer*, 20th Anniversary Edition, by David Thomas and Andrew Hunt (Addison-Wesley Professional)
- *A Philosophy of Software Architecture* by John Ousterhout (Yaknyam Press)

In summary, here are some ways to think about how to write good code:

Simplicity
Your code should avoid repetition, unnecessary complexity, and unneeded lines of code.

Modularity
Your code should be broken down into logical functions, with well-defined inputs and outputs.

Readability
Your code should follow the PEP8 standard for formatting, contain well-chosen names, and be well documented.

Performance
Your code should not take an unnecessarily long time to run or use up more resources than are available.

Robustness

Your code should be reproducible, raise useful error messages, and handle unexpected inputs without failing.

In the next chapter, I'll look in more detail at one aspect of good code: performance.

## CHAPTER 2

Analyzing Code Performance

In Chapter 1, I set out some of the aspects of writing good code, and in this chapter I'll take a deep dive into one aspect: performance. If you're writing code that forms part of a larger system, it is very important that your code is performant. It should return its outputs in a timely manner, and it shouldn't exceed the computing resources available.

But first, the most important thing is that your code should work. Before applying any of the techniques in this chapter or the next, make sure that your code solves the problem that it needs to solve and returns the outputs that you expect. Any optimization or speedup should happen after the code is already running correctly.

Second, ask whether there is a requirement for improved performance. You'll need to know the expectations of the larger system your code is interfacing with. Does your code need to return a result within a specific amount of time? Is your user waiting to take some action based on the results of your code? If so, the faster it works, the better the user's experience.

For example, your machine learning model may need to return its prediction within 100 ms so that the prediction can be shown to the user. If your code already returns its result within the time allowed, there may be no need to spend time optimizing its performance.

It is, however, a really good idea to be aware of the principles in this chapter. It's useful to know when you're writing code that's inefficient (for example, if you need to hack something together in a hurry) so that you can come back to it later and optimize it. I'll cover how to choose the most efficient data structure for your code in Chapter 3.

As a data scientist, you'll be familiar with the idea that what you measure matters. The first step in improving your code's performance is to find out which parts of it are the slowest or taking up the most memory. Once you've collected this data you'll know whether these slow or memory-hungry parts are things you can fix. The slow-down may come from inefficiencies in your code or it may already be as efficient as possible, but you'll need data to know which of these is the case. I'll cover how to measure the performance of your code in "Timing Your Code" on page 17 and "Profiling Your Code" on page 20.

Premature Optimization

...premature optimization is the root of all evil (or at least most of it) in programming.
—Donald Knuth, *The Art of Computer Programming*

This quote from Donald Knuth is a classic phrase that is often repeated in the software engineering world. And while many other things in the data science world could be described as evil, this is still a useful piece of advice. I interpret it as a recommendation not to optimize your code before you know the time or memory requirements for that code, or before you know where the bottlenecks are.

Methods to Improve Performance

I'll define good performance here as minimizing the amount of computer resources your code uses. I won't go into any details of computer architecture here, because that's a huge topic on its own. But you can measure the effect of different code on the time that it takes to complete a task or the amount of computer memory needed. So, performant code means code that is faster or takes up a smaller memory footprint, although often there's a trade-off where faster code takes up more memory.

Your choice of methods to improve your code performance depends on the programming language you're using, among other factors. In Python, the main options available are the following:

Your choice of algorithm
> Choices you make in the code you write can make a huge difference to its performance. For example, avoid nested loops where possible so that you don't iterate through a list twice when you need to iterate through it just once.

Your choice of data structure
> Depending on the task you need to accomplish, different data structures may have different trade-offs. For example, it's much quicker to look up a value in a dictionary than to search for it in a list. I'll cover this in detail in Chapter 3.

Using built-in functions

If a built-in function exists to solve your problem, it's almost always more efficient to use that function than to write your own. Many of these built-in functions are implemented in C, which is generally faster than recreating the same function in Python.

Compiling Python

You may be able to get your code to run faster by compiling Python to a lower-level language using tools like Cython (*https://cython.org*), Numba (*https://numba.pydata.org*), and PyPy (*https://www.pypy.org*). Your choice of which you use will depend on your use case. Numba contains a subset of Python; Cython is a superset of Python with additional options in C; and PyPy is a reimplementation of Python using just-in-time compilation.

Asynchronous code

You may be able to speed up your code by having it accomplish a task while it waits for the outcome of another. For example, your code might be waiting for an API to return a response over a slow network.

Parallel and distributed computing

Parallel computing means running your code on more than one processor within a computer. You can run your code on multiple CPUs at once using the `multiprocessing` module. Distributed computing means running your code on multiple different machines at the same time.

In this book I focus on what you can do to improve the code you write routinely, without needing to take the time to learn a lot of new tools and techniques. So I won't cover all the options from the list above. In this chapter, I'll concentrate on how to measure performance and how to choose your algorithm. Knowing how to measure your code's performance will let you know when built-in functions give you an improvement. I'll also cover how to choose the best data structure for your use case in Chapter 3. And I'll briefly mention parallel and distributed computing in "Array Operations Using Dask" on page 41.

If you'd like to take a deep dive into code performance, I highly recommend the book *High Performance Python: Practical Performant Programming for Humans* by Micha Gorelick and Ian Osvald (O'Reilly, 2020) as a next step. This book also includes extensive details on different compilers for Python. You can find my favorite introduction to asynchronous code in the FastAPI documentation (*https://oreil.ly/JtZED*).

Timing Your Code

The simplest way of figuring out which parts of your code are slow is to measure the time taken to run a function or a line of code, make a change, then measure it again.

It's good practice to make only one change at a time because otherwise you can't tell what caused the speedup or slowdown.

 In this chapter, I use examples of some simple statistical functions. I don't recommend that you use this code or implement these functions yourself (they're available in the `statistics` package or in NumPy). I'm just using them to illustrate my points.

The following example shows a simple piece of code that calculates the statistical mode of a list of numbers. Let's take a look at how you can measure the running time of your code using this as an example:

```
def slow_way_to_calculate_mode(list_of_numbers):
    result_dict = {}
    for i in list_of_numbers:
        if i not in result_dict:
            result_dict[i] = 1
        else:
            result_dict[i] += 1

    mode_vals = []
    max_frequency = max(result_dict.values())
    for key, value in result_dict.items():
        if value == max_frequency:
            mode_vals.append(key)

    return mode_vals
```

Next, let's generate a list of 100,000 random integers to input into this function:

```
import numpy as np

random_integers = np.random.randint(1, 1_000_000, 1_000_000)
```

The simplest way to measure how long this function takes to run is by using the `time` module. You can record the time on the computer's clock before and after running the function, then just print out the difference:

```
import time

start = time.time()
slow_way_to_calculate_mode(random_integers)
end = time.time()

print(end-start)
```

However, the runtime of a function can vary, so it's good to measure this multiple times to get a robust result. You can do this using the `timeit` module. If you're working in the Jupyter Notebook, there's a neat way of doing it using the `%%timeit` cell magic command:

```
>>> %%timeit
... slow_way_to_calculate_mode(random_integers)

267 ms ± 23.4 ms per loop (mean ± std. dev. of 7 runs, 10 loops each)
```

In this case, `timeit` looped through the code 10 times, and it repeated the set of 10 loops 7 times, then returned the summary statistics of those runs. `timeit` defaults to the number of runs and loops that will fit into a 2-second window, but you can specify the number of runs using the `-r` flag and the number of loops using the `-n` flag.

If you're using a standalone script, you can use `timeit` as shown in this example:

```
import numpy as np
import timeit

random_integers = np.random.randint(1, 100_000, 1000)

def slow_way_to_calculate_mode(list_of_numbers):
    result_dict = {}
    for i in list_of_numbers:
        if i not in result_dict:
            result_dict[i] = 1
        else:
            result_dict[i] += 1

    mode_vals = []
    max_frequency = max(result_dict.values())
    for key, value in result_dict.items():
        if value == max_frequency:
            mode_vals.append(key)

    return mode_vals

mode_timer = timeit.Timer(stmt="slow_way_to_calculate_mode(random_integers)",
                          setup="from __main__ import"\
                          "slow_way_to_calculate_mode,random_integers")

time_taken = mode_timer.timeit(number=10)

print(f"Execution time: {time_taken} seconds")
```

But is this code any good? Is 267 ms fast or slow? Because this is just an example without real-world requirements for speed, I'll compare it with another way of calculating the mode and see if that improves the performance. Here's another way to carry out the same calculation:

```
from collections import Counter

def mode_using_counter(list_of_numbers):
    c = Counter(list_of_numbers)
    return c.most_common(1)[0][0]
```

And again using `timeit` to measure how long it takes to run:

```
>>> %%timeit
... mode_using_counter(random_integers)

23.2 ms ± 737 µs per loop (mean ± std. dev. of 7 runs, 10 loops each)
```

As you can see, this version of the code takes much less time to run. Instead of an average of approximately 267 ms, it takes only approximately 23 ms. The standard deviation is also much lower, which helps guarantee an upper bound to the runtime.

You can take two points from this example: first, different code can perform exactly the same function, but one version can be much faster than another. Second, using built-in functions (in this case `Counter` from the `collections` module) is often much faster than writing your own version. Both the `collections` and `itertools` modules have many built-in functions that can help you speed up common functions.

Profiling Your Code

Timing your code using `%%timeit` is great for single lines of code, but if you have a longer function or a whole script, it's tedious to break out each line into its own notebook cell and time it separately. This is where a profiler comes in. Profilers can tell you which part of a function takes the most time and give you extra levels of detail, making it easier to find the bottlenecks in your code. I'll also include details of how to profile the memory usage of your code in this section.

cProfile

`cProfile` is the built-in profiler for Python, and you can use it to get a basic overview of the locations of bottlenecks in a longer script. In this example, I'll put the random number generator inside the mode function from the previous section so that there's more to see in the profiler:

```python
import numpy as np
from collections import Counter

def mode_using_counter(n_integers):
    random_integers = np.random.randint(1, 100_000, n_integers)
    c = Counter(random_integers)
    return c.most_common(1)[0][0]
```

To run the profiler, use the command:

```
%%prun
mode_using_counter(10_000_000)
```

This should give you an output like this:

```
         25 function calls in 2.585 seconds

   Ordered by: internal time

   ncalls  tottime  percall  cumtime  percall filename:lineno(function)
        1    2.467    2.467    2.467    2.467 {built-in method
                                             _collections._count_elements}
        1    0.104    0.104    0.104    0.104 {method 'randint' of
                                             'numpy.random.mtrand.RandomState'
                                             objects}
        1    0.007    0.007    2.584    2.584 <string>:1(<module>)
        1    0.006    0.006    0.006    0.006 {built-in method builtins.max}
        1    0.000    0.000    2.467    2.467 __init__.py:649(update)
        1    0.000    0.000    2.585    2.585 {built-in method builtins.exec}
        1    0.000    0.000    0.000    0.000 {method 'reduce' of
                                             'numpy.ufunc' objects}
        1    0.000    0.000    2.577    2.577 3744758285.py:
                                             (mode_using_counter)
        1    0.000    0.000    2.467    2.467 __init__.py:581(__init__)
        1    0.000    0.000    0.000    0.000 fromnumeric.py:69(_wrapreduction)
        1    0.000    0.000    0.006    0.006 heapq.py:521(nlargest)
        1    0.000    0.000    0.006    0.006 __init__.py:600(most_common)
        1    0.000    0.000    0.000    0.000 <__array_function__ internals>:177
                                             (prod)
        1    0.000    0.000    0.000    0.000 {built-in method
                                             _abc._abc_instancecheck}
        1    0.000    0.000    0.000    0.000 fromnumeric.py:2927(prod)
        1    0.000    0.000    0.000    0.000 abc.py:117(__instancecheck__)
        1    0.000    0.000    0.000    0.000 {built-in method
                                             builtins.isinstance}
        1    0.000    0.000    0.000    0.000 {built-in method numpy.core.
                                             _multiarray_umath.
                                             implement_array_function}
        1    0.000    0.000    0.000    0.000 {built-in method builtins.getattr}
        1    0.000    0.000    0.000    0.000 fromnumeric.py:70(<dictcomp>)
        2    0.000    0.000    0.000    0.000 {method 'items' of 'dict' objects}
        1    0.000    0.000    0.000    0.000 {built-in method builtins.iter}
        1    0.000    0.000    0.000    0.000 {method 'disable' of
                                             '_lsprof.Profiler' objects}
        1    0.000    0.000    0.000    0.000 fromnumeric.py:2922
                                             (_prod_dispatcher)
```

The tottime column in this output shows where the computer spent most of the time when running this code: in the built-in method _collections._count_elements function, which is the Counter function. The next most time-consuming part was method 'randint' of 'numpy.random.mtrand.RandomState' objects, which is the step that created the list of random numbers. All the other steps took very little time. The disadvantage of using cProfile is that you need to map each of these function calls back to lines within your code.

You can also use the SnakeViz package to give you a graphical display of the results from cProfile.

You can install SnakeViz with the following command:

```
$ pip install snakeviz
```

Then, if you're working in the Jupyter Notebook you can use the SnakeViz extension. You can load the extension with the following command:

```
>>> %load_ext snakeviz
```

And then you can run SnakeViz using:

```
>>> %%snakeviz
>>> mode_using_counter(10_000_000)
```

This gives the result shown in Figure 2-1.

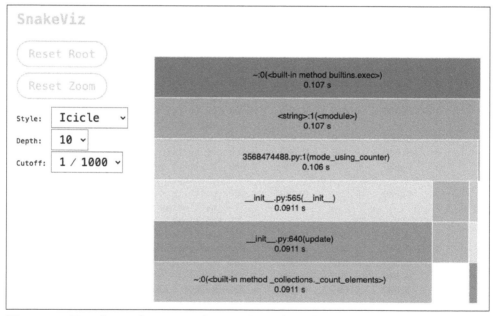

Figure 2-1. Visualizing the output of cProfile with SnakeViz

This can be easier to interpret than the default output of cProfile.

line_profiler

cProfile gives you a detailed breakdown of how the computer spends its time, including details of Python's internal workings. However, its output is not particularly easy to read and may dive too deep into Python built-in methods called by your code. The package line_profiler (*https://oreil.ly/KcGKg*) gives a much more readable breakdown of your code.

line_profiler isn't installed by default, so you can install it using:

```
$ pip install line_profiler
```

Next, you need to load this as a separate extension in the Jupyter Notebook:

```
>>> %load_ext line_profiler
```

You need to explicitly tell line_profiler which function to look at using the -f flag, and you can run the function using this command:

```
>>> %lprun -f mode_using_counter mode_using_counter(10_000_000)
```

This is the output for the mode_using_counter function:

```
Timer unit: 1e-09 s

Total time: 2.60904 s
File: .../3744758285.py
Function: mode_using_counter at line 1

Line # Hits          Time       Per Hit  % Time  Line Contents
==============================================================
     1                                           def mode_using_counter
                                                     (n_integers):
     2     1    124198000.0   124198000.0    4.8  some_list = np.random.randint
                                                     (1, 100000, n_integers)
     3     1   2479064000.0  2479064000.0   95.0  c = Counter(some_list)
     4     1      5780000.0     5780000.0    0.2  return c.most_common(1)[0][0]
```

This output is much easier to read than the output of cProfile. It's clear that approximately 5% of the time in this function is spent generating the list of random numbers, and 95% of the time is spent counting them using the Counter built-in function. This tells you that if you wanted to improve the performance of this function you should focus on the line containing the Counter. Being able to identify the line that takes the most time is particularly important in longer functions and scripts.

You can also use line_profiler with a script using decorators to identify the functions you want to profile, and you can find more details on how to do this in the line_profiler documentation (*https://oreil.ly/xwGkQ*).

Memory Profiling with Memray

You can profile your code's memory usage as well as the time it takes to run. Memory usage is something you also may need to optimize, depending on your code's requirements. It's important to consider this as the size of your data increases, because you may hit the upper limits of the hardware you are using. Additionally, the CPU has to work harder to manage memory. This could increase the runtime of your code if the CPU is spending too much time managing the memory instead of executing code.

Memray (*https://oreil.ly/n-HqF*) is a memory profiling tool developed by Bloomberg that can give you different reports on the memory usage of your code. You can install Memray using this command:

```
$ pip install memray
```

Let's look at how to use Memray with a standalone Python script containing the `mode_using_counter` function. Here's the complete script:

```
import numpy as np
from collections import Counter

def mode_using_counter(n_integers):
    random_integers = np.random.randint(1, 100_000, n_integers)
    c = Counter(random_integers)
    return c.most_common(1)[0][0]

if __name__ == '__main__':
    print(mode_using_counter(10_000_000))
```

You'll need to run Memray using the following command to collect data on your script's memory usage:

```
$ memray run mode_using_counter.py
```

You should see this output:

```
Writing profile results into memray-mode_using_counter.py.17881.bin
26008
[memray] Successfully generated profile results.

You can now generate reports from the stored allocation records.
```

Memray has generated a binary file (*.bin*) with the results. You can now run other commands to generate a variety of reports from this binary file. The `flamegraph` command is the most useful:

```
$ memray flamegraph memray-mode_using_counter.py.17881.bin
```

You'll need to replace *memray-mode_using_counter.py.17881.bin* with the filename that Memray has generated for you. This will generate an HTML file, and if you open it you should see something like the Figure 2-2.

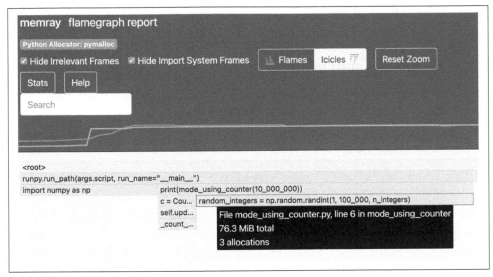

Figure 2-2. Flamegraph report from Memray

You can look at the memory usage of each line of code. In this example, the highest usage was by the line `random_integers = np.random.randint(1, 100_000, n_integers)` with a memory usage of 76.3 MB. This is a simple example, but with a longer script this tool becomes extremely useful to track down the lines of code that have the highest memory usage. This lets you know where you should focus your efforts if you need to optimize the memory usage of your script.

You can also use Memray in a Jupyter notebook with the `memray` extension, and you can find details of this in the Memray documentation (*https://oreil.ly/i-E-J*).

Whichever method you use to measure the performance of your code, it's important to do this before you optimize your code using the methods described in "Methods to Improve Performance" on page 16. This way, you will know where the bottlenecks are, and you'll be able to focus your efforts in the correct place.

Time Complexity

In the previous section, I introduced how to find bottlenecks in your code. This tells you how your code is performing on the amount of data you currently have, but what happens if you expect the amount of data to grow in the future? Or what if parts of your code take so long to run that it's not feasible to measure them? The concept of time complexity can help you here.

Time complexity describes how the running time of an algorithm grows as the size of the input increases. This means an overall trend, not specific to any hardware. To make this more concrete, consider this question: if you run your code on a list of numbers, then double the length of the list, what happens to the runtime of the code? Does it stay the same, or does it double, or something else?

How to Estimate Time Complexity

Here's an example. This function calculates a weighted mean, taking as input a list of numbers and a list of weights to apply to those numbers:

```
def weighted_mean(list_of_numbers, weights):
    running_total = 0
    for i in range(len(list_of_numbers)):
        running_total += (list_of_numbers[i] * weights[i])
    return (running_total/sum(weights))
```

If the length of num_list doubles, the number of iterations in the for loop also doubles. The other lines in this function (initializing the running total and dividing it by the length of the list) don't increase their runtime. You could think about this as an equation for the runtime of the code in terms of the number of steps in this function, where each step is some operation carried out by the code. Initializing the running total is one step, each time the running total is added to constitutes another step, and returning the result is another step. The equation would be:

number_of_steps = n + 2, where n is the length of the input lists.

So as the size of n increases, the number of steps grows linearly but the 2 remains constant.

The following function accepts two lists as inputs and calculates their covariance (a measure of the strength of the correlation between two random variables). Again, this isn't the best way to calculate this; the function is just to illustrate the point:

```
def covariance(X, Y):
    cov_sum = 0
    for i in range(len(X)):
        for j in range(len(Y)):
            cov_sum += 0.5 * (X[i] - X[j]) * (Y[i] - Y[j])
    return cov_sum / (len(X) ** 2)
```

Because there are two nested (one inside the other) for loops in this function, if the sizes of both X and Y double, the number of steps taken to calculate the result increases fourfold. X and Y both must be the same length in this function. The running time of the code increases proportionally to the square of the increase in the size of the dataset.

This suggests a way to improve your code: what if it's possible to use a faster method to carry out this same calculation? The following function also calculates the covariance, but it uses only one for loop:

```
def covariance_fast(X, Y):
    avg_X = sum(X) / len(X)
```

```
avg_Y = sum(Y) / len(Y)

result = 0
for i in range(len(X)):
    result += (X[i] - avg_X) * (Y[i] - avg_Y)

return result / len(X)
```

An additional point I want to note here is that the timing and profiling methods introduced in "Timing Your Code" on page 17 and "Profiling Your Code" on page 20 may also tell you that the nested for loops were the most time-consuming part of the function. So this is a great place to look for more efficient algorithms.

Big O Notation

> Big O is how code slows as data grows.
>
> —Ned Batchelder, PyCon 2018

Big O notation is a more formal way of describing the patterns of how the runtime of your code increases as the size of your data grows, as I introduced in the previous section. The letter O in this case refers to the order of the function, another way of referring to the growth rate of the function. It's a useful way of describing different classes of algorithms depending on how they behave as datasets get larger. It's also independent of the hardware you are using. A function may run much faster on a more powerful machine but slower on a less powerful machine. This analysis lets you predict the performance of your code regardless of what machine you run it on.

Big O notation is similar to the equation for the number of steps in the weighted mean example from the previous section, but the coefficients are left out. In big O notation, the runtime is described as a function of the size of the input, n, and it's written as $O(f(n))$. $f(n)$ is an upper bound on the number of operations performed by the algorithm as a function of n. So the weighted mean example would be classed as $O(n)$.

You might be wondering why the weighted mean example is $O(n)$ and not $O(n + 2)$, given that I showed that the equation for it is number of steps = n + 2. Big O notation considers the limit of this equation as n becomes large, and at this point the extra two steps are insignificant. It's an approximation that helps you compare different approaches, not an exact measure of how long your code takes to run. Similarly, if code takes $n^2 + n$ steps to run, this is approximated to $O(n^2)$.

Some common classes in big O notation include:

$O(1)$

   This is also known as "constant time," and it means that the runtime is independent of the size of the dataset. An example of this is looking up a particular element in a list. Returning the last element in a list still takes the same amount of time even if the list is very large.

$O(n)$

This is also known as "linear time," and it means that the runtime increases linearly with the size of the dataset, as shown in the weighted mean example.

$O(n^2)$

This is also known as "quadratic time," and it means that the runtime increases in proportion to the square of the size of the dataset, as shown in the slow covariance example.

These three classes are plotted in Figure 2-3, along with exponential time $O(2^n)$, logarithmic time $O(\log n)$, and $O(n \log n)$. Exponential time means that running time increases proportional to 2 to the factor of the size of the dataset, and recursive algorithms often give you a time complexity of $O(2^n)$. Logarithmic time means that the runtime increases in proportion to the log of the size of the dataset, and many search algorithms have this time complexity.

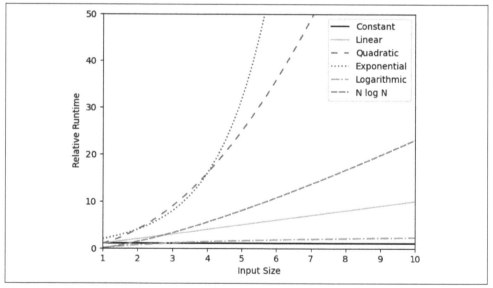

Figure 2-3. Relative runtime compared to input size

As you can see from the plot, $O(n^2)$ and $O(2^n)$ get very slow very quickly. So if you need your code to be more performant, try to avoid these.

You should also consider what is a realistic range of n for your use case to avoid premature optimization. For example, if n is never greater than 5, it doesn't matter too much if the runtime of your code increases linearly or exponentially.

You'll see an example of how big O notation can be very useful when I discuss choosing different data structures in the next chapter.

Key Takeaways

When considering code performance, you first need to know when it's appropriate to optimize. If the amount of data is small, or your code already meets all the requirements, don't spend time optimizing it.

But if you need to improve your code's performance, your first step should be to measure it, to find where the bottlenecks are. The simplest way of doing that is to time how long the function or the line of code takes to run. If you need more detail, or you want to get the time breakdown of a longer script, use a profiler.

It also can be useful to think about the number of steps your code will take, and how this will scale as the amount of data grows. You'll often see big O notation used to describe this. Overall, remember that there are many options for writing the same piece of code, and some will give you better performance than others!

## CHAPTER 3

Using Data Structures Effectively

In the previous chapter, you saw how to measure the performance of your code. In this chapter, I'll show you how your choice of data structure can affect your code's performance, and I'll discuss how to choose the best data structure for the problem you're working on.

As a data scientist, when you're writing code, you'll need to use a variety of data structures to store your data. You will have a lot of choices for which data structure to use, and it's likely that some are appropriate for the problem you're working on, and others are less good choices.

> *...a large part of performant programming is knowing what questions you are trying to ask of your data, and picking a data structure that can answer those questions quickly.*
>
> —Micha Gorelick and Ian Osvald, *High Performance Python*

It's important to use the correct data structure for the problem you're working on for two main reasons: first, the data structure is optimized for that use case, and second, useful methods are associated with it. So if you choose the correct data structure, your code performs better and is also easier to use. It also means that your code is more predictable and easier to understand.

In this chapter, I'll go through some of the more common data structures that you'll use when writing data science code: Python lists, tuples, dictionaries, and sets; NumPy arrays; and pandas DataFrames. I'll describe the advantages and disadvantages of each and discuss which ones give you better performance in terms of both time and memory usage. I'll also discuss how to best use the different data structures for optimal performance.

In many books and articles you'll see a lot of data structures that I won't cover here, for example, linked lists, heaps, queues, binary search trees, and many more. These tend to be more important in software engineering than in data science, particularly in programming languages other than Python. If you'd like to learn more about data structures, I recommend *A Common-Sense Guide to Data Structures and Algorithms in Python* by Jay Wengrow (Pragmatic Bookshelf).

Native Python Data Structures

In this section, I want to discuss four fundamental data structures in Python: lists, tuples, dictionaries, and sets. You're likely using these in your code already. I want to give you some insight into how these data structures are implemented and some details of the time complexity for common operations. I'll use big O notation for this, which I described in "Time Complexity" on page 25. It's valuable to have an intuition for what these data structures do quickly, and where they're slow. This will help you choose the best data structure for your use case and give you some ideas for where to focus your efforts if you need to optimize your code.

Lists

Lists are an essential data structure in Python, and you'll see them frequently. Lists in Python are a type of array: a data structure that has some order. This means you can look up the first, third, or any other element of the list.

A Python list is a dynamic array, and this means that it can resize if more elements are added. It can also store elements of different types, so, for example, a list could contain both strings and integers.

Python allocates a continuous chunk of memory according to the size of the list, with one element of a list in the next door memory location to the next element. This has important implications: it's very easy to look up an element in a list. The Python interpreter knows the memory location of the start of the list, then if you're looking up the fifth element in the list, it simply retrieves the element that's in the fifth memory location from the start.

You can measure how the time taken to look up an element in a list changes as a list grows. First, create a list with 10 elements:

```
small_list = list(range(10))
```

Then you can use `%%timeit` (which I introduced in "Timing Your Code" on page 17) to measure the length of time taken to look up the last element in the list:

```
>>> %%timeit
>>> last_element = small_list[-1]

... 19.6 ns ± 0.13 ns per loop (mean ± std. dev. of 7 runs,
10,000,000 loops each)
```

Next, create a list of 10,000 elements to run the same experiment on:

```
large_list = list(range(10_000))
```

Finally, measure the time it takes to look up the last element:

```
>>> %%timeit
>>> last_element = large_list[-1]

... 18 ns ± 0.0944 ns per loop (mean ± std. dev. of 7 runs,
100,000,000 loops each)
```

The time taken is approximately the same for both lists, even though the second is 1,000 times the size of the first. List lookups are *O(1)* (constant time). This is the big O notation, which I explained in Chapter 2. However big your list is, it still takes approximately the same amount of time to look up an element in it.

Each time you add an element to a list it takes up extra space in memory. Python allocates some extra space beyond the length of the original list, but once this space is full, the entire list needs to be copied into a new memory location with more consecutive space. Appending at the end of a list is *O(1)* but with some overhead due to copying the list once the extra space is full.

If you insert something in the middle of a list, everything after that new element needs to move to a new memory location. So the insert operation is *O(n)*. Deleting an element from the middle of a list is also *O(n)*. Inserting and deleting are both *O(n)* because the list must always be in a continuous chunk of memory.

If you know you'll be adding elements to a list up to a specific length, .append() may not be the most efficient way to do this. It may be better to use a list comprehension (*https://oreil.ly/ZqTu0*) or create a list of zeros of the correct length, then update the values in it. If you want to append items to the start and end of a list, you can use the deque (*https://oreil.ly/7a7CU*) (double-ended queue) data structure from the collections module.

If you need to search for an element in a list, you'll need to compare the element you're searching for with every item in the list. You can measure how this changes as the list grows using the lists from the previous code examples.

First, you can measure how long it takes to search the list containing 10 elements:

```
>>> %%timeit
>>> 4200 in small_list

... 75.8 ns ± 0.298 ns per loop (mean ± std. dev. of 7
runs, 10,000,000 loops each)
```

Then, you can measure the same thing for the list of 10,000 elements:

```
>>> %%timeit
>>> 4200 in large_list
```

```
... 23.8 µs ± 1.9 µs per loop (mean ± std. dev. of 7 runs,
10,000 loops each)
```

It takes approximately 1,000 times as long. Searching a Python list in this way is *O(n)*. There are more efficient ways of searching a list, including binary search, which is *O(log n)*. But if you need to frequently search if something is present it's probably better to use a dictionary or a set, as I'll explain below.

Tuples

Tuples in Python are also an array, but they have a static size. They are immutable— once you've created a tuple, you can't change it. You can't append extra elements to the end of a tuple, for example.

Tuples are useful when you have only a few items you want to store in a data structure, and those items are not going to change. One thing to note is that a tuple is cached in the Python runtime, rather than stored in memory, so it's even faster to look up an element in a tuple than in a list. Looking up an element in a tuple is *O(1)*.

Dictionaries

Dictionaries are another essential data structure in Python, and they are based on key and value pairs. This means there are pairs of data elements that have some link between them, for example, the name of a person and their street address. Dictionaries are best for data that has no inherent ordering.

Under the hood, Python dictionaries are powered by hash tables. These use a hash function to turn a key into the index for a list. Figure 3-1 shows how this works: in this case the key `'Heather Hancock'` is transformed by the hash function into the index 3, and this lets you retrieve the address associated with this person's name.

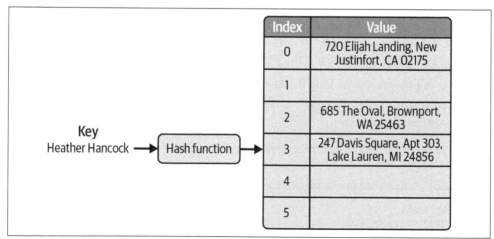

	Index	Value
	0	720 Elijah Landing, New Justinfort, CA 02175
	1	
	2	685 The Oval, Brownport, WA 25463
Key Heather Hancock → Hash function →	3	247 Davis Square, Apt 303, Lake Lauren, MI 24856
	4	
	5	

Figure 3-1. Dictionary lookup using a hash table

A hash function maps strings or integers, whatever is in the dictionary key, to an integer that is the relevant index in the list of values. There are many different types of hash functions. Taking the modulus of an integer is a simple example. The hash function in a Python dictionary is much more complex.

The hash function must return the same integer every time it is applied to the same key. Keys in the dictionary also must be unique so that it's possible to return the correct value. A dictionary key needs to be a hashable type such as a string, an integer, or a float. A Python list can't be hashed.

The hash table provides a useful feature: looking up the value corresponding to a particular key in a dictionary is $O(1)$. You get the same performance as looking up an element in a list, but you don't need to know the order in the list. Inserting, updating, and deleting a key and value pair are all $O(1)$. Items can be inserted in any order in the hash table.

You can run an experiment to check for yourself that dictionary lookups stay constant. The Faker (*https://oreil.ly/4JRuL*) library is very useful for this: it creates fake data that seems realistic, including personal data such as names, addresses, email addresses, and so on.

You can initialize a Faker generator to produce fake data with the following command:

```
from faker import Faker

fake = Faker()
```

Then, use this to populate a dictionary to run experiments on:

```
small_dict = {}

for i in range(10):
    small_dict[fake.name()] = fake.address()
```

You can time how long lookups take in this small dictionary with 10 key and value pairs:

```
>>> %%timeit
>>> small_dict['Erin Hogan']

... 21.7 ns ± 0.125 ns per loop (mean ± std. dev. of 7 runs,
10,000,000 loops each)
```

Then, you can make a dictionary of 10,000 key and value pairs:

```
large_dict = {}

for i in range(10_000):
    large_dict[fake.name()] = fake.address()
```

And you can measure the time taken to look up a value from a key in this dictionary:

```
>>> %%timeit
>>> large_dict['Nicole Morgan']

... 23.9 ns ± 0.449 ns per loop (mean ± std. dev. of 7 runs,
10,000,000 loops each)
```

It's approximately the same amount of time, even though this dictionary is 1,000 times larger than the previous one. It's extremely efficient to look things up in a dictionary. The downside is that they often have a large memory footprint.

Sets

A set is another data structure that is useful for data with no inherent order. Sets are implemented in Python using a hash table, similar to dictionaries. However, instead of key and value pairs, they just have a set of unique keys. This means that all the elements in a set must be unique.

Sets share the property with dictionaries that inserting, deleting, and updating items are all *O(1)*. Looking up an element in a set is also *O(1)*. Converting a list to a set and then looking up the length is an efficient way to count the number of unique elements in a list.

Because set lookups are *O(1)* but list lookups are *O(n)*, is it more efficient to convert a list to a set, then perform the lookup? Let's run an experiment to find out.

Using the large list of 10,000 elements from earlier, you can measure the time taken for a list lookup:

```
>>> %%timeit
>>> 4200 in large_list

... 23.8 µs ± 1.9 µs per loop (mean ± std. dev. of 7 runs,
10,000 loops each)
```

Next, you can measure the time taken to convert that list to a set then perform the lookup:

```
>>> %%timeit
>>> large_set = set(large_list)
>>> 4200 in large_set

... 76.7 µs ± 1.28 µs per loop (mean ± std. dev. of 7 runs,
10,000 loops each)
```

Converting a list to a set then performing the lookup takes more than three times as long as the list lookup due to the time needed to convert the list to the set. However, once you have converted the list to a set, subsequent lookups are fast:

```
>>> %%timeit
>>> 4592 in large_set

... 22 ns ± 0.188 ns per loop (mean ± std. dev. of 7 runs,
10,000,000 loops each)
```

The set lookup is 1,000 times faster than the list lookup. Converting to a set is a great option when you want to repeatedly check whether items are present in a list but it isn't worthwhile if you want to do it only a small number of times. As with everything in this chapter, it's worth experimenting and measuring what is faster for the particular problem you're working on.

If you would like to learn more about the internal workings of dictionaries and sets, I recommend this blog post from Luciano Ramalho (*https://oreil.ly/MFOuT*).

 There are a couple of other native Python data structures I haven't covered here that you may find helpful, depending on your use case. Named tuples (*https://oreil.ly/TxRJc*) are tuples that allow you to look up elements by an assigned name rather than just a position. Dataclasses (*https://oreil.ly/qtVog*) are a type of class (which I'll cover in Chapter 4) optimized for storing data.

NumPy Arrays

In this section, I want to move on from native Python data structures to look at NumPy arrays. NumPy is one of the most commonly used Python libraries for data science, and this is because of its core data structure: the ndarray or *n*-dimensional array.

I'm not going to cover the details of how to create and use NumPy arrays or all the actions you can take using them. For that, I recommend *Python for Data Analysis* by Wes McKinney (O'Reilly, 2021), which has a full reference guide on how to use NumPy.

I'll give you an overview of some of the reasons you might choose to use NumPy arrays and why they're so popular in data science. I'll give you an overview of what you can do with NumPy arrays, and I'll take a look at some performance considerations.

NumPy Array Functionality

NumPy arrays are n-dimensional arrays, and this gives you an excellent clue as to the best time to use one: when your data is multidimensional—something that you'll encounter frequently. In machine learning, many calculations are performed on data that's in a matrix or two-dimensional array structure. NumPy arrays make it much easier to deal with this data compared to native Python lists, and many ML libraries work very smoothly with NumPy arrays.

It is possible to make a multidimensional data structure from nested Python lists, but it quickly becomes difficult to perform calculations on them. I'll illustrate this with an example: given a two-dimensional array, how can you look up the values in the first column?

To do this using nested lists, you would need to write a line of code to go through all the rows and extract the first value. Here's one way of doing that, using a list comprehension:

```
python_2d_list =[[1, 3, 5], [2, 4, 6], [7, 9, 11]]

first_column = [python_2d_list[i][0] for i in range(len(python_2d_list))]
```

But if you have a NumPy array, you can simply look up the values in the first column using NumPy's array slicing syntax:

```
import numpy as np

np_2d_array = np.array([[1, 3, 5], [2, 4, 6], [7, 9, 11]])

first_column = np_2d_array[:, 0]
```

 If you look up elements in a list and assign a new variable name to the selection, this creates a new copy of those elements. But if you do the same with a NumPy array, this is a view of the original array. So if you change the values in the np_2d_array object in the above example, this will also change the corresponding values in the first_column object. Creating a view is faster and more memory efficient than creating a copy, and this is another way NumPy arrays give better performance than lists.

In the same vein, many other operations on multidimensional data are much easier using NumPy arrays than nested lists. These include matrix multiplication, concatenating arrays, transposing arrays, and reshaping arrays.

However, one consideration with NumPy arrays (as I'll talk about much more in the next section) is that they can contain data of only one type. So they are not a valid choice if your data contains mixed types (for example, you need your data structure to contain both strings and integers).

NumPy Array Performance Considerations

As I mentioned in the previous section, NumPy arrays allow data of only a single type. This might seem like a limitation, but it actually has huge performance benefits. This is in contrast to Python lists, where this code is a valid option:

```
mixed_type_list = ["one", 2, 3.14]
```

A Python list can contain strings, integers, and floats in the same data structure. You can try to create a NumPy array to store the same data, like so:

```
mixed_type_array = np.array(["one", 2, 3.14])
```

And this line of code runs without errors. But if you look at this array, you'll see that all the elements have been converted to strings:

```
>>> print(mixed_type_array)
... ['one' '2' '3.14']
```

NumPy has converted all the elements so that they are the same type.

The type of the elements in a NumPy array is stored with it and can be looked up using the .dtype attribute:

```
>>> integer_array = np.array([1, 2, 3])

>>> print(integer_array.dtype)
... dtype('int64')
```

The type is int64 rather than the standard Python int. NumPy uses types different from the standard Python types, which can also lead to some performance gains. I'll discuss this later in this section.

Knowing that every element in a NumPy array is the same type leads to large performance gains, in particular for what's known as vectorized calculations. In a regular Python for loop, the type of every element needs to be checked so that the Python interpreter knows what function to apply to it. But NumPy can skip this step and go straight to optimized C code for many mathematical operations. It operates on every element in an array at once, instead of iterating through every element. This process is termed vectorization. If you would like to learn more about vectorization, I recommend this article by Itamar Turner-Trauring (*https://oreil.ly/DumcS*).

Here's an example of the performance gains you can make by using NumPy arrays compared to Python lists. First, I'll generate an array of 100,000 random integers using NumPy and then convert it to a regular Python list:

```
random_int_array = np.random.randint(1, 100_000, 100_000)
random_int_list = list(random_int_array)
```

Then you can sum the list using the regular Python sum(), and use %%timeit, introduced in "Timing Your Code" on page 17, to measure how long it takes:

```
>>> %%timeit -r 7 -n 100
>>> sum(random_int_list)

... 1.96 ms ± 463 µs per loop (mean ± std. dev. of 7 runs, 100 loops each)
```

Next, you can perform the same operation using np.sum(), which is a vectorized operation, and again measure how long it takes:

```
>>> %%timeit -r 7 -n 100
>>> np.sum(random_int_array)

... 13.9 µs ± 3.63 µs per loop (mean ± std. dev. of 7 runs, 100 loops each)
```

It's approximately 100 times faster! This is an enormous performance boost. If the operation you want to perform is available as a vectorized NumPy array method, you should definitely use this rather than a native Python method or writing your own code. You can consult the NumPy documentation (*https://oreil.ly/11vRd*) to find out if the operation is available.

When using NumPy arrays, you also need to consider whether you'll need to add more elements to an array later. Unlike a regular Python list, when NumPy allocates space for an array, it doesn't allow any extra room. So if you append more elements to a NumPy array the entire array needs to be moved to a new memory location every time. This means appending to a NumPy array is *O(n)*. It's definitely worthwhile to initialize your array with the correct amount of space, and an easy way to do this is to use np.zeros, like so:

```
array_to_fill = np.zeros(1000)
```

You can then replace the zeros with the new elements instead of appending to the array.

You also can save a lot of memory space with NumPy arrays by taking advantage of NumPy's different types. NumPy arrays are loaded into memory, so reducing their size may be helpful when you are dealing with large arrays.

You can generate an array of random integers as before:

```
random_int_array = np.random.randint(1, 100_000, 100_000)
```

You can look up the number of bytes this takes up by inspecting the .nbytes attribute:

```
>>> random_int_array.nbytes
... 800000
```

This array takes up 800,000 bytes of space.

You can find out the type from the .dtype attribute:

```
>>> random_int_array.dtype
... dtype('int64')
```

In this case it's int64. Referring to the NumPy documentation (*https://oreil.ly/beqRz*), this is a 64-bit integer with an allowed range of -9,223,372,036,854_775,808 to 9,223,372,036,854_775,808.

If you don't expect to need this full range of integers, you can convert your array to a 32-bit integer type, which has an allowed range of -2,147,483,648 to 2,147,483,648. You also could use a 16-bit integer if your data range is small enough.

You can convert your array by using the .astype method:

```
random_int_array_32 = random_int_array.astype(np.int32)
```

If you inspect the number of bytes, you'll see it takes up half the space:

```
>>> random_int_array_32.nbytes
... 400000
```

You also can do this out of the box by specifying the dtype when you initialize the array:

```
small_array = np.array([1, 3, 5], dtype=np.int16)
```

The NumPy documentation (*https://oreil.ly/uHITq*) has a complete list of all the available types.

Array Operations Using Dask

If you have tried the strategies in the previous section for improving your code's performance using NumPy arrays, but your code still needs to be optimized further, the Dask (*https://www.dask.org*) library is a great option. It lets you carry out array operations in parallel, for faster computation and for data that doesn't fit in your computer's memory. Dask provides an interface that is very similar to standard NumPy arrays, but it does add a little extra complexity, so it is worth using only if you need the performance boost. It lets you run computations on multiple cores at once on your laptop and on distributed systems (clusters).

Dask works by dividing an array into chunks, running computations on one or several chunks at once, then combining the results. For example, if you want to find the maximum value of a very large array, you could split that array into some number of chunks, find the maximum of each chunk, then find the maximum of all the results of each chunk combined. Not every operation can be parallelized like this, but if this applies to the problem you're working on, it can make your code much more efficient.

Dask also lets you run computations on data that's larger than your system's memory. Because not all the chunks are loaded and evaluated at one time, you don't need to load the whole array into memory, and each chunk can be evaluated sequentially.

You can install Dask with the following command:

```
$ python -m pip install "dask[complete]"
```

You can run the same operation with NumPy and with Dask, and compare the amount of time it takes.

One experiment you can do is to find the maximum value of a large array. You can create a NumPy array filled with random integers using `np.random.randint()`, and the code below creates an array of 1 billion integers:

```
large_np_array = np.random.randint(1, 100000, 1000000000)
```

You can measure the time it takes to do this calculation on a standard NumPy array:

```
>>> %%timeit -r 1 -n 7
>>> np.max(large_np_array)
... 30.7 s ± 0 ns per loop (mean ± std. dev. of 1 run, 7 loops each)
```

The Dask array is a data structure different from a NumPy array. Many NumPy methods are replicated in Dask, so you can create a Dask array of random integers with this code:

```
import dask.array as da

large_dask_array = da.random.randint(1, 100_000, 1_000_000_000)
```

You also can create a Dask array from a NumPy array, like so:

```
large_dask_array = da.from_array(large_np_array)
```

There's an extra step with Dask compared to NumPy. You first need to initialize the operation, in this case with the `.max()` method. Then you need to compute the operation using the `.compute()` method. You can measure the time for this step, to compare with the NumPy array:

```
>>> %%timeit -r 1 -n 7
>>> array_max = large_dask_array.max()
>>> array_max.compute()
... 1.51 s ± 0 ns per loop (mean ± std. dev. of 1 run, 7 loops each)
```

Finding the maximum in a Dask array is approximately 20 times faster than with a NumPy array!

The computation on each chunk also can be done by a different core or machine. Dask Distributed (*https://oreil.ly/yTAkI*) schedules the tasks for you. You need to create a `Client` object to use this:

```
from dask.distributed import Client

client = Client(n_workers=4)
client
```

Figure 3-2 shows a local client that is prepared to use all the cores on a laptop.

Figure 3-2. Dask local cluster dashboard

Once this client is ready, you can use Dask arrays as above, and the computations will be distributed across the number of workers you specify.

If you would like to learn more about Dask, see the Dask documentation (*https:// oreil.ly/ES1I9*) for some great examples.

Arrays in Machine Learning

Array multiplication is a large part of many machine learning algorithms. Data in ML is often stored in matrices (two-dimensional arrays) or tensors (higher-dimension arrays), whether that's categorical, image, or text data. As ML models have become larger there's been a lot of effort to make array operations more efficient so that models train faster.

The two most popular training frameworks for ML models, TensorFlow and PyTorch, offer optimized data structures for ML that take advantage of speedups gained by training on GPUs. You can easily convert NumPy arrays for either of these frameworks.

Create a NumPy array as before:

```
np_tensor = np.random.rand(4,4)
```

Then convert it to TensorFlow `tensor` format, like so:

```
import tensorflow as tf

tf_tensor = tf.convert_to_tensor(tensor_numpy)
```

Or to PyTorch `tensor` format:

```
import torch

pytorch_tensor = torch.from_numpy(np_tensor)
```

ML data structures are optimized for GPUs because these processors can run many tensor operations in parallel. Many ML algorithms are very easy to parallelize, including backpropagation in neural networks.

I also want to mention sparse matrices here. These are memory-efficient data structures for storing matrices that are mostly zeros. A common example of where these are useful is counting the frequency of different words in text data. For any given block of text, if the vocabulary you are using is large, most of the features are zeros. In scikit-learn, the `CountVectorizer` uses a SciPy sparse matrix. You can convert this to or from a NumPy array, but the sparse matrix is much more memory efficient.

Optimizing your ML model training is a huge topic that I won't cover here. If you want to get started with this, both PyTorch (*https://oreil.ly/Bz2H0*) and TensorFlow (*https://oreil.ly/zhG6e*) offer a profiler for figuring out where the bottlenecks are in your training code.

pandas DataFrames

pandas is one of the most popular libraries for doing data science in Python. It's a key library for manipulating and analyzing data. pandas has a reputation for being slow and memory intensive, but in this section I'll demonstrate a variety of ways you can improve its performance.

pandas was originally built on top of NumPy, which is an important thing to remember when you're working with it. Many of the principles that apply to NumPy arrays also apply to pandas DataFrames, but there are features specific to pandas. The 2.0 release of pandas in April 2023 added the option to use PyArrow (*https://oreil.ly/vVzYz*) data structures as a backend.

As with NumPy arrays, I won't cover all the functions associated with pandas DataFrames, and I again recommend *Python for Data Analysis* by Wes McKinney (O'Reilly, 2021) for full details.

DataFrame Functionality

pandas has two key data structures: DataFrames and Series. A DataFrame is made up of one or more Series. A Series is similar to a one-dimensional NumPy array, with the key addition that it also has an index. This lets you look up an item in a Series by its index as well as its location.

You can create a Series, like so:

```
usa_data = pd.Series([13.33, 14.02, 14.02, 14.25],
                     index=["2000", "2001", "2002", "2003"])
```

This gives you the following structure, where the year is the index:

```
2000    13.33
2001    14.02
2002    14.02
2003    14.25
dtype: float64
```

As with a NumPy array, a Series is created as a continuous block of memory. This means that some of the same performance considerations apply. For example, it's slow to append new items to the end of a Series because the whole structure must be moved to a new memory location. I'll talk in detail about performance considerations in the next section.

A pandas DataFrame is a two-dimensional arrangement of pandas Series structures, with a column index as well. You can construct one from pandas Series like so:

```
india_data = pd.Series([9.02, 9.01, 8.84, 8.84],
                       index=["2000", "2001", "2002", "2003"])

df = pd.DataFrame({'USA': usa_data, 'India': india_data})
```

This gives you the following DataFrame:

```
        USA     India
2000    13.33   9.02
2001    14.02   9.01
2002    14.02   8.84
2003    14.25   8.84
```

Unlike NumPy arrays, each column within a DataFrame can be a different type. pandas also offers an `object` column type so that you can mix data of different types within a Series. pandas also has more functions to handle missing data than NumPy.

pandas data structures are particularly useful for two-dimensional tabular data with row and column information. They're great for spreadsheet-style data as well. They can also be used similarly to database tables, giving you the option to join or query data, but this works best when your project is too small to be worth setting up a full database. pandas also offers many specialized functions for working with time series.

DataFrame Performance Considerations

Like NumPy, the pandas library has many vectorized operations that apply calculations to all the elements in an array at once. Many of these use NumPy under the hood. If you're doing something where a vectorized operation is available, this will almost always give you the best performance.

For example, arithmetic operations are vectorized:

```
>>> %%timeit
>>> df["India_fraction"] = df["India"] / 100

... 65.7 µs ± 1.01 µs per loop (mean ± std. dev. of 7 runs,
    10,000 loops each)
```

In addition to the vectorized operations available in NumPy, pandas includes vectorized string operations (*https://oreil.ly/CwzmR*). These include `lower`, `strip`, `split`, and so on. It's faster to use `df['column_name'].str.lower()` than the regular Python `.lower()` method.

If what you're trying to do isn't available as an inbuilt function, you can use `apply` with any function you define (more about `apply` in the next chapter). As you can see below, it adds some overhead to a calculation:

```
>>> %%timeit
>>> df["India_fraction"] = df["India"].apply(lambda x: x / 100)

... 87.7 µs ± 302 ns per loop (mean ± std. dev. of 7 runs,
    10,000 loops each)
```

If you want to perform some operation on every row of your DataFrame, it might seem intuitive to iterate through all the rows. And pandas provides the `iterrows` method for this. But as you can see below, this is much slower than using a vectorized operation or using `apply`, so it's something you should avoid:

```
>>> %%timeit
>>> df["India_fraction"] = [row['India'] / 100 for index, row in df.iterrows()]

... 348 µs ± 4.14 µs per loop (mean ± std. dev. of 7 runs,
    1,000 loops each)
```

By default, a pandas DataFrame is loaded into memory. So if your DataFrame is larger than your computer's memory, you have a problem. It's also difficult to estimate how much memory your data processing will take, so even if your DataFrame is smaller than your computer's memory you might still have a problem. Memory management in pandas is improving rapidly, but there are a few basic things that you can do if your DataFrame is larger than your computer's memory. First, you can simply only load the columns you want to work on. For example, you can specify the columns you want to read in a CSV file using the `usecols` argument in `read_csv`. Second, you can use the `chunksize` argument to create an iterator that will let you work on only a subset of rows at a time. The recent introduction of PyArrow as an optional pandas backend also gives support for more memory-efficient data types (*https://oreil.ly/kCzMf*).

Another option for larger amounts of data is to use the Dask library. As you saw with NumPy, if your data is much too large to fit in memory, Dask can split it up. It's also a great option if your data processing is slow and you want to parallelize it on multiple cores or machines. Dask has its own DataFrame (*https://oreil.ly/yv913*) data structure, and you can create one directly from your data or from an existing pandas DataFrame.

You also can consider switching to the Polars (*https://www.pola.rs*) library for improved performance with DataFrames. This is a less mature project than pandas, but it's faster and more memory efficient. The underlying code is written in Rust and uses Apache Arrow, but it has an interface very similar to pandas.

Key Takeaways

In this chapter, you've seen how to use data structures effectively for a variety of different use cases. As well as thinking about the expected performance you'll get from each of these data structures, it's important to measure their performance in the code you're writing and experiment with different options to see what will work best for the problem you're working on.

Often, Python's built-in data structures are all you need to solve your problem. Lists are an efficient choice if you need to look up items by their index, but searching for items in a list is relatively slow. Dictionaries are a good choice for frequent lookups using keys, and sets can be an efficient way of checking whether items are present.

NumPy arrays are perfect for multidimensional data. Because these arrays contain only one type of data, NumPy can go straight to fast, compiled C code for vectorized operations. This gives an enormous speedup, so if a vectorized method is available for the calculation you want to perform, definitely use it!

You can also take advantage of NumPy's types to reduce memory footprint and use Dask for larger memory arrays or for parallelized computations. In ML projects, you may find it advantageous to use data structures optimized for GPUs, and sparse matrices are also helpful.

pandas DataFrames are perfect for tabular data and for doing basic data analysis. They have similar performance considerations to NumPy arrays, and you should always use vectorized operations if they are available. It's very inefficient to iterate through the rows in a DataFrame. If you need more efficient performance than standard pandas, you can look into the Dask library or the Polars library.

If you'd like to learn more about the concepts in this chapter, I recommend these resources:

- *Python in a Nutshell* by Alex Martelli, Anna Martelli Ravenscroft, Steve Holden, and Paul McGuire (O'Reilly, 2023) for a good overview of Python data structures.
- *Python for Data Analysis* by Wes McKinney (O'Reilly, 2021) for more details on NumPy arrays and pandas DataFrames.
- *High Performance Python* by Micha Gorelick and Ian Osvald (O'Reilly, 2020) for much more detail on optimizing Python performance.
- *Scaling Python with Dask* by Holden Karau and Mika Kimmins (O'Reilly 2023) for more on how to use Dask for data science.
- Data science articles on the Python Speed website (*https://oreil.ly/ptdyp*).

## CHAPTER 4

Object-Oriented Programming and Functional Programming

In this chapter, I want to introduce you to two styles of programming that you'll likely encounter in your data science career: object-oriented programming (OOP) and functional programming (FP). It's extremely helpful to have an awareness of both. Even if you don't ever write code in either of these styles, you'll encounter packages that use one or other of them extensively. These include standard Python data science packages such as pandas and Matplotlib. I'd like to equip you with an understanding of OOP and FP so that you can use the code you encounter more effectively.

OOP and FP are programming paradigms based on underlying computer science principles. Some programming languages support only one of them or strongly favor one over the other. For example, Java is an object-oriented language. Python supports both. OOP is more popular as an overall style in Python, but you'll also see the occasional use of FP.

These styles also give you a framework for ways to break down your code. When you're writing code, you could just write everything you want to do as one single long script. This would still run just fine, but it's hard to maintain and debug. As discussed in Chapter 1, it's important to break code down into smaller chunks, and both OOP and FP can suggest good ways to do this.

In my code, I don't stick strictly to the principles of either functional or object-oriented programming. I sometimes define my own classes following OOP principles, and occasionally I write functions that conform to FP principles. Most modern Python programs occupy a middle ground combining both paradigms. In this chapter, I'll give you an overview of both styles so that you gain an understanding of the basics of both.

Object-Oriented Programming

Object-oriented programming is very common in Python. But what is an "object" in this context? You can think of an object as a "thing" that can be described by a noun. In data science code some common objects could be a pandas DataFrame, a NumPy array, a Matplotlib figure, or a scikit-learn estimator.

An object can hold data, it has some actions associated with it, and it can interact with other objects. For example, a pandas DataFrame object contains a list of column names. One action associated with a DataFrame object is renaming the columns. The DataFrame can interact with a pandas Series object by adding that series as a new column.

You can also think about an object as a custom data structure. You design it to hold the data you want so that you can do something with it later. Taking a pandas Data-Frame as an example again, the designers of pandas came up with a structure that could hold data in a tabular format. You can then access the data in rows and columns and operate on the data in those forms.

In the next section, I'll introduce the main terminology in OOP and show some examples of how you may already be using it.

Classes, Methods, and Attributes

Classes, methods, and attributes are important terms that you'll encounter in OOP. Here's an overview of each:

- A class defines an object, and you can think of it as a blueprint for making more objects of that variety. An individual object is an instance of that class, and each object is an individual "thing."

- Methods are something that you can do to objects of that class. They define the behavior of that object and may modify its attributes.

- Attributes are variables that are some property of that class, and each object can have different data stored in those attributes.

That's all very abstract, so I'll give you a more concrete example. Here's a way that object-oriented terminology could be adapted to the real world. The book you're currently reading, *Software Engineering for Data Scientists*, is an object of the class "Book." One of the attributes of this object is its number of pages and another is the name of the author. A method you could call on this object is to "read" it. There are many instances of the "Book" class, but they all have a certain number of pages, and they can all be read.

In Python, a class is usually named using CamelCase, so you would name a class MyClass rather than my_class. This convention helps you identify classes more easily. You can look up an attribute using the format class_instance.attribute. You can call a method using class_instance.method() (note that this includes parentheses). Methods may take arguments, but attributes cannot.

For example, let's consider a pandas DataFrame. You're likely to be familiar with the syntax for creating a new DataFrame:

```
import pandas as pd

my_dict = {"column_1": [1, 2], "column_2": ["a", "b"]}

df = pd.DataFrame(data=my_dict)
```

Looking at this from an object-oriented perspective, when you run the line df = pd.DataFrame(data=my_dict) you've initialized a new object of type DataFrame, and you've passed in some data that will be used to set up the attributes of that DataFrame.

You can look up some of the attributes of that DataFrame, like so:

```
df.columns
```

```
df.shape
```

.columns and .shape are attributes of the df object.

And you can call many methods on that DataFrame object, for example:

```
df.to_csv("file_path", index=False)
```

.to_csv() is the method in this example.

Another familiar example of creating a new object and calling a method comes from scikit-learn. If you're training a machine learning model on two arrays, with X_train containing the training features and y_train containing the training labels, you'd write some code like this:

```
from sklearn.linear_model import LogisticRegression

clf = LogisticRegression()
clf.fit(X_train, y_train)
```

In this example, you're initializing a new LogisticRegression classifier object and calling the .fit() method on it.

Here's another example. This is the code that creates Figure 2-3 in Chapter 2. Two objects are created here, a Matplotlib figure object and a Matplotlib axes object. Several methods are then called to do various operations to those objects, as I'll explain in the code annotations:

```
import matplotlib.pyplot as plt
import numpy as np

n = np.linspace(1, 10, 1000)
line_names = [
    "Constant",
    "Linear",
    "Quadratic",
    "Exponential",
    "Logarithmic",
    "n log n",
]
big_o = [np.ones(n.shape), n, n**2, 2**n, np.log(n), n * (np.log(n))]

fig, ax = plt.subplots() ❶
fig.set_facecolor("white") ❷

ax.set_ylim(0, 50) ❸
for i in range(len(big_o)):
    ax.plot(n, big_o[i], label=line_names[i])
ax.set_ylabel("Relative Runtime")
ax.set_xlabel("Input Size")
ax.legend()

fig.savefig(save_path, bbox_inches="tight") ❹
```

❶ Initialize `figure` and `axes` objects.

❷ Call the `set_facecolor` method on the `fig` object with an argument `white`.

❸ All the methods in the next few lines operate on the `ax` object.

❹ Saving the figure is a method called on the `fig` object.

The `figure` and `axes` objects have many methods that you can call to update these objects.

> Matplotlib sometimes feels confusing because it has two types of interface. One of these is object oriented, and the other is designed to imitate plotting in MATLAB. Matplotlib was first released in 2003, and its developers wanted to make it familiar to people who were accustomed to using MATLAB. These days, it's much more common to use the object-oriented interface as I've shown in the previous code example. But because people's code depends on both types of interface, they both still need to exist. The article "Why You Hate Matplotlib" (*https://oreil.ly/rYXUJ*) has more details on this topic.

Even if the terminology surrounding OOP is unfamiliar, you'll already be using it frequently in a lot of common data science packages. The next step is to define your own classes so that you can use an object-oriented approach in your own code.

Defining Your Own Classes

If you want to write your own code in an object-oriented style, you'll need to define your own classes. I'll show you a couple of simple examples for how to do this. The first one repeats some text a set number of times. The second one uses the UN Sustainable Development Goals data that I've used in other examples throughout this book. You can find more details about this data in "Data in This Book" on page 11.

In Python, you define a new class with the `class` statement:

```
class RepeatText():
```

It's very common to store some attributes every time a new instance of an object is initialized. To do this, Python uses a special method called `__init__`, which is defined like this:

```
def __init__(self, n_repeats):
    self.n_repeats = n_repeats
```

The first argument in the `__init__` method refers to the new instance of the object that gets created. By convention, this is usually named `self`. In this example, the `__init__` method takes one other argument: `n_repeats`. The line `self.n_repeats = n_repeats` means that each new instance of a `RepeatText` object has an `n_repeats` attribute, which must be provided each time a new object is initialized.

You can create a new `RepeatText` object like this:

```
repeat_twice = RepeatText(n_repeats=2)
```

Then you can access the `n_repeats` attribute with the following syntax:

```
>>> print(repeat_twice.n_repeats)
... 2
```

Defining another method looks similar to defining the `__init__` method, but you can give it any name you like, as if it were a normal function. As you'll see below, you still need the `self` argument if you want each instance of your object to have this behavior:

```
def multiply_text(self, some_text):
    print((some_text + " ") * self.n_repeats)
```

This method will look up the `n_repeats` attribute of the instance of the class that it acts on. This means you need to create an instance of a `RepeatText` object before you can use the method.

There are special methods in Python that don't take the `self` parameter as an argument: classmethods and staticmethods. Classmethods apply to a whole class, not just an instance of a class, and staticmethods can be called without creating an instance of the class. You can learn more about these in *Introducing Python* by Bill Lubanovic (O'Reilly, 2019).

You can call your newly created method like this:

```
>>> repeat_twice.multiply_text("hello")
... 'hello hello'
```

Here's the complete definition of the new class:

```python
class RepeatText():

    def __init__(self, n_repeats):
        self.n_repeats = n_repeats

    def multiply_text(self, some_text):
        print((some_text + " ") * self.n_repeats)
```

Let's look at another example. This time let's use the UN Sustainable Development Goal data introduced in Chapter 1. In the example below, I'm creating a `Goal5Data` object to hold some data relevant to Goal 5 (*https://oreil.ly/tw77-*), "Achieve gender equality and empower all women and girls." This particular object will hold data for one of the targets associated with this goal, Target 5.5: "Ensure women's full and effective participation and equal opportunities for leadership at all levels of decision-making in political, economic and public life."

I want to be able to create an object to store the data for each country so that I can easily manipulate it in the same way. Here's the code to create the new class and hold the data:

```python
class Goal5Data():
    def __init__(self, name, population, women_in_parliament):
        self.name = name
        self.population = population
        self.women_in_parliament = women_in_parliament  ❶
```

❶ This attribute holds a list of the percentage of seats in the country's governing body held by women, by year.

Here's a method that prints a summary of this data:

```python
def print_summary(self):
    null_women_in_parliament = len(self.women_in_parliament) -
    np.count_nonzero(self.women_in_parliament)
    print(f"There are {len(self.women_in_parliament)} data points for
    Indicator 5.5.1, 'Proportion of seats held by women in national
```

```
            parliaments'.")
        print(f"{null_women_in_parliament} are nulls.")
```

In the same way as the previous example, you can create a new instance of this class, like so:

```
usa = CountryData(name="USA",
                  population=336262544,
                  women_in_parliament=[13.33, 14.02, 14.02, ...])
```

Calling the `print_summary` method gives the following result:

```
>>> usa.print_summary()
... "There are 24 data points for Indicator 5.5.1,
    'Proportion of seats held by women in national parliaments'.
    0 are nulls."
```

Writing this as a method ensures the code is modular, well organized, and easy to reuse. It's also very clear what it is doing, which will help anyone who wants to use your code.

I'll use this class in the next section to show you another principle of classes: inheritance.

OOP Principles

You'll often encounter these terms in OOP: encapsulation, abstraction, inheritance, and polymorphism. I'll define all of these in this section and show some examples of how inheritance can be useful to you.

Inheritance

Inheritance means that you can extend a class by creating another class that builds on it. This helps reduce repetition, because if you need a new class that's closely related to one you have already written, you don't need to duplicate that class to make a minor change.

You may not need to use inheritance when defining your own classes, but you might need to use it with classes from an external library. You'll see a couple of examples of inheritance for data validation later in the book, in "Data Validation with Pydantic" on page 107 and in "Adding Functionality to Your API" on page 174. In this section, I want to help you spot and understand inheritance when you encounter it.

You can spot a class that uses inheritance because it will have the following syntax:

```
class NewClass(OriginalClass):
    ...
```

The NewClass class can use all the attributes and methods of the OriginalClass, but you can override any of these that you want to change. The term "parent" is often used to refer to the original class, and the new class that inherits from it is often called the "child" class.

Here's an example of a new class, Goal5TimeSeries that inherits from the Goal5Data class in the previous section, turning it into a class that can work with time series data:

```
class Goal5TimeSeries(Goal5Data):
    def __init__(self, name, population, women_in_parliament, timestamps):
        super().__init__(name, population, women_in_parliament)
        self.timestamps = timestamps
```

The __init__ method looks a little different this time. Using super() means that the parent class's __init__ method gets called, and this initializes the name, population, and women_in_parliament attributes.

You can create a new Goal5TimeSeries object, like so:

```
india = Goal5TimeSeries(name="India", population=1417242151,
                        women_in_parliament=[9.02, 9.01, 8.84, ...],
                        timestamps=[2000, 2001, 2002, ...])
```

And you can still access the method from the Goal5Data class:

```
>>> india.print_summary()
... "There are 24 data points for Indicator 5.5.1,
    'Proportion of seats held by women in national parliaments'. 0 are nulls."
```

You also can add a new method that's relevant to the child class. For example, this new fit_trendline() method fits a regression line to the data to find its trend:

```
from scipy.stats import linregress

class Goal5TimeSeries(Goal5Data):
    def __init__(self, name, population, women_in_parliament, timestamps):
        super().__init__(name, population, women_in_parliament)
        self.timestamps = timestamps

    def fit_trendline(self):
        result = linregress(self.timestamps, self.women_in_parliament)  ❶
        slope = round(result.slope, 3)
        r_squared = round(result.rvalue**2, 3)  ❷
        return slope, r_squared
```

❶ Use the linregress function from scipy to fit a straight line through the data using linear regression.

❷ Calculate the coefficient of determination (R-squared) to determine the goodness of fit of the line.

Calling the new method returns the slope of the trendline and the normalized root mean squared error of the fit of the line to the data:

```
>>> india.fit_trendline()
... (0.292, 0.869)
```

If you're using inheritance in your own classes, it lets you extend the capabilities of the classes you create. This means less duplication of code and it helps keep your code modular. It's also very helpful to inherit from classes in an external library. Again, this means that you don't duplicate their functionality but you can add extra features.

Encapsulation

Encapsulation means that your class hides its details from the outside. You can see only the interface to the class, not the internal details of what's going on. The interface is made up of the methods and attributes that you design. It's not so common in Python, but in other programming languages classes are often designed with hidden or private methods or attributes that can't be changed from the outside.

However, the concept of encapsulation is still applied in Python, and many libraries and applications take advantage of it. pandas is a great example of this. pandas uses encapsulation by providing methods and attributes that let you interact with data while keeping the underlying implementation details hidden. A DataFrame object encapsulates data and provides various methods for accessing, filtering, and transforming it. As I mentioned in Chapter 3, pandas DataFrames use NumPy under the hood, but you don't need to know this to use them. You can use the pandas Data-Frame interface to achieve your tasks, but if you need to dive deeper you can still use NumPy methods as well.

 Interfaces are extremely important because other code or classes will often depend on the existence of some attribute or method, so if you change that interface some other code may break. It's fine to change the internal workings of your class, for example, to change the calculations within some method to make it more efficient. But you should make the interface easy to use from the start and try not to change it. I'll discuss interfaces in more detail in Chapter 8.

Abstraction

Abstraction is closely linked to encapsulation. It means that you should deal with a class at the appropriate level of detail. So you might choose to keep the details of some calculation within a method, or you might allow it to be accessed through the interface. Again, this is more common in other programming languages.

Polymorphism

Polymorphism means that you can have the same interface for different classes, which simplifies your code and reduces repetition. That is, two classes can have a method with the same name that produces a similar result, but the internal workings are different. The two classes can be a parent and child class, or they can be unrelated.

scikit-learn contains a great example of polymorphism. Every classifier has the same `fit` method to train the classifier on some data, even though it's defined as a different class. Here's an example of training two different classifiers on some data:

```
from sklearn.linear_model import LogisticRegression
from sklearn.ensemble import RandomForestClassifier

lr_clf = LogisticRegression()
lr_clf.fit(X_train, y_train)

rf_clf = RandomForestClassifier()
rf_clf.fit(X_train, y_train)
```

Even though `LogisticRegression` and `RandomForestClassifier` are different classes, both of them have a `.fit()` method that takes the training data and training labels as arguments. Sharing the name of the method makes it easy for you to change the classifier without changing much of your code.

This was a brief overview of the main features of object-oriented programming. It's a huge topic, and I recommend *Introducing Python* by Bill Lubanovic (O'Reilly, 2019) if you would like to learn more.

Functional Programming

While Python supports the functional programming paradigm, it's not common to write Python in a purely FP style. Many software engineers have the opinion that other languages are more suitable for FP, such as Scala. However, useful FP features available in Python are very much worth knowing about, which I'll discuss below.

Functional programming, as the name suggests, is all about functions that don't change. These functions shouldn't change any data that exists outside the function or change any global variables. To use the correct terminology, the functions are immutable, "pure," and free of side effects. They don't affect anything that isn't reflected in what the function returns. For example, if you have a function that adds an item to a list, that function should return a new copy of the list rather than modifying the existing list. In strict FP, a program consists only of evaluating functions. These may be nested (where one function is defined within another) or functions may be passed as arguments to other functions.

Some advantages of FP include:

- It's easy to test because a function always returns the same output for a given input. Nothing outside the function is modified.
- It's easy to parallelize because data is not modified.
- It enforces writing modular code.
- It can be more concise and efficient.

Common Python concepts in a functional style include lambda functions and the map and filter built-in functions. In addition, generators are often written in this style, and list comprehensions can also be thought of as a form of FP. Other libraries worth knowing about for FP include itertools (*https://oreil.ly/ldikd*) and more-itertools (*https://oreil.ly/qOMsA*). I'll take a closer look at lambda functions and map() in the next section.

Lambda Functions and map()

Lambda functions are small, anonymous Python functions that you can use for quick one-off tasks. They are termed "anonymous" because they aren't defined like a normal Python function with a name.

A lambda function has the syntax:

```
lambda arguments: expression
```

A lambda function can take as many arguments as you like, but it can have only one expression. Lambda functions are frequently used with built-in functions like map and filter. These take functions as arguments and then can apply the function to every element in an iterable (such as a list).

Here's a simple example. Using the Goal 5 data from "Defining Your Own Classes" on page 53, you can convert a list of the percentages of women in government positions to a list of proportions from 0 to 1 using the following function:

```
usa_govt_percentages = [13.33, 14.02, 14.02, 14.25, ...]

usa_govt_proportions = list(map(lambda x: x / 100, usa_govt_percentages))
```

There's a lot going on in one line here. The lambda function in this case is lambda x: x/100. In this function, x is a temporary variable that isn't used outside the function. map() applies the lambda function to every element in the list. And finally, list() creates a new list based on the map.

This gives the following result:

```
>>> print(usa_govt_proportions)
... [0.1333, 0.1402, 0.1402, 0.1425, ...]
```

Note that the original data was not changed by applying this function. A new list was created with the altered data.

Applying Functions to DataFrames

In a similar way to the `map()` built-in function above, you can also apply functions to DataFrames. This can be particularly useful if you want to create a new column based on an existing column. Again, you can use a function that takes another function as an input. In pandas, this is `apply()`.

Here's an example of applying a lambda function to a column in a DataFrame:

```
df["USA_processed"] = df["United States of America"].apply(lambda x:
                                            "Mostly male"
                                            if x < 50
                                            else "Mostly female")
```

In this example, the column `United States of America` is the data on women in government positions that I've been using throughout the chapter. The lambda function takes the percentage of women in government positions and returns `"Mostly male"` if that figure is under 50%, or `"Mostly female"` if it is 50% or greater.

You can also use `df.apply()` with a named function defined elsewhere as well. Here's the same function as before but as a named function:

```
def binary_labels(women_in_govt):
    if women_in_govt < 50:
        return "Mostly male"
    else:
        return "Mostly female"
```

You can call this function on every row in a column by passing the function name as an argument to the `apply` function:

```
df["USA_processed"] = df["United States of America"].apply(binary_labels)
```

This is a better solution than writing a lambda function because you may want to reuse the function in the future, and you can also test and debug it separately. You can also include more complex functionality than in a lambda function.

 The `apply` function in pandas is slower than built-in vectorized functions because it iterates through every row in a DataFrame. So best practice is to use `apply` only for something that's not already implemented. Simple numeric operations like getting the maximum of a list or simple string options such as replacing one string with another are already available as faster vectorized functions, so you should use these built-in functions where possible.

Which Paradigm Should I Use?

To be honest, if you're just writing a small script or working on a short project on your own, you don't need to fully buy in to either of these paradigms. Just stick to modular scripts that work.

For larger projects, however, it's a great idea to think about the type of problem you're dealing with and whether one of these paradigms is a good fit. You might reach for OOP if you find yourself thinking about a set of things that need something done to them. You can turn your problem space into instances that need to have similar behavior but different attributes or data. An important point here is that you should have many instances of some class. It isn't worth writing a new class if you have only one instance of it; that just adds extra complexity you don't need.

If you find yourself wanting to do new things to some data that remains fixed, FP might be a good choice for you. It's also worth looking at FP if you have a large amount of data and you want to parallelize the operations you do to it.

There's no right or wrong here, though. You can go with your personal preference if you're working alone, or go with what's predominantly used in your team to keep things standardized. It's good to recognize when these paradigms are being used, use them in other people's code, and make decisions about what would work best for your specific problem.

Key Takeaways

OOP and FP are programming paradigms that you'll encounter in the code you read. OOP is concerned with objects, which are custom data structures, and FP is concerned with functions that don't change the underlying data.

In OOP, a class defines new objects, which can have attributes and methods. You can define your own classes to keep associated methods and data together, and this is a great approach to use when you have many instances of similar objects. You can use inheritance to avoid repeating code, and you can use polymorphism to keep your interfaces standardized.

In FP, ideally everything is within the function. This is useful when you have data that doesn't change and you want to do lots of things to it, or you want to parallelize what you are doing to the data. Lambda functions are the most commonly used example of FP in Python.

Your choice of paradigm depends on the problem you are working on, but you'll find it useful to have an awareness of both.

## CHAPTER 5

Errors, Logging, and Debugging

In this chapter, I'll introduce some techniques for making your code more robust. Robustness is one of the principles of writing good code that I discussed in Chapter 1. First, I'll discuss how to handle errors in your code so that your code behaves predictably even if something goes wrong. Next, I'll show you how to save information about what your code is doing by logging it, which will help other people reason about your code and also help when an unexpected error occurs. Finally, I'll talk about debugging, which is how to track down sources of problems in your code. I'll explain some strategies and tools for efficient debugging.

Errors in Python

An error is when your code stops unexpectedly before the program has completed all the tasks it is supposed to do. If this happens, whatever depends on your code may also stop. Sometimes, this is what you want to happen, but sometimes you want something else to happen so that your code continues running. This is known as handling the error. Your code should be predictable for the set of things that you expect to happen, and this makes it robust.

In this section I'll discuss how to read Python error messages, how to handle them, and how to raise your own errors.

Reading Python Error Messages

Python error messages may look cryptic, but they are full of useful information. There are two types: syntax errors and exceptions. Syntax errors arise when you write code that isn't completely correct Python language, for example, failing to close parentheses or forgetting def in a function definition. These can't be correctly parsed by the Python interpreter, and the code stops and returns an error.

Exceptions comprise all other errors, for example, a missing input to a function or trying to look up the value for a key that doesn't exist in a dictionary.

In this next example, I'll deliberately generate an error to show how to interpret Python error messages. Here's the trendline code you saw in Chapter 4 as a separate function, but the `data` argument is missing in the function definition:

```
from scipy.stats import linregress

def fit_trendline(year_timestamps):
    result = linregress(year_timestamps, data)
    slope = round(result.slope, 3)
    r_squared = round(result.rvalue**2, 3)
    return slope, r_squared
```

You could try and run the function with only one argument:

```
fit_trendline(timestamps)
```

But this gives the following error:

```
---------------------------------------------------------------------
NameError                                Traceback (most recent call last)
Cell In[7], line 1
----> 1 fit_trendline(timestamps)

Cell In[6], line 2, in fit_trendline(year_timestamps)
      1 def fit_trendline(year_timestamps):
----> 2     result = linregress(year_timestamps, data) ❶
      3     slope = round(result.slope, 3)
      4     r_squared = round(result.rvalue**2, 3)

NameError: name 'data' is not defined ❷
```

❶ The line in the code that is the source of the error

❷ The type of error and a suggestion for how to correct it

Python errors are printed as tracebacks. They show all the functions that were called that produced the error. Sometimes this includes details of Python internals or libraries you are using, so it looks a bit overwhelming, but they contain lots of useful information to help you figure out the cause of the error.

A good strategy for dealing with Python error messages is to start at the end of the message. The last line tells you what type of error you are dealing with (for example, `NameError`) and some information on how to fix the error, if Python thinks it can help you. Above the details of the type of error, you'll see your code with an arrow pointing to the line that caused the error. This is a good starting point for looking for the problem, but as this example shows, the problem is actually in the previous line where the `data` argument is missing in the function definition.

Errors can also arise from modules that you have imported, for example, if you give the wrong type of input to an imported function. These can look more confusing because, in addition to highlighting the line in your code where the error came from, the error message includes the line in the imported function, plus any other functions it called. Even if the error message is very long, the same strategy applies: start at the end and work backward to try and solve the problem.

 Error messages in Python have seen substantial improvements in versions 3.10 (*https://oreil.ly/QpddI*) and 3.11 (*https://oreil.ly/J7nxs*). The newer versions are much more readable and informative, and improvements include syntax errors that point to the correct location in your code, rather than the previous line in many cases. It's worth upgrading to a recent version of Python if you are able.

Handling Errors

In many situations, you may not want your code to stop when it encounters an error. This is important if some other function is depending on your function to return a result: if your function raises an error, it may cause a cascade of errors in a larger system. If this is the case, you should "handle" the error so that your code behaves predictably.

Python uses the keywords `try` and `except` to handle errors. This takes the form of two code blocks:

```
try:
    # some code that you want to run
except KeyError:
    # what you want to happen instead
    # if an error of this type is raised
```

The `try` block contains some code that you want to run but may encounter an error. The `except` block states what you want to happen in the event of a certain type of error, in this case a `KeyError`. For example, you might have some code that looks up a value for some key in a dictionary. If the key is not present in the dictionary, you might choose to return a default value instead of stopping the code with an error.

You can have multiple `except` blocks, with code that you want to run in the event of particular types of exception, or you can handle multiple types of error in one `except` block. This takes the following syntax: `except (KeyError, ValueError):`.

You can also have an `else` block, which must be after the except block. This contains code that runs after the `try` block if no error is raised. Another feature of Python error handling is a `finally` block that runs whether or not an error is raised, and this must go after the `try`, `except`, and optional `else` blocks. The `finally` block is most often used to release a resource, such as closing an open file. Figure 5-1 shows this flow. The Python documentation (*https://oreil.ly/GkThO*) contains more details about error handling syntax.

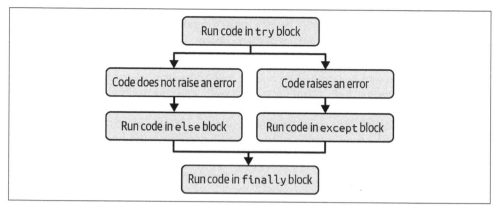

Figure 5-1. Sequence of execution for the try, except, else, and finally blocks

I'll illustrate error handling using the trendline function from "Reading Python Error Messages" on page 63, with the correct arguments this time:

```
from scipy.stats import linregress

def fit_trendline(year_timestamps, data):
    result = linregress(year_timestamps, data)
    slope = round(result.slope, 3)
    r_squared = round(result.rvalue**2, 3)
    return slope, r_squared
```

I'll run it with some incorrect inputs to cause it to throw an exception:

```
timestamps = ["2000", "2001", "2002"]
data = [18.36, 18.36, 17.91]

fit_trendline(timestamps, data)
```

This gives a `ValueError` because both lists must consist of floats or integers. You can handle this error so that the code runs without raising an error using try, except, and else blocks, like so:

```
def fit_trendline(year_timestamps, data):
    try:
        result = linregress(year_timestamps, data)
    except TypeError:
        print(f"Both lists must contain only float or integers,
        got {data.dtype} and {year_timestamps.dtype}")
    else:
        slope = round(result.slope, 3)
        r_squared = round(result.rvalue**2, 3)
        return slope, r_squared
```

If an error is raised, the code prints the message "Both lists must contain only floats or integers" and includes the details of what type of data was provided. If no error is raised in the first line, the else block runs.

It's important that your error messages are informative and easy to read. Good error messages can save you and anyone else who works on your code a lot of time by providing clear guidance on what went wrong and where in the code the error occurred. Your error message should describe what the problem was and ideally also what should be done to fix it.

You can also return some default value in the except block. It's a good idea to keep this in the same format as the function returns if it is successful. This keeps the interface to your function consistent. If you have some other code that depends on this function returning answers of some specific type, it will still run regardless of whether this function encountered this error.

Here's an example where the except block returns a default value:

```
def fit_trendline(year_timestamps, data):
    try:
        result = linregress(year_timestamps, data)
    except TypeError:
        print("Both lists must contain floats or integers.")
        return 0.0, 0.0
    else:
        slope = round(result.slope, 3)
        r_squared = round(result.rvalue**2, 3)
        return slope, r_squared
```

This function now returns a tuple of two floats whether it encounters an error or not.

When I was thinking about this book, I looked at some code that I wrote before I got my first data science job. This code illustrates how you should not handle errors:

```
except:
    return
```

Please don't do this! This code will silence all the errors it encounters, and you won't know that a function hasn't worked. It's much better for your function to behave predictably, even when it receives an incorrect input.

Raising Errors

In some circumstances, you might want your code to raise an error when something unexpected happens. You might want any code that depends on your function to also stop. In this situation, you can use the raise keyword in Python to raise an error even if it wouldn't normally trigger an error, and you can customize what that error is.

In this next example, I'll check if any of the inputs to the `fit_trendline` function are empty lists and raise an error if this occurs:

```
from scipy.stats import linregress

def fit_trendline(year_timestamps, data):
    if not year_timestamps or data:
        raise ValueError("Timestamps and data cannot be empty lists")
    result = linregress(year_timestamps, data)
    slope = round(result.slope, 3)
    r_squared = round(result.rvalue**2, 3)
    return slope, r_squared
```

You can provide a custom error message using the syntax `raise {error}('Message')`.

You can run this function with an empty list:

```
fit_trendline([], [18.36, 18.36, 17.91])
```

It returns the following result, including the custom error message:

```
---------------------------------------------------------------------
ValueError                                 Traceback (most recent call last)
Cell In[27], line 1
----> 1 fit_trendline([], [18.36, 18.36, 17.91])

Cell In[26], line 3, in fit_trendline(year_timestamps, data)
      1 def fit_trendline(year_timestamps, data):
      2     if not year_timestamps or data:
----> 3         raise ValueError('Timestamps and data cannot be empty lists')
      4     result = linregress(year_timestamps, data)
      5     slope = round(result.slope, 3)

ValueError: Timestamps and data cannot be empty lists
```

The error message should be informative to the person who reads it, and this is part of making your code readable. "An error occurred" is not a useful error message.

Here's an example of a useful error message I encountered while writing Chapter 2:

```
"UsageError: Cell magic `%%lprun` not found (But line magic `%lprun` exists,
did you mean that instead?)."
```

It told me what was wrong, and what I should do to correct the error.

You can also define custom errors if none of the Python errors covers what you want. This is also good practice for large projects, because you can give errors custom names to allow the code's users to easily tell where the error has come from. Defining a new error takes the form:

```
class NewException(Exception):
```

This is an example of "Inheritance" on page 55, where the new error class inherits from the Exception class. You can read more about defining custom errors in this article (*https://oreil.ly/P0bj9*).

Using custom errors can make your code easier to read and maintain. When errors are well defined, other parts of the code can handle specific errors and respond appropriately. This ensures that errors from different parts of the codebase do not get mixed up. This level of granularity in error handling helps prevent unintended consequences. It also makes debugging and troubleshooting more efficient.

Logging

Logging is a method of recording what your code has done in a separate file while it runs. This means that your code can communicate to other people what is going on, and this helps other people reason about your code. It helps make your code more readable and more robust because there is a record of what happens if it goes wrong.

Logging lets you save a record of what your code has done. It's different from just getting your code to print out messages, because you can save things to a separate file that you can search. This is particularly useful for long-running processes or code that has been deployed to a production system. In these situations, you don't want to stop your code to find out what is happening or what has gone wrong.

I'll give a basic introduction to logging here, but if you'd like to dive into more detail I recommend the logging tutorials (*https://oreil.ly/8s5Ey*) in the Python docs.

What to Log

The logging module in Python lets you record whatever message you would like. What's useful to log? This will depend on your exact use case and project but could include:

- A message to say that a long-running task has started or finished
- Error messages so that you know what has gone wrong in a production system
- Which functions called some other functions
- The inputs and outputs of a function
- The file path where some data has been saved

Logging is hugely helpful in debugging a production system or a long-running task, and I'll talk about this much more in "Debugging" on page 73.

Logging can also serve as evidence that your code has done what it was supposed to do. If this is useful to your project, include log messages that state a task has happened and the result. An example of this could be logging the accuracy of a machine learning model when it has finished training.

A good strategy is to err on the side of logging more, not less. If your messages are structured in a standardized way or include specific keywords, you can search the log file and easily find what you're looking for. It's also important to be specific in your log messages. A message that reads `"started saving file"` is not useful. What are the contents of the file? What is the filename? F-strings are a neat way of handling this use case:

```
f"Saving {variable_name} data to {file_name}"
```

In the next sections, I'll describe how to log messages using the Python `logging` module.

Logging Configuration

The `logging` module from the Python standard library is big and extensive, but you need only a small subset of the functions within it. The library handles saving any messages you log to a separate file, so you don't need to worry about how to save it. But you do need some configuration settings.

The first configuration setting to consider is the severity level of the logs that get recorded. The Python logging module has five different severity levels, from `DEBUG` (least severe) to `CRITICAL` (most severe). This allows you to filter the logs to easily find the messages you're looking for or only log messages above a certain level, depending on your use case. For example, you might want to log messages at the `DEBUG` level when you're developing your code but then only log errors and more severe messages when your code is running in production.

Table 5-1 from the Python documentation describes all five levels of logging:

Table 5-1. Python logging levels[a]

Level	When it's used
DEBUG	Detailed information, typically of interest only when diagnosing problems.
INFO	Confirmation that things are working as expected.
WARNING	An indication that something unexpected happened, or indicative of some problem in the near future (for example, "disk space low"). The software is still working as expected.
ERROR	Due to a more serious problem, the software has not been able to perform some function.
CRITICAL	A serious error, indicating that the program itself may be unable to continue running.

[a] Source: *https://oreil.ly/6iVoR*

The default logging level in the Python logging module is WARNING, so anything at this level or more severe gets logged automatically. This means that if you write messages at the INFO level without changing the logging level, they won't get saved.

Before you log anything, set the level using:

```
import logging

logging.basicConfig(level=logging.DEBUG)
```

In this case, because the level is set to DEBUG, every level from DEBUG to CRITICAL will be logged. This line needs to go at the start of your Python script, before you start logging anything.

The other default setting you will likely want to override is where the logs are saved. The default is to print the logs to the console, but logs are most useful if they are saved in a file so that you can consult them after your code has finished running.

If you want to save your logs to a separate file, add this setting to the configuration at the start of your script:

```
logging.basicConfig(filename='chapter_5_logs.log', level=logging.DEBUG)
```

The default setting when writing to a file is to append the logs to the file each time the code runs. If you want to overwrite the file, use filemode='w':

```
logging.basicConfig(filename='chapter_5_logs.log', filemode='w',
                    level=logging.DEBUG)
```

As well as saving messages to a file, log viewers can pick up the output from the Python logging module and save or display it elsewhere. There are built-in solutions for this in production systems using cloud providers such as Amazon Web Services (AWS), and these will often use the handlers (*https://oreil.ly/apGQb*) in the Python logging module. Standalone tools such as Kibana (*https://oreil.ly/Cgkn7*) and Prometheus (*https://prometheus.io*) also will pick up logs generated by your code.

How to Log

Once you've set your logging configuration at the start of your script, the next step is to decide what to log. I'll add a couple of lines of logging to the fit_trendline function at the INFO level using the logging.info function, which takes the message you want to log as an argument:

```
from scipy.stats import linregress

def fit_trendline(year_timestamps, data):
    logging.info("Running fit_trendline function")
```

```
result = linregress(year_timestamps, data)
slope = round(result.slope, 3)
r_squared = round(result.rvalue**2, 3)
logging.info(f"Completed analysis. Slope of the trendline is {slope}.")
return slope, r_squared
```

You can run this function as before:

```
fit_trendline(timestamps, data)
```

It will produce this in the log file:

```
INFO:root:Running fit_trendline function
INFO:root:Completed analysis. Slope of the trendline is 0.836.
```

It can be useful to add a timestamp to your logs so that you know when you ran that particular line of code and for easier searching later. You can do this in the configuration settings at the start of the script using the format argument:

```
logging.basicConfig(filename="chapter_5_logs.log",
                    level=logging.DEBUG,
                    format='%(asctime)s %(message)s') ❶
```

❶ The format argument has many options, which are described in the Python logging documentation (*https://oreil.ly/wUJdq*).

This gives the following messages:

```
2023-05-26 11:37:43,951 Running fit_trendline function
2023-05-26 11:37:43,953 Completed analysis. Slope of the trendline is 0.836.
```

It's a good idea to log error messages, and you can do this using logging.exception as shown here:

```
def fit_trendline(year_timestamps, data):
    logging.info("Running fit_trendline function")
    try:
        result = linregress(year_timestamps, data)
    except TypeError as e:
        logging.error("Both lists must contain floats or integers.") ❶
        logging.exception(e) ❷
    else:
        slope = round(result.slope, 3)
        r_squared = round(result.rvalue**2, 3)
        logging.info(f"Completed analysis. Slope of the trendline is {slope}.")
        return slope, r_squared
```

❶ Logs a message at level "Error"

❷ Records the entire traceback in the logs

logging.exception() is very useful because the entire traceback is recorded in the logs, and you can then use this for debugging.

You can use the logging module in a Jupyter notebook, which can preserve your results in a log file so that you don't need to rerun the notebook. This may be a better option than copying and pasting your results into a Markdown cell, but it means you have another file to keep track of. You can also use experiment tracking solutions such as the ones I describe in "Documenting Machine Learning Experiments" on page 141.

Debugging

Debugging means finding and removing bugs in your code. A bug is when your code is throwing unexpected errors or producing results that you don't expect. Debugging is an essential skill for writing code, and you'll want to have a variety of techniques when you're dealing with larger codebases so that you have something to suit any situation. In this section, I'll describe some strategies for finding bugs and then describe some tools for debugging.

Strategies for Debugging

My favourite way to get information about buggy code is to run the buggy code and experiment on it. (Add print statements! Make a tiny change!).

—Julia Evans

As you gain experience, you'll probably come up with your own favorite strategies for tracking down difficult bugs. However, a great starting point, as recommended in Julia Evans's quote, is to do what a data scientist does best: run an experiment! You can make a small change to your code and see how this affects the results while being sure to change only one thing at a time.

I'll cover this in Chapter 7, but tests are super useful here. A test will let you know whether a change that you make produces the result you expect from your code (the test passes) or not (the test fails).

Another top tip is to save a copy of whatever caused the error, whether this is the inputs to your function or the results of a particular database query. This is where logging can be very helpful, because you have a record of what has happened.

You're also probably not the first person to make the mistake that's causing your error message. A wealth of information is available on the internet to help you solve your problems. Searching for your error message on Google is a great starting point.

Talking to other people about your code is another great strategy for finding bugs. Explaining it to your teammate or just talking about it out loud to a rubber duck makes you think through what you've been doing a little differently than just looking at your code, and you may well find the solution. Other people can also share their experiences and help you out.

Everyone has bugs in their code and, even though not all workplace cultures encourage this, it should be acceptable to say you don't know something or that you have made a mistake. I certainly write code that has a lot of bugs. Some of them are subtle and difficult to find; others are simple but can be frustrating to track down. Even as I write this book, someone has already emailed me to let me know they spotted a mistake in the code in the early online edition of the book!

Another excellent debugging strategy is to take a break from coding. Make a cup of tea, go for a walk, work on something else. The solution might come to you while you're doing something completely different or when you come back to your code with fresh eyes. A break also helps you think of different possible causes for your bug.

Sometimes you need to delve into your code in detail, and the tools in the next section will be very helpful to you.

Tools for Debugging

Tools for debugging help you track exactly what is going on in your code. If you can get information on the values associated with a named variable in your code, this is extremely useful in checking that your code is indeed doing what you think it should be doing. The simplest possible way of doing this is to add `print` statements to your code, but you can get more information by using debugging tools. These provide a way to pause your code and display the value of any particular variable, then move through that code one step at a time.

I'll illustrate this with some of the example code from Chapter 2. In this example, the `weighted_mean` function contains a bug, and it won't return the correct result:

```
def weighted_mean(num_list, weights):
    running_total = 0
    for i in range(len(num_list)):
        running_total += (num_list[i] * weights[0])  ❶
    return (running_total/len(num_list))
```

❶ The mistake is in this line: instead of `weights[0]` it should be `weights[i]`.

Adding a `print` statement might help you find the bug, like so:

```
def weighted_mean(num_list, weights):
    running_total = 0
    for i in range(len(num_list)):
        running_total += (num_list[i] * weights[0])
        print(f"The running total at step {i} is {running_total}")
    return (running_total/len(num_list))
```

Running this function gives you the following output:

```
>>> print(weighted_mean([1, 6, 8], [1, 3, 2]))
... The running total at step 0 is 1
... The running total at step 1 is 7
... The running total at step 2 is 15
...
... 5.0
```

This tells you your running total is not being calculated correctly. It should be 19 at step 1 and 35 at step 2.

However, it's not best practice to clutter your code with `print` statements. These make it harder to pick out the result of your code and if your code is running on a production system, you may not have access to the output.

Another option is to log the intermediate values of your code as described in "Logging" on page 69. Here's an example:

```python
import logging

logging.basicConfig(filename="chapter_5_logs.log",
                    level=logging.DEBUG,
                    format='%(asctime)s %(message)s')

def weighted_mean(num_list, weights):
    running_total = 0
    for i in range(len(num_list)):
        running_total += (num_list[i] * weights[0])
        logging.debug(f"The running total at step {i} is {running_total}")
    return (running_total/len(num_list))
```

This will produce the following output in the log file:

```
2023-06-01 17:14:56,976 The running total at step 0 is 1
2023-06-01 17:14:56,980 The running total at step 1 is 7
2023-06-01 17:14:56,980 The running total at step 2 is 15
```

This output is saved in a separate file, which means that you could access it on a production system.

`print` statements or logging might be fine for small programs like this one, but what if you have tens of variables in your function? What if some of the variables you want to log large dictionaries? You can see how this would quickly become unwieldy. Luckily this is a problem software engineers often come across, and there is a range of tools (debuggers) to help you in this situation.

Debuggers use the concept of breakpoints. Breakpoints are points you select where you want to pause code execution and inspect the state of some variable (or a saved file or database). You can check that everything is what you expect, and then step through your code to see how the variables change, and this will help you find the source of your bug.

Integrated development environments commonly include a debugger. I'll illustrate how to use one using the debugger in VS Code, but it's very similar in other IDEs.

In the next example, I'll show you how to debug the following runnable script:

```
def weighted_mean(num_list, weights):
    running_total = 0
    for i in range(len(num_list)):
        running_total += (num_list[i] * weights[0]) ❶
    return (running_total/len(num_list))

weighted_mean([1, 6, 8], [1, 3, 2])
```

❶ I've added a breakpoint to this line of code.

Using the debugger, you can easily step through what each variable is at any point in the function. It highlights the changes with each step in the loop.

Figure 5-2 shows the first iteration through the loop.

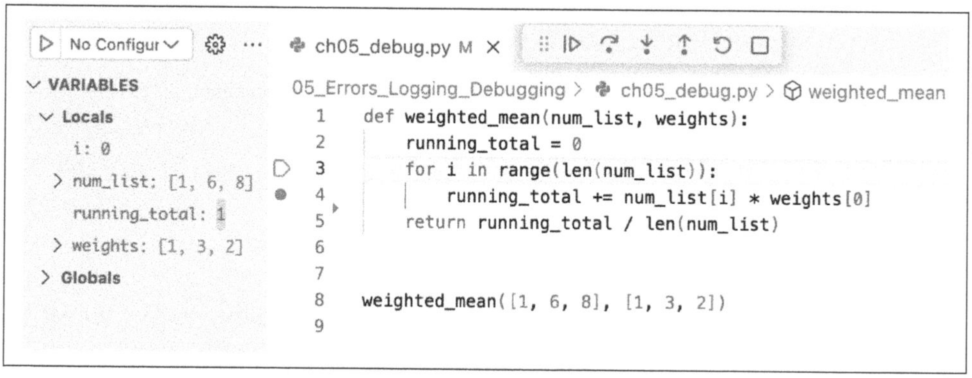

Figure 5-2. Showing the variables in an IDE debugger, iteration 1

The debugger shows that the value of running_total is 1 when the value of i is 0.

Next, I'll step through the lines of code to the second iteration, when i has a value of 1. As you can see in Figure 5-3, the running total is incorrect at this point. It should be (1 * 1) + (3 * 6) = 19, but instead it's 7.

```
 ▷  No Configur ∨   ⚙  ⋯      ⬡ ch05_debug.py M  ✕     ⠿ |▷  ⤳  ↧  ↑  ↺  ☐

∨ VARIABLES                    05_Errors_Logging_Debugging > ⬡ ch05_debug.py > ◈ weighted_mean
 ∨ Locals                       1   def weighted_mean(num_list, weights):
    i: 1                        2       running_total = 0
   > num_list: [1, 6, 8]     ▷  3   |   for i in range(len(num_list)):
                             ●  4   |       running_total += num_list[i] * weights[0]
    running_total: 7            5   |▸  return running_total / len(num_list)
   > weights: [1, 3, 2]         6
 > Globals                      7
                                8   weighted_mean([1, 6, 8], [1, 3, 2])
                                9
```

Figure 5-3. Showing the variables in an IDE debugger, iteration 2 (note that the values of i *and* running_total *have changed)*

The bug is in the fourth line of the function. Here's the corrected line:

```
running_total += (num_list[i] * weights[i])
```

The exact details of how to use the debugger will depend on which IDE you are using, but all will have similar features. You can find more details in the VS Code documentation (*https://oreil.ly/j9K2a*) and the PyCharm documentation (*https://oreil.ly/xQkOW*).

You can also use the debugging functionality if you're running a Jupyter notebook in an IDE, as shown in Figure 5-4.

```
 F |▷  No Configur ∨   ⚙  ⋯     ▤ chapter_05.ipynb  ✕     ⠿ |▷  ⤳  ↧  ↑  ↺  ⬀

∨ VARIABLES                    05_Errors_Logging_Debugging > ▤ chapter_05.ipynb > Mↆ Errors, logging and debugging
 ∨ Locals                       + Code  + Markdown  |  ☐ Interrupt  ↺ Restart  ≡ Clear All Outputs  ⟳ Go To  |
    i: 1
   > num_list: [1, 6, 8]     ▷       def weighted_mean(num_list, weights):
    running_total: 7         ▷           running_total = 0
   > weights: [1, 3, 2]      ●           for i in range(len(num_list)):
 > Globals                               |   running_total += num_list[i] * weights[0]
                                         return running_total / len(num_list)
                             [1]   ✓  0.0s

                                     weighted_mean([1, 6, 8], [1, 3, 2])
∨ WATCH                       [2]   ⟳
```

Figure 5-4. Debugging a notebook in an IDE

You can simply add a breakpoint in the same way as in a standalone script.

You also can still use a debugger even if you're not using an IDE. pdb (*https://oreil.ly/78KQu*) is a command line debugger that is included in the Python standard library.

To use it, add the `breakpoint()` method in your code, like so:

```
def weighted_mean(num_list, weights):
    running_total = 0
    for i in range(len(num_list)):
        running_total += (num_list[i] * weights[0])
        breakpoint()
    return (running_total/len(num_list))

weighted_mean([1, 6, 8], [1, 3, 2])
```

Then simply run your script as normal:

```
$ python ch05_debug.py
```

The code will run until it reaches the breakpoint and then open up the pdb debugger, giving you an output that looks like this:

```
> /Users/.../ch05_debug.py(3)weighted_mean()
-> for i in range(len(num_list)):
(Pdb)
```

You can show the value of any variable with p *variable_name*:

```
(Pdb) p running_total
1
(Pdb) p weights
[1, 3, 2]
```

And go to the next line with n:

```
(Pdb) n
> /Users/.../ch05_debug.py(4)weighted_mean()
-> running_total += (num_list[i] * weights[0])
(Pdb) n
> /Users/.../ch05_debug.py(5)weighted_mean()
-> breakpoint()
(Pdb) n
> /Users/.../ch05_debug.py(3)weighted_mean()
-> for i in range(len(num_list)):
(Pdb) p running_total
7
```

When you're done, you can stop debugging with q, and this exits your script:

```
(Pdb) q
```

When you've finished using pdb, you'll need to go through your code and delete all the `breakpoint()` calls; otherwise pdb will start every time you run your script. In Chapter 12 I'll show you a way to automatically remove these.

Table 5-2 lists command shortcuts for pdb based on this article by Nina Zakharenko (*https://oreil.ly/z1sx2*).

Table 5-2. pdb commands

Command shortcut	Function
p expr	Print the value of the expression
l	Print the lines of code around the current line
n	Step to the next line
c	Continue to the next breakpoint
r	Continue until the current function returns
q	Quit and finish debugging

pdb gives you the same functionality as the debugger in an IDE, but it's good to be aware of a few different tools so that you can use the one that suits your situation. If you're developing code in an IDE, it's easiest to use the debugger that's included with it, but if you're running your script at the command line, pdb is better suited.

Key Takeaways

This chapter has been all about making your code more robust, and logging also makes it more readable. I've also given a brief overview of skills for finding and solving problems in your code.

Proper handling of errors keeps your code robust to unexpected inputs, and you should raise your own custom errors when necessary.

Logging saves a record of what your code has done, which is particularly useful for production code or scripts that take a long time to run. The Python built-in logging module contains all the functionality you need.

It's very useful to have a variety of strategies and tools for tracking and removing bugs from your code. Debugging tools range from `print` statements, through logging, to specific debugging tools, and I'll also talk about how you can use tests for debugging in Chapter 7.

## CHAPTER 6

Code Formatting, Linting, and Type Checking

This chapter covers tools you can use to help you with some of the more tedious aspects of writing code. Code formatting, linting, and type checking tools analyze your code to check for mistakes or areas for improvement. Code formatting tools concentrate on how your code looks, while linting and type checking tools ensure that your code functions correctly.

You might be wondering why the formatting of your code gets so much attention. Why does it matter what your code looks like? Why do people spend their precious time setting standards for the number of spaces around a + sign? It's because consistent, standardized formatting makes your code much easier to read. And, as discussed in Chapter 1, if your code is more readable it's much more likely to get reused. Formatting tools mean that you don't have to spend time updating the aesthetics of your code manually.

Linting and type checking tools help ensure that your code is robust. When you run Python code, syntax errors will crash your code straight away wherever they are in the script, but if you have another mistake (for example, a misspelled variable name) the error will not show up until this line. If your script takes a long time to run, this is frustrating. Linters and associated tools can help you find some of these mistakes before you run your code.

My key message in this chapter is that you should use tools rather than checking your code manually. The details of your code formatting are very boring. This is not where you want to spend your time. I'll show you how to set up your tools and make good use of your IDE so that the standards you need to conform to are automatically applied.

Many of the tools I describe in this chapter don't work in the Jupyter Notebook. They're not appropriate for code that's divided into separate cells; instead they're designed for use on longer scripts. So in this chapter, I'll give examples of how to run the tools on standalone scripts.

Code Formatting and Style Guides

Formatting your code according to a style guide is an important part of writing good code. A style guide can be set by a company, for example Google's style guide (*https:// oreil.ly/8yGQU*), or if your company doesn't have its own style guide, the default is to use PEP8, described in the next section.

Code formatting alters the appearance of your code, but it does not change anything about how the code works. Formatting includes things like the location of line breaks in your code, whitespace around an equals sign, or the number of blank lines in a script between different functions.

Applying a consistent style makes your code more readable. It's faster to read new code if it's in a consistent style, because it's easier to read code if you know what you are expecting. This consistency also makes it less likely that you will inadvertently introduce syntax errors, for example, with missing or mismatched parentheses. Again, this is because it's easier to know what to expect with standardized code.

Another major benefit of a consistent style is that there's no need to discuss formatting with your team when you're reviewing code. This means you can concentrate on reviewing the code's functionality and whether it meets your team's requirements.

The Great Tabs Versus Spaces Debate

Do you use tabs or spaces to indent your code? It's become a cliché that this is something that developers argue about, and there are lengthy internet debates about which of these is better. Spaces show up consistently on any computer, while tabs don't, but tabs are faster to type and reduce the file size, because there are fewer characters to save. In 2016, Felipe Hoffa, then a developer advocate at Google, analyzed 1 billion files of code (*https://oreil.ly/d2K4X*) (14 terabytes!) to discover whether tabs or spaces were more popular. Spaces were overwhelmingly the most popular.

This also gives you insight about the mindset of some software engineers: they can be very focused on the fine details of the code they are writing. However, this debate has recently been solved to some extent. Many IDEs automatically use spaces to indent code when the user presses the tab button. This means you get the speed advantage of using tabs but the consistency across different computers of using spaces, and the process has been automated.

In the next section, I'll describe the main features of PEP8, how to format code imports, and how you can automate the process of formatting your code.

PEP8

Python Enhancement Proposal 8, or PEP8 (*https://oreil.ly/RqeYi*), is the document that sets the standards for Python formatting. It is a style guide written by Guido van Rossum, Barry Warsaw, and Nick Coghlan in 2001 as a style guide for the Python standard library as Python first started to become popular. It has been adopted as a default style guide by the Python developer community to increase consistency across everyone writing code in Python.

As PEP8 states:

> A style guide is about consistency. Consistency with this style guide is important. Consistency within a project is more important. Consistency within one module or function is the most important.

PEP8 is full of guidelines for what to do and not do in your code. Here's an example of one of these guidelines—that you should have a line break after an `if` statement:

```
# Correct:
if foo == 'blah':
    do_blah_thing()

# Wrong:
if foo == 'blah': do_blah_thing()
```

The code still runs if you use the "wrong" option, but it's much easier to read if you use the "correct" option.

PEP8 has a lot to say about whitespace, because it really helps keep your code readable. For example, PEP8 describes best practices for spacing around = signs, and the number of blank lines around a function definition, whether it's inside a class (one) or on its own (two). It also suggests how to write comments and choose variable names, which I will cover in Chapter 9. It suggests you use spaces for indentation, not tabs, for consistency across environments.

There's a lot more detail in PEP8, but you don't need to read the whole thing. You can use one of the tools in this chapter to make sure your code conforms with the style guide. Flake8 or Pylint can highlight your code in your IDE so that you know where you need to make changes, and I'll describe these in "Linting" on page 87. I'll also describe the Black code formatter in "Automatic Code Formatting with Black" on page 85, which is compliant with PEP8 but also includes its own style preferences.

Import Formatting

Importing external modules frequently causes bugs. It's really easy to forget to update the modules you import when you update your code, so it's good to have a clear list of the modules you are using.

PEP8 sets standards for how to group your imports:

> Imports should be grouped in the following order:
>
> 1. Standard library imports.
>
> 2. Related third-party imports.
>
> 3. Local application/library specific imports.

Fortunately, this is not something you need to do manually. You can use a tool such as isort (*https://oreil.ly/7oNhq*) to sort your module imports into the correct order.

You can install isort with the following command:

```
$ pip install isort
```

Before running isort, your imports might look something like this:

```
import time
from sklearn.metrics import mean_absolute_error

import sys, os
import numpy as np
from sklearn.model_selection import train_test_split
import pandas as pd

from sklearn.neural_network import MLPRegressor
import matplotlib.pyplot as plt

from sklearn.pipeline import Pipeline
from sklearn.preprocessing import StandardScaler
from sklearn.preprocessing import FunctionTransformer, OneHotEncoder
```

You can run isort with the following command:

```
$ isort my_script.py
```

Afterward, your imports will look like this:

```
import os
import sys
import time

import matplotlib.pyplot as plt
import numpy as np
import pandas as pd
from sklearn.metrics import mean_absolute_error
from sklearn.model_selection import train_test_split
```

```
from sklearn.neural_network import MLPRegressor
from sklearn.pipeline import Pipeline
from sklearn.preprocessing import (FunctionTransformer, OneHotEncoder,
                                    StandardScaler)
```

This is much easier to read and conforms to PEP8. You can also use isort as a plug-in in your IDE. `reorder-python-imports` (*https://oreil.ly/ggPBW*) is an alternative to isort that places only one import on each line.

Automatic Code Formatting with Black

Black is a tool for automating the code formatting process. It enforces a code style, so there's no need for a human to review it. The idea behind Black is that you can write ugly code quickly, then you can save your file and it is magically made consistent. Black applies a uniform coding style specified by the tool's authors, which is the reason for the name of this tool: it's taken from Henry Ford's famous quote about being able to choose any color car, as long as it's black.

Black uses a subset of PEP8 with some minor differences. For example, instead of limiting the length of all lines of code to 79 characters, Black will try and find a sensible place to split longer lines so that they are around 90 characters. Black doesn't let you change many of its configuration options, but you can override this choice of line length as detailed in the Black documentation (*https://oreil.ly/V1l_7*).

You can install Black with:

```
$ pip install black
```

If you also want to run Black on Jupyter notebooks, install it with:

```
$ pip install "black[jupyter]"
```

I'll use the following script to show how Black works in practice, and I'll also use it to demonstrate the linting tools in "Linting" on page 87. This is the code that produces Figure 2-1, the plot of common big O classes from Chapter 2, but it has one syntax error, a missing import, and several places where the formatting does not conform with PEP8. Example 6-1 is what the code looks like before running Black.

Example 6-1. plot_big_o.py

```
import matplotlib.pyplot as plt

def plot_big_o(save_path)

    n = np.linspace(1, 10, 1000)
    line_names = ['Constant','Linear','Quadratic','Exponential','Logarithmic']
    big_o = [np.ones(n.shape), n, n**2, 2**n, np.log(n)]

    fig, ax = plt.subplots ()
```

```
fig.set_facecolor("white")

ax.set_ylim(0,50)
for i in range(len(big_o)):
    ax.plot(n, big_o[ i], label= line_names[i ])
ax.set_ylabel('Relative Runtime')
ax.set_xlabel('Input Size')
ax.legend()

fig.savefig(save_path, bbox_inches='tight')
```

Run Black to format the script with the following command:

```
$ black plot_big_o.py
```

Black throws an error at this, because it cannot reformat files with syntax errors. It gives the following output:

```
error: cannot format plot_big_o.py: Cannot parse: 3:25: def plot_big_o(save_path)

Oh no! ☄ 💔 ☄ File failed to reformat.
```

In this case, the function definition is missing its finishing colon and should read def plot_big_o(save_path):.

After fixing this error and rerunning Black, the script looks like this:

```
import matplotlib.pyplot as plt

def plot_big_o(save_path):  ❶
    n = np.linspace(1, 10, 1000)
    line_names = ["Constant", "Linear", "Quadratic", "Exponential", "Logarithmic"]  ❷
    big_o = [np.ones(n.shape), n, n**2, 2**n, np.log(n)]

    fig, ax = plt.subplots()  ❸
    fig.set_facecolor("white")

    ax.set_ylim(0, 50)
    for i in range(len(big_o)):
        ax.plot(n, big_o[i], label=line_names[i])
    ax.set_ylabel("Relative Runtime")
    ax.set_xlabel("Input Size")
    ax.legend()

    fig.savefig(save_path, bbox_inches="tight")
```

❶ The blank line following the function definition has been removed.

❷ Strings have been enclosed by double quotes instead of single quotes.

❸ Extra spaces have been removed.

Black has corrected the formatting throughout the script, as detailed in the annotations. For example, the line `ax.plot(n, big_o[ i], label= line_names[i ])` has been changed to `ax.plot(n, big_o[i], label=line_names[i])`, which conforms to the PEP8 style guide.

You can also preview the changes that Black will make with the following command:

```
$ black plot_big_o.py --diff
```

If there are any lines of code that you don't want Black to change, you can add the comment `# fmt: skip` at the end of the line. You can also skip a block of code by putting the comment `# fmt: off` at the start of the block, and the comment `# fmt: on` at the end of the block.

Black cleaned the formatting in Example 6-1, but it didn't do anything about the missing import. For that, you'll need to use a linter, which I'll describe in the next section. I'll return to Black later in the book when I describe how to run it automatically in "Pre-Commit Hooks" on page 183.

Linting

Linting means checking your code for errors before it runs. The strange name comes from the lint (fuzz) trap in a clothes dryer, and the first tool to do this function was called lint because it removed fuzz from code. The original lint tool was developed for the C language in 1978, but now linters are common for all programming languages.

Python linters will analyze your code and warn you of some of the things that would cause your code to fail when you run it. An example could be misspelling a variable name or forgetting to import a module, both of which would cause your code to throw an error when you run it.

Common linting tools for Python include Flake8 (*https://oreil.ly/JSJTW*), Pylint (*https://oreil.ly/zVVN2*), and Ruff (*https://oreil.ly/5v5fu*). All of these tools check the formatting of your code for compliance with a style guide, which is either PEP8 or a subset of it. Pylint and Flake8 don't change your code if they spot a formatting issue; they highlight it instead. This means you can manually review formatting suggestions before making the changes yourself. You also can combine these with running Black to make formatting changes first so that the linter only picks up potential errors. Ruff lints code and also updates the formatting, similar to Black.

Linting Tools

Let's look at how to use linting tools on the Example 6-1 script from before.

You can install Pylint with the following command:

```
$ pip install pylint
```

Run Pylint on Example 6-1 from the command line, which gives the following result:

```
$ pylint plot_big_o.py

************* Module plot_big_o
plot_big_o.py:3:26: E0001: Parsing failed: 'invalid syntax (<unknown>, line 3)'
(syntax-error)
```

Because there is a syntax error, Pylint does not complete its analysis of the entire script. It doesn't say exactly what the error is, but the 3:26 means that the error is in line 3, column 26. In this case, the function definition is missing the trailing :.

Fixing this error and rerunning Pylint gives the following output:

```
$ pylint plot_big_o.py

************* Module plot_big_o
plot_big_o.py:19:0: C0304: Final newline missing (missing-final-newline)
plot_big_o.py:1:0: C0114: Missing module docstring (missing-module-docstring)
plot_big_o.py:3:0: C0116: Missing function or method docstring
(missing-function-docstring)
plot_big_o.py:5:4: C0103: Variable name "n" doesn't conform to
snake_case naming style (invalid-name)
plot_big_o.py:5:8: E0602: Undefined variable 'np' (undefined-variable)
plot_big_o.py:7:13: E0602: Undefined variable 'np' (undefined-variable)
plot_big_o.py:7:46: E0602: Undefined variable 'np' (undefined-variable)
plot_big_o.py:9:9: C0103: Variable name "ax" doesn't conform to
snake_case naming style (invalid-name)
plot_big_o.py:13:4: C0200: Consider using enumerate instead of iterating
with range and len (consider-using-enumerate)
```

This time, Pylint is able to scan the rest of the script. It reveals a number of errors (messages starting with E, such as E0602) and places where the code does not follow conventions (messages starting with C, such as C0304). You can then use these messages to update the code and fix the errors. If it's not clear what the correct version of the code should be, the Pylint documentation (*https://oreil.ly/MurWR*) provides help.

Flake8 operates in a very similar way to Pylint. You can install it using the following command:

```
$ pip install flake8
```

Running Flake8 on Example 6-1 gives the following output:

```
$ flake8 plot_big_o.py

plot_big_o.py:3:25: E999 SyntaxError: invalid syntax
```

This is the same behavior as Pylint: it does not complete the analysis of the script, but it stops and flags the syntax error. However, fixing the syntax error and rerunning Flake8 gives a different output:

```
$ flake8 plot_big_o.py

plot_big_o.py:3:1: E302 expected 2 blank lines, found 1
plot_big_o.py:5:9: F821 undefined name 'np'
plot_big_o.py:6:29: E231 missing whitespace after ','
plot_big_o.py:6:38: E231 missing whitespace after ','
plot_big_o.py:6:50: E231 missing whitespace after ','
plot_big_o.py:6:64: E231 missing whitespace after ','
plot_big_o.py:7:14: F821 undefined name 'np'
plot_big_o.py:7:47: F821 undefined name 'np'
plot_big_o.py:9:27: E211 whitespace before '('
plot_big_o.py:12:18: E231 missing whitespace after ','
plot_big_o.py:14:26: E201 whitespace after '['
plot_big_o.py:14:37: E251 unexpected spaces around keyword / parameter equals
plot_big_o.py:14:50: E202 whitespace before ']'
plot_big_o.py:19:48: W292 no newline at end of file
```

Flake8 flags different formatting issues than Pylint because it is using a different style guide.

Ruff is a newer linter that has been designed to be extremely fast. You can install Ruff with the following command:

```
$ pip install ruff
```

Ruff separates its linting and formatting checks. You can run Ruff to lint your code with the following command:

```
$ ruff check plot_big_o.py
```

In the same way as Flake8, Ruff stops at the syntax error. Fixing this and rerunning gives the following output:

```
plot_big_o.py:5:9: F821 Undefined name `np`
plot_big_o.py:7:14: F821 Undefined name `np`
plot_big_o.py:7:47: F821 Undefined name `np`
```

You can run Ruff again to update your code's formatting with the following command:

```
$ ruff format plot_big_o.py
```

This updates the formatting for you, but it does not tell you what it has changed.

Because each linter uses a slightly different style guide, it's important to choose one linter and stick to it to ensure your code remains consistent. You should agree within your team which linter you all will use.

Linting in Your IDE

Instead of running a separate tool to lint and format your code, some IDEs also check your code while you are writing it. Figure 6-1 shows an example from VS Code using the `pylance` extension.

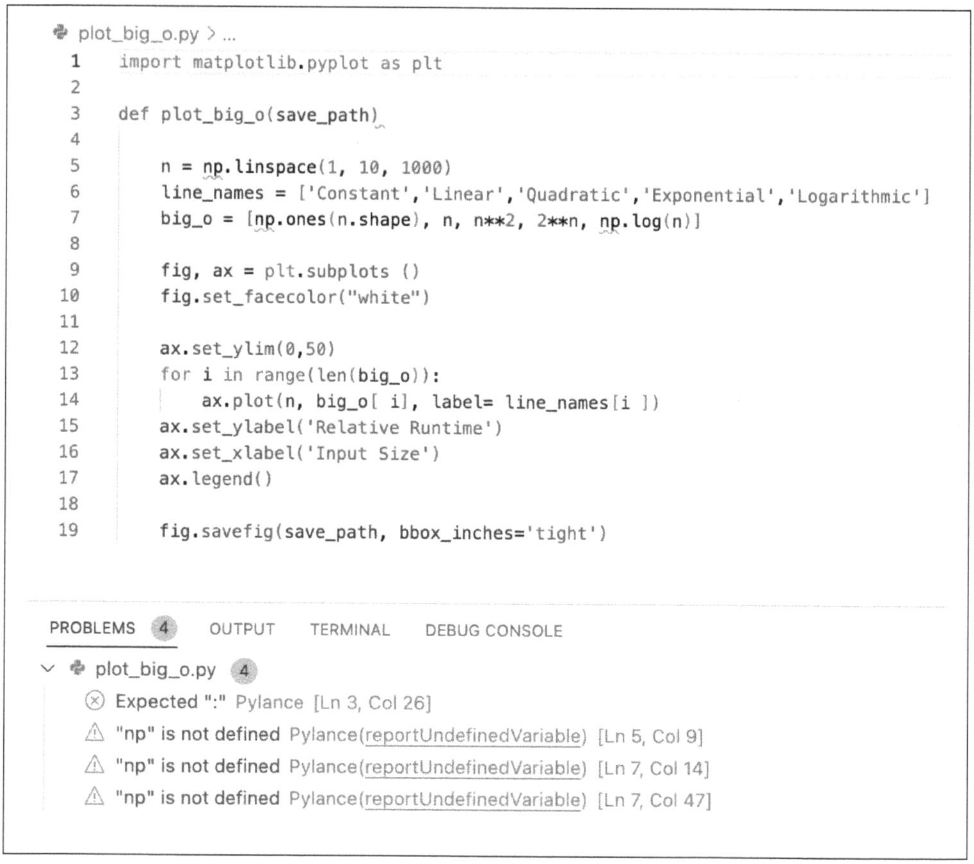

```
plot_big_o.py > ...
1    import matplotlib.pyplot as plt
2
3    def plot_big_o(save_path)
4
5        n = np.linspace(1, 10, 1000)
6        line_names = ['Constant','Linear','Quadratic','Exponential','Logarithmic']
7        big_o = [np.ones(n.shape), n, n**2, 2**n, np.log(n)]
8
9        fig, ax = plt.subplots ()
10        fig.set_facecolor("white")
11
12        ax.set_ylim(0,50)
13        for i in range(len(big_o)):
14            ax.plot(n, big_o[ i], label= line_names[i ])
15        ax.set_ylabel('Relative Runtime')
16        ax.set_xlabel('Input Size')
17        ax.legend()
18
19        fig.savefig(save_path, bbox_inches='tight')
```

PROBLEMS 4   OUTPUT   TERMINAL   DEBUG CONSOLE

∨ plot_big_o.py 4

⊗ Expected ":" Pylance [Ln 3, Col 26]

⚠ "np" is not defined Pylance(reportUndefinedVariable) [Ln 5, Col 9]

⚠ "np" is not defined Pylance(reportUndefinedVariable) [Ln 7, Col 14]

⚠ "np" is not defined Pylance(reportUndefinedVariable) [Ln 7, Col 47]

Figure 6-1. Linting while coding in VS Code

This tool underlines errors that will occur at runtime and provides a list of more details. It can also be configured to use Pylint, Flake8, or many other linters. You can configure it to ignore warnings that aren't relevant to your use case. And you can use this extension to lint Jupyter notebooks in VS Code.

Whichever tool you choose, linting your code will save you a lot of time by identifying many errors before they happen and making your code consistent.

Type Checking

Type checking is another way of catching bugs before they cause errors in your code. The term "type" refers to categories of objects used by Python such as integers (`ints`), strings, floats, and so on. A mismatch between the type of the input that a function is expecting and the type of the input that it receives will cause an error.

For example, this code sends a string to the function `math.sqrt()` when it is expecting a numeric type (such as an integer or a float):

```
import math

my_int = "100"
print(math.sqrt(my_int))
```

This gives the following error: `TypeError: must be real number, not str`.

Additionally, Python is a dynamically typed language, which means that the type of a variable can change. This is as opposed to other languages like Java, where once you set the type of a variable it is fixed and cannot change.

For example, this code runs without errors and changes the type of the variable:

```
>>> my_variable = 10
>>> my_variable = "hello"
>>> type(my_variable)
... str
```

`my_variable` starts out as an integer, but then becomes a string.

Types are an extremely common source of bugs. A function may receive a different type than it is expecting or output a result of an incorrect type. This is so common that tools have been developed to spot these for you so that you don't need to write a whole bunch of tests (which I'll cover in the next chapter) to check for them.

Type Annotations

Type annotations, also called type hints, were introduced in Python 3.5 to help reduce the number of bugs caused by incorrect types. They tell anyone reading code what type of input a function expects or returns. This helps to make the code much more readable, because the type annotation communicates the expected behavior of the function. Additionally, type annotations help with consistency and standardization in a larger codebase.

Type annotations are relatively new to Python, and they are still somewhat controversial. Some people find that they help with readability, but other people find that they make code harder to read. There's also extra work involved in adding the annotations and checking them. The developers of Python have stated (in PEP 484) that type annotations will remain optional in Python. If your team or company has a recommendation on whether to use them or not, you should follow that recommendation.

Type annotations follow the format `my_variable: type`. For example, to define the type that a function returns, use the following format:

```
--- -
def my_function(some_argument: type) -> return_type:
--- -
```

In Example 6-2, I've added type annotations to one of the functions from Chapter 2. This function expects a list as input and returns a float, as you can now see in the function definition:

Example 6-2. mode_using_counter.py

```
from collections import Counter

def mode_using_counter(list_of_numbers: list) -> float:
    c = Counter(list_of_numbers)
    return c.most_common(1)[0][0]
```

You could also specify that the input list needs to contain only floats by using the following syntax:

```
from collections import Counter
from typing import List

def mode_using_counter(list_of_numbers: List[float]) -> float:
    c = Counter(list_of_numbers)
    return c.most_common(1)[0][0]
```

You can also create type annotations using types from outside the Python standard library. Here's an example of how you can write a type annotation using a NumPy array:

```
import numpy as np

def array_operation(input_array: np.ndarray) -> np.ndarray:
    ...
```

 If you're checking the type of a data structure from a library that's not part of the Python standard library, the library must provide the type. This is an optional feature, and if the library doesn't provide it the type checker will detect the type Any.

Type annotations don't actually make any difference to the functioning of your code. For example, in Example 6-3 one type annotation is incorrect: the input is annotated as a float when it should be a list. The code still runs correctly:

Example 6-3. mode_using_counter_incorrect.py

```
from collections import Counter

def mode_using_counter(list_of_numbers: float) -> float:
    c = Counter(list_of_numbers)
    return c.most_common(1)[0][0]
```

Type annotations are useful only if they are used with type checking tools, and the idea is that you run the type checker before running or deploying your code. The type checker analyzes your code and checks for mismatched types. You could also write tests to do this, but it's easier and faster with a type checker.

The most popular type checking tool at the time of writing is mypy (*https://mypy-lang.org*), and I'll describe how to use this in the next section. Other tools for type checking include Pyright (*https://oreil.ly/2BIR2*), which is increasing in popularity, and also Pyre (*https://pyre-check.org*). Your IDE also may support type checking, either through built-in functionality or by installing an extension such as Pyright. Once you start using type annotations, your IDE may autocomplete these for you and tell you when the types are mismatched.

Type Checking with mypy

You can install mypy with the following command:

```
$ pip install mypy
```

Then you can run it on any script with the following command:

```
$ mypy my_script.py
```

Running mypy on Example 6-2, where the type annotations are correct, gives the following output:

```
Success: no issues found in 1 source file
```

But running mypy on Example 6-3 with incorrect type annotations gives this output:

```
mode_using_counter_incorrect.py:4: error: No overload variant of "Counter"
matches argument type "float"  [call-overload]
mode_using_counter_incorrect.py:4: note: Possible overload variants:
mode_using_counter_incorrect.py:4: note:     def [_T] Counter(self, None = ..., /)
-> Counter[_T]
mode_using_counter_incorrect.py:4: note:     def [_T] Counter(self, None = ..., /,
**kwargs: int) -> Counter[str]
mode_using_counter_incorrect.py:4: note:     def [_T] Counter(self,
```

```
SupportsKeysAndGetItem[_T, int], /) -> Counter[_T]
mode_using_counter_incorrect.py:4: note:   def [_T] Counter(self, Iterable[_T],
/) -> Counter[_T]
Found 1 error in 1 file (checked 1 source file)
```

Mypy has found the error in the type annotation, so this can be corrected. Then, anyone using this function will know what type it should accept and return.

Key Takeaways

In this chapter, I described how code formatting, linting, and type checking can improve the quality of your code and help increase your productivity when writing code. Formatting according to a style guide makes your code more readable. Linting and type checking identify potential errors before your code is deployed to production, ensuring that your code is robust.

A key takeaway here is that you should comply with your team or company's standards or introduce standards if they don't already exist. Standardized formatting helps prevent bugs, because it's easier to understand what the code is doing. It also means that you can spend your time working on your code's functionality rather than the details of its style.

The most important thing you should remember about code formatting, linting, and type checking is: use tools to carry out these tasks for you. It's not a valuable use of your time to do them manually. These tools may take some time to set up at the start, but investing time in them will definitely pay off over the long term. In Chapter 12 I'll show you how to automate these tools so that they take up even less of your time.

In the next chapter, I'll explain another key aspect of ensuring that your code is robust: testing.

## CHAPTER 7

Testing Your Code

Writing tests is an important skill in learning to write good code. A test is code that calls a function and checks that it does what it is supposed to do. It gives you evidence and confidence that your code is working correctly. Similar to logging in the previous chapter, tests take some effort to set up at first, but that effort pays off as your project grows.

If your code is truly a tiny one-off experiment, tests may be less important. But what if your code is part of a larger system? What if other people are changing your code? What if other code depends on your code to return a certain result? Testing gives you some guarantees that your code is working, and you'll know if a change that you or someone else makes breaks your code.

Tests are also important when you are the only one working on your code. They're a safety net that will help ensure that your code keeps working when you change it, rather than needing to rely on your memory. They also give you examples of how your code should work, and this makes your code easier to read and maintain.

It may seem challenging to get started with testing, because some experience in knowing what might go wrong is helpful. But you can start by testing that your code is doing what you think it is doing, as I'll describe in "A Basic Test" on page 98. Then you can add more tests as you find occasions when your code doesn't work.

There are two major types of testing in building software: automated code testing and user testing of the entire software product. User testing is likely to be handled by a separate team, but if you are writing production code you should write automated tests. I'll cover only automated testing in this book.

In this chapter, I'll go into depth about the motivations for writing tests, then I'll describe how to write a very simple test and a more complex one. I'll show you how to automate your tests so that you don't need to run them manually. I'll also take a detailed look at data validation and testing for machine learning.

 To clarify, when I refer to testing in this book, this does not include A/B testing. In an A/B test, you're running an experiment to discover which variation of something is preferable, for example, two different versions of a software feature. The tests covered here are to check whether your code works as expected.

Why You Should Write Tests

You often work on your code until it produces the results you expect. And then your job is done, right? But what if the input data changes in the future, or you haven't tried all the possible inputs to your code? I've often had the experience that my code works fine at one point, then something unexpected happens and it breaks. This means my code is not robust. And if my code is part of a larger system, this is a problem.

Many things can change that could affect your code and cause it to break. There might be a new version of a library or a language, you might upgrade your computer's operating system, or, commonly, some code that your code depends on changes. For a long list of reasons why your code may break in the future, check out this article (*https://oreil.ly/oG4oq*). Testing helps future-proof your code.

Additionally, your code may not work correctly in a different environment from the one where you developed your code. Examples include an online dashboard, on someone else's machine, in a Docker container, or in a production environment. If you have tests for your code, you can move your code to another environment, run the tests, and confirm that your code also works there.

Testing provides some assurance that your code does what you say it should do. This helps other people to trust your code, and it's a signal that it is robust and good quality. You also might need to make some guarantees about what your code should do, for example, if you are working in a high-stakes situation like the medical field, or if a large number of users depend on your code.

Testing also gives you confidence to make changes without being afraid that your code will break in some way that's hard to spot. It gives you a good signal that, if you make a change, your code still functions correctly. This is extremely useful for debugging (as I discussed in Chapter 5) and refactoring (which I'll cover in Chapter 8).

Test-Driven Development

Test-driven development (TDD) is a software development process where a developer writes the tests before writing the functions that actually achieve the objectives of the project. The aim is to use the tests to describe the requirements of the code, and the tests specify the expected behavior and the function's inputs and outputs. Then, the developer writes code to pass the test. This encourages developers to make their code modular and break down complex problems into easily testable pieces.

This approach isn't appropriate for many data science projects because, at the start of a typical data science project, you don't know exactly what functions you'll need. You'll often start with exploratory work, and you'll know how your code should be structured only toward the end of the project. However, if you'd like to know more about TDD, *Expert Python Programming* by Michal Jaworski and Tarek Ziadé (Packt, 2021) covers Python development from a TDD perspective.

When to Test

In data science projects, it can be difficult to know exactly when to start writing tests. Testing generally isn't worth the time it takes in the exploratory phase of your project, because you don't know what code will be useful in the future. But when you need to reuse your code and modify it, that can be a good time to add a test. It's also less important to add tests to your code in one-off analyses. There's a trade-off between getting results quickly and taking time to make sure that the results are correct.

Writing tests early in your project can help you catch simple mistakes such as inconsistent names, missing imports, spelling errors, or syntax errors. Sometimes these aren't caught by your code editor.

It's most important to write tests before your code is deployed to a production environment or before someone else uses it, to give you confidence that your code is robust and reproducible. Another time to add a test is when something goes wrong in your code and you get an unexpected error. Adding a test can help you find the source of the error. Tests are also extremely helpful if you need to refactor your code.

Remember that you only need to test your own code. You don't need to test imported libraries or dependencies. These aren't your responsibility and they should have their own tests already.

How to Write and Run Tests

Let's look at what goes into a simple test: how to structure it and how to write it. I'll explain how to test unexpected inputs as well as what you expect your code to handle and discuss how to run tests automatically. I'll also show examples of two common types of tests: unit tests and integration tests.

A Basic Test

The simplest test checks that a function runs correctly with the kind of inputs that you expect if everything is working correctly. If you're struggling to figure out what to include in a test, a good starting point can be things that you repeatedly want to display in a Jupyter notebook as you're developing your function.

Tests can be structured in four stages, as described in the Pytest documentation (*https://oreil.ly/slpmH*):

1. Arrange: Set up everything you'll need to run the function, for example, load some data.
2. Act: Run the function you're testing.
3. Assert: Check that the result of running the function is what you expect.
4. Cleanup: Make sure the test doesn't leave any trace behind. For example, if you have opened a file, make sure to close it.

I'll use the `weighted_mean` function from Chapter 2 here and write a test to check that it's working as expected. Here's the function again:

```
def weighted_mean(num_list, weights):
    running_total = 0
    for i in range(len(num_list)):
        running_total += (num_list[i] * weights[i])
    return (running_total/sum(weights))
```

Here's a test that goes along with this function to confirm some simple inputs:

```
from ch07_functions import weighted_mean ❶

def test_weighted_mean(): ❷

    list_a = [1, 2, 4]
    list_b = [1, 2, 4] ❸

    result = weighted_mean(list_a, list_b) ❹

    assert result == 3 ❺
```

❶ The test function is in a separate Python file from the function; the function is imported from the *ch07_functions.py* file. The file containing the test should have a name of the format *test_*.py* or **_test.py*.

❷ The convention is that the test function name begins with `test_`.

❸ The arrange step, where you generate the input data for the function you're testing.

❹ The act step, where you call your function with the input data you've chosen.

❺ The assert step, where you check that the result that the function has produced is what you expect.

In this test, I've started with a typical set of inputs to the function. Then I've run the function and checked that the result is correct using the `assert` statement.

The next step is to run the test and check that it passes; you can do this using a testing framework such as Pytest, which I will describe in "Running Automated Tests with Pytest" on page 101. If your test passes, you know that your code is working correctly for at least these input data values. If your test fails, you need to check two things. First, confirm that your test is accurate and that the value you're checking in the assertion step is indeed what you'd expect for that set of inputs. Second, look for the mistake in your code that's causing your test to fail, and fix that mistake so that your test passes.

Here's another example, this time using the `fit_trendline` function you've seen in other chapters:

```
from scipy.stats import linregress

def fit_trendline(year_timestamps, data):
    result = linregress(year_timestamps, data)
    slope = round(result.slope, 3)
    r_squared = round(result.rvalue**2, 3)
    return slope, r_squared
```

And here's a test that goes with it:

```
def test_fit_trendline():

    data = [1, 2, 3]
    timestamps = [2020, 2021, 2022]

    slope, r_squared = fit_trendline(timestamps, data)

    assert slope == 1
    assert r_squared == 1
```

In this case, I've chosen to use fake data. I know this should produce a trendline with a slope of 1 and an R² value that is also 1. This serves as a sanity check that the function is indeed doing exactly what you expect. I'll cover other inputs that you should consider testing in the next section.

It's common practice to put your tests in a separate folder and to start the names of the Python files containing your tests with `test_`. This keeps the tests separate from the rest of the code and allows automated test runners to find your tests, as I'll explain in "Running Automated Tests with Pytest" on page 101.

Testing Unexpected Inputs

As well as testing that your code works with the inputs you expect, it's useful to make your code robust by testing whether your code can handle unexpected inputs. These are also known as edge cases, which are extreme or unusual examples of an input that require special handling. Examples include empty strings or data of an incorrect type.

Here's an example of how you could update the `weighted_mean` test to check that the code is robust to an unexpected input:

```
def test_weighted_mean():

    result = weighted_mean([1, 2, 4], [1, 2, 4])

    assert result == 3

    empty_list_result = weighted_mean([], [])

    assert not empty_list_result
```

In this test I'm stating that I expect the `weighted_mean` function to return None if it receives empty lists as input. So for this test to pass, I need to update the `weigh ted_mean` function to handle this input:

```
def weighted_mean(num_list, weights):
    if not (num_list or weights):
        return None
    running_total = 0
    for i in range(len(num_list)):
        running_total += (num_list[i] * weights[i])
    return (running_total/sum(weights))
```

Next, I want to add a test to check that my function behaves correctly if it receives data of an incorrect type as input. Here's the updated test that checks that the `weigh ted_mean` function will return None if it receives a string in one of the input lists:

```
def test_weighted_mean():

    result = weighted_mean([1, 2, 4], [1, 2, 4])
    assert result == 3

    empty_list_result = weighted_mean([], [])
    assert not empty_list_result

    wrong_types_result = weighted_mean(['one', 2, 4], [1, 2, 4])
    assert not wrong_types_result
```

I would then update the code to get the expected behavior. You can see how adding a test and updating your function go together, and you often iterate around the loop of updating the test then updating the code.

Testing with unexpected inputs is hard to do when your code is working fine, because it's tough to anticipate how it'll break. But when your code breaks and you update your code to handle the error, you should add a test to make sure your code won't break next time the same thing happens. You also might consider what code inputs would have major consequences and test for these, but don't drive yourself crazy trying to anticipate every possible input.

I want to mention a couple of libraries that may be useful to you. The Faker (*https://oreil.ly/A7Wb-*) library can produce fake data in different formats such as timestamps, email addresses, and so on, which saves you from needing to read in real data. This is important if you are dealing with personal or sensitive data that shouldn't be visible in test code. Another is Hypothesis (*https://oreil.ly/uTNW0*), which can help you find edge cases where your code doesn't work. It performs property-based testing, where you can write tests that describe a range of scenarios and then the Hypothesis library will try these out.

Running Automated Tests with Pytest

Pytest (*https://oreil.ly/z1MRC*) is a framework that handles finding, collecting, and running your tests. If you use Pytest or another similar framework, you don't have to run every single test function if you have many functions or write boilerplate code to run all the tests.

Pytest is not part of the Python standard library; install it using the following command:

```
$ pip install pytest
```

You can run a single test file with the following command:

```
$ pytest test_weighted_mean.py
```

If you want to run all the tests in a folder, simply use the command `pytest` on its own. Pytest will recursively search all the files in the folder where you run this command, and it will run tests from files that match the pattern *test_*.py* or **_test.py*. Inside these files, it will run any test functions that start with `test_`. You can find more details on how Pytest discovers tests in the Pytest documentation (*https://oreil.ly/fGAj0*).

If all your tests pass, you'll get a readout that looks like this:

```
================================ test session starts =============================
platform darwin -- Python 3.10.4, pytest-7.4.0, pluggy-1.2.0
rootdir: /Users/.../book_code
collected 1 item

test_weighted_mean.py .                                            [100%]

================================= 1 passed in 0.01s ==============================
```

However, if your test fails you'll get an output like this:

```
================================ test session starts =============================
platform darwin -- Python 3.10.4, pytest-7.4.0, pluggy-1.2.0
rootdir: /Users/.../book_code
collected 1 item

test_weighted_mean.py F                                            [100%]

===================================== FAILURES ===================================
_____ test_weighted_mean _____

    def test_weighted_mean():

        result = weighted_mean([1, 2, 4], [1, 2, 4])

>       assert result == 3
E       assert 2.3333333333333335 == 3

test_weighted_mean.py:7: AssertionError
============================== short test summary info ===========================
FAILED test_weighted_mean.py::test_weighted_mean -
assert 2.3333333333333335 == 3
================================ 1 failed in 0.49s ===============================
```

Pytest prints a message to show that the test has failed, and it highlights the exact line that failed. It also prints out the assertion error and shows the incorrect value that the code generated.

Pytest has many more advanced features, such as the ability to skip tests or handle logs, and you can find more details in the Pytest documentation (*https://oreil.ly/eSN4m*).

> ### Other Testing Frameworks
>
> Pytest is a popular testing framework because it's fully featured and easy to use. However, there are several other options. `unittest` (*https://oreil.ly/uRZyg*) is included in the Python standard library, helpful if you want your code to have fewer dependencies. It's a little more complex to set up than Pytest, however.
>
> `tox` (*https://tox.wiki/en*) is another tool worth being aware of. It's a test runner that includes setting up a virtual environment, installing your application, and managing dependencies and Python versions. This tool is extremely useful for confirming that your code runs correctly in other environments.

I also want to mention the concept of test coverage. This is the proportion of the lines of code in a file that is executed when all the tests are run. You can measure test coverage using the `pytest-cov` (*https://oreil.ly/BYfJR*) plug-in for Pytest. This helps you check that all your functions have been tested, but it only checks what lines have been run, not what lines have been tested.

You should run your tests before you commit your code to version control (which I'll discuss in Chapter 10). I'll talk about this more and describe how to run your tests automatically in Chapter 12.

Types of Tests

There's a wide range of terminology to describe different tests. In *Robust Python* (O'Reilly, 2021), Patrick Viafore identifies six types of tests commonly used in software engineering:

Unit tests
Check that units of code, such as functions or classes, do what a developer expects.

Integration tests
Check that a larger system is connected correctly.

Acceptance tests
Check that the system does what the user expects.

Load tests
Check that the system still functions correctly if the amount of data or the number of users increases.

Security tests
Check that the system is resistant to attacks.

Usability tests
   Check that the system is intuitive to use.

I'm going to concentrate on unit tests and integration tests, because these are likely to be the most useful to you in writing data science code.

Unit Tests

All the tests I've shown so far in this chapter have been unit tests. A unit test takes a small component of your code and runs a test on it, for example, testing a function or a class. You'd usually write these while developing your code or while debugging.

Unit tests should be quick to run, so it's best to use small datasets. Avoid operations that take a long time to run such as connecting to a database; it's better to use fake data instead. Unit tests also should be deterministic. They should always give the same result with the same inputs, so don't include anything that has some random component to it.

Integration Tests

Integration tests confirm that a larger system functions correctly. They test a whole script or a larger chunk of a project, combining the functionality of multiple units and running them together.

To demonstrate an integration test, I'll use two of the functions from earlier chapters: `process_sdg_data` and `fit_trendline`. Together, these two functions accept an Excel file and output the slope and R^2 of the trendline, with some code to tie them together:

```
from scipy.stats import linregress
import pandas as pd

def process_sdg_data(excel_file, columns_to_drop):
    df = pd.read_excel(excel_file)
    df = df.drop(columns_to_drop, axis=1)
    df = df.set_index("GeoAreaName").transpose()
    return df

def fit_trendline(year_timestamps, data):
    result = linregress(year_timestamps, data)
    slope = round(result.slope, 3)
    r_squared = round(result.rvalue**2, 3)
    return slope, r_squared
```

Here's an integration test that goes with these two functions, including the code to tie them together:

```
from ch07_functions import process_sdg_data, fit_trendline

def test_processing_trendline():
    df = process_sdg_data(
        "../data/SG_GEN_PARL.xlsx",
        [
            "Goal",
            "Target",
            "Indicator",
            "SeriesCode",
            "SeriesDescription",
            "GeoAreaCode",
            "Reporting Type",
            "Sex",
            "Units",
        ],
    )
    timestamps = [int(i) for i in df.index.tolist()]
    uk_parl = df["United Kingdom of Great Britain and Northern Ireland"]
                .tolist()

    slope, r_squared = fit_trendline(timestamps, uk_parl)

    assert slope == 0.836
    assert r_squared == 0.868
```

This test checks that the output of the two functions together is what is expected. Note that this is testing with only one particular dataset, but eventually you might want functions to work with many different datasets. You should make sure that the datasets you use for integration testing are representative or provide a range of values as explained in "Testing Unexpected Inputs" on page 100.

Data Validation

Data validation is an important type of testing in data science projects. It's a process to confirm that your data is what you expect. It's not quite the same as the other tests I've introduced in this chapter, because you're testing the data you're working with rather than the code you're writing.

Data validation may be handled by a data engineering team, it may be a step in your machine learning pipeline, or you may wish to include it as part of your testing process. *Building Machine Learning Pipelines* by Catherine Nelson and Hannis Hapke (O'Reilly Media, 2020) contains more details about data validation as part of a machine learning pipeline. In this section, I'll discuss some of the ways you might want to validate your data and introduce a couple of tools you can use for this.

Data Validation Examples

Data validation is important because data can change often during the lifespan of a data science project. This means it's good practice to test the properties of the data rather than exact values. Common data validation steps include:

- Testing that all the columns you need in a dataset are present.
- Testing that the data in each column is the correct type.
- Testing that columns are not all null values or don't have more than a certain proportion of null values.
- Checking that the statistical properties of the data are as expected (for example, the mean, standard deviation, or range of the data).
- Related to the previous point, checking that the data distribution is similar to the data version from the previous day, week, or other relevant time period.
- Checking for anomalous data.

In the next section, I'll describe how you can use the Pandera module to validate your data. Great Expectations (*https://oreil.ly/6dp8t*) is another excellent tool for data validation, with more advanced functionality, but it's a little more time consuming to set up than Pandera. In the section after that, I'll cover Pydantic, an option for data validation that uses type annotations.

Using Pandera for Data Validation

The Pandera module is a lightweight data validation option that uses a schema to validate pandas DataFrames or similar data structures, including Dask DataFrames. I'll give a very quick overview, but more features are described in the Pandera documentation (*https://oreil.ly/xvOrN*).

You can install Pandera as follows:

```
$ pip install pandera
```

Figure 7-1 shows part of a DataFrame to validate, using the same data as in Chapter 4.

	Year	India	United States of America
0	2000	9.02	13.33
1	2001	9.01	14.02
2	2002	8.84	14.02
3	2003	8.84	14.25
4	2004	8.84	14.25

Figure 7-1. DataFrame to validate

To validate the data, you can define a schema that states what columns the DataFrame should include, along with the types of data in each column:

```
import pandera as pa

schema = pa.DataFrameSchema({
    "Year": pa.Column(int),  ❶
    "India": pa.Column(float),  ❷
    "United States of America": pa.Column(float)  ❸
})
```

❶ There should be a column named "Year" that contains integers.

❷ There should be a column named "India" that contains floats.

❸ There should be a column named "United States of America" that contains floats.

Then validate the data with the following command:

```
schema(df)
```

This validates the data according to the schema, checking that all the columns are present and validating the data types in each column. Pandera will throw an error if not all columns specified in the schema are present, but it won't complain if an extra column is present.

You can also validate properties of the values in the columns. You can check that all the values are within the range you expect using the checks= argument. This accepts a variety of Pandera Check objects:

```
schema = pa.DataFrameSchema({
    "Year": pa.Column(int, checks=pa.Check.in_range(2000, 2023)),
    "India": pa.Column(float, checks=pa.Check.in_range(0, 100)),
    "United States of America": pa.Column(float, checks=pa.Check.in_range(0, 100))
})
```

If the data validation passes, you'll have confirmed that all the columns you require are present, the data in each column is of the correct type, and the data is in the range you expect. This is just a simple example, but you can build from this to validate your own dataset.

Data Validation with Pydantic

You can validate your data at runtime using Pydantic (*https://oreil.ly/ey_Op*). This is an incredibly useful library that is becoming increasingly popular in the Python community. Pydantic uses type annotations, which I introduced in "Type Checking" on page 91 to validate data, but it is not a static analysis tool like mypy. Instead, the validation happens when you run your code; you don't need to run a separate tool. This is particularly useful if you deploy your code in an API, as I'll explain in Chapter 11.

You can install Pydantic with the following command:

```
$ pip install pydantic
```

Pydantic uses the concept of data schemas to validate data. First, you define a schema that describes the format of your data; then you can use that schema to check that new data is in the correct format. Here's an example of defining a schema for the UN Sustainable Development Goals data from Chapter 1. You'll see that you can define the type of your data and whether it is required (an error is raised if it is not present) or optional:

```
from pydantic import BaseModel
from typing import Optional
from datetime import datetime

class CountryData(BaseModel):
    country_name: str  ❶
    population: int  ❷
    literacy_rate_2020: Optional[float]  ❸
    timestamp: Optional[datetime] = None  ❹
```

❶ The country name is required and must be a string or something that can be cast to a string without raising an error.

❷ The population is required and must be an integer.

❸ The literacy rate is optional and must be a float or something that can be cast to a float.

❹ The timestamp is optional and must be a datetime object or something that can be cast to a datetime object, and the default value is None if no data is passed in.

Next, here's an example of data that will be validated as correct:

```
sample_data_correct = {
    'country_name': 'India',
    'population': 1417242151,
    'literacy_rate_2020': 79.43,
    'timestamp': datetime.now()
}
```

You can then use this data to create a new CountryData object. If the data is of the correct format no error is raised:

```
india = CountryData(**sample_data_correct)
```

You can look up any of these pieces of data:

```
>>> india.timestamp
... datetime.datetime(2023, 3, 7, 16, 3, 41, 423508)
```

However, if you pass in data that does not fit the requirements, like this:

```
sample_data_incorrect = {
    'country_name': 'United States',
    'population': None,
    'literacy_rate_2020': None,
    'timestamp': None
}

united_states = CountryData(**sample_data_incorrect)
```

In this case, the `population` field is missing. Pydantic raises the following error:

```
ValidationError: 1 validation error for CountryData
population
  Input should be a valid integer [type=int_type, input_value=None,
  input_type=NoneType]
```

Pydantic is extremely useful for checking that the input data into a large project is what you're expecting. I'll give an example of how to use it in an API in "Adding Functionality to Your API" on page 174.

Testing for Machine Learning

Machine learning code needs to be tested a little differently from most other code. This is because you don't know exactly what model you'll get from a given dataset, because most machine learning algorithms include randomization in some way. But this doesn't mean you can't test machine learning code. This is a complex topic, but I'll give you an overview in this section and describe some useful strategies.

Figure 7-2 shows the structure of a common machine learning project. I'll go through the test possibilities for all of these steps in turn and focus on a couple in particular.

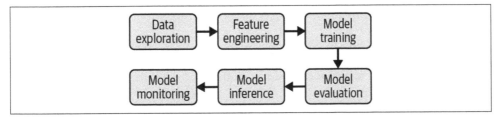

Figure 7-2. Steps in a machine learning project

Data exploration
> There's no need to write tests in the exploratory phase of a project, unless you write code that you expect to reuse elsewhere.

Feature engineering
> You can write unit tests for feature engineering code and include data validation in this step.

Model training
> I'll cover this in detail in the following section.

Model evaluation
> Model evaluation assesses the performance of your trained model on a dataset. This in itself is a kind of test, but the results will be slightly different for every model training run. You could, for example, formalize this into a test by enforcing that the accuracy must always be greater than a certain percentage.

Model inference
> I'll cover this in detail in the following section.

Model monitoring
> Model monitoring in production is often handled by external tools or libraries, but if you write your own code you can add unit tests.

Testing Model Training

Testing model training is difficult because, given some input data, you don't know the expected output. You don't know exactly what the weights of the neural network should be, and you don't know all the parameters that go into your saved model file. You can't test whether a particular dataset gives you a particular model structure. But there are definitely things you can test, and your strategy will depend on whether you're using a large model that takes a long time to train (let's say more than a few minutes) or a small model.

If your model takes a long time to train, it's impractical to test whether the model outputs are correct or the final model accuracy. Instead, you should check that training is running as you expect, and that the model trains without crashing. You can do this by writing a test for your training code that compares model weights before and after a training step, to ensure that they have changed.

Another option for neural networks is to check that the loss decreases over the first few training steps. You can also write tests that check that the model accepts input tensors of the correct shape and produces outputs of the correct shape, as this is a common source of errors.

For smaller models, you could also write an integration test that checks that a model exists at the end of the training process. You could use a small part of your training data for speed or use fake data.

Testing Model Inference

After you have trained your model, you should check that it returns predictions correctly. There are two main strategies for testing a model that is running inference in production. First, you should write unit and integration tests that check that the inference code is working correctly. Does it return a prediction given some fake input data? Does it handle empty inputs correctly? Does it handle errors gracefully? If your model is very large, you may want to run some tests on a smaller sample model, and some on the full version of the model.

Second, you can send particular data examples to your model and confirm that the model predictions are what you expect. This is different from model evaluation because you'll use just a few data examples, rather than a whole evaluation dataset. For a regression model, you could check that the model's output for a given data example is within the correct range. Or for a classification model you can give it some inputs that should always be a specific class. You want your model to be deployed to production only if it makes those predictions correctly.

If you would like to learn more about testing for ML, check out this article by Jeremy Jordan (*https://oreil.ly/FUtlq*).

Key Takeaways

Writing tests is an important part of writing good code, and in particular, it helps you write more robust code. You should write tests to ensure correct behavior even when your code changes, to confirm your code works in other environments, to give you confidence your code is doing what you expect, to help people trust your code, and to help with debugging and refactoring.

The simplest possible test checks that your function returns the result you expect with some simple inputs. Structure your tests with arrange, act, assert, and cleanup steps. Next, add edge cases. Don't run your tests manually; use a test framework such as Pytest.

You can validate your data using its overall properties to confirm that the data in your project is what you expect. Pandera is an easy-to-use option for validating pandas DataFrames.

ML requires a different approach because you don't know exactly what model will be generated from a given dataset. But you still should write tests, including unit tests where possible.

## CHAPTER 8

Design and Refactoring

In this chapter, I want to move away from thinking about the finer details of each line of code you write and toward the bigger picture: how to design your projects, how to arrange your code, and how to refactor your code when that design changes. I'll include some ideas for how to organize and standardize the high-level structure of your projects and I'll suggest how to break your code into modular, reusable functions.

Good design, whether at the level of a whole project or at the level of individual functions, has a number of benefits for your code. If your project design is somewhat standardized, it removes some of the mental load of switching from one project to another. It's easier for someone to work on your project if they have seen something similar before. If your code is well designed, it is easier to reuse pieces of it in other projects, and it is easier to add new features.

In my experience as a data scientist, I've seen many projects in which all the code is in one giant Jupyter notebook. I've created projects like this myself. A Jupyter notebook is a fantastic way to get started on a project, draft your ideas, and try things out. But notebooks can be limiting when your project scales up or becomes more complex. You can see a framework for turning your notebooks into Python scripts in "From Notebooks to Scalable Scripts" on page 122.

It's sometimes difficult in data science to know exactly when to design the structure of your project. You may not have any clue what the outcome of the project will be when you begin it. But it's generally still worthwhile to take the time to deliberately design it when you start to get a sense of where it is going, and this may be at the point where you switch from notebooks to scripts.

You shouldn't expect to get the design of your project exactly right the first time. It's likely to be something you iterate on. And it's almost certain that the details of your code will change during your project. Refactoring, the process of adjusting the structure of your code while keeping its behavior the same, is a normal part of software engineering, and it will likely be very useful for you as a data scientist. I'll provide details of how to do this in "Refactoring" on page 126.

Project Design and Structure

There are no hard and fast rules about project design and structure. Both depend so much on what you're working on, the business you're in, the timescale of the project, and many other factors. A machine learning project will likely require a completely different structure than that of an analysis powering some decision.

That said, in this section I want to give you some ideas for how to design your projects well. Keeping your design somewhat standardized is very helpful. This means anyone who uses your projects has some idea of what to expect, and it reduces the cognitive load of switching to a new project. Also, it's easier to pick up work that someone else on your team has done if you share a standard design for your projects.

In this section, I'll discuss how to structure your projects at the overall level, setting up the different files and the folder structure. I'll give an example of a machine learning project and discuss some tools for automatically creating new projects with a given structure.

Project Design Considerations

How do you take a whole project plan and turn that into well-structured code? In some cases you may need to start the project and try some initial ideas to set the overall project direction before you set out the structure. If this is the case, it's worth spending some time thinking about your project plan as early as possible. This can help you turn a big mass of notebook code into a well-structured project.

These questions will help you design your project:

- What are the overall goals or aims of your project? What is the overall problem you need to solve? You should always have the big picture in mind to ensure that all the code you write is helping you reach this goal, rather than getting sidetracked on less important details.

- What are the overall inputs and outputs of your project? For example, a machine learning project may take raw data as an input and output model predictions.

- Who are the stakeholders in the project? How much work do you need to do before you check in with them? These could be project managers, other teams, or even the customer of your product.

- What is the timeline for your project? What are the milestones or the deadlines? Knowing this will help you figure out whether this is a project where you need to get a result quickly and tidy up the code afterward, or whether you can take your time to write the code well upfront and spend some time designing it.

- What are the ideas you are going to try out? How much time can you spend on exploration and experimentation versus solving the problem you need to solve? If it is heavy on exploration, you may find it useful to think about how you can reuse code from this phase. Can you set up your machine learning experiments in a standardized way so that you can easily run many of them?

- What is the likelihood that the scope of this project might change? Or that at some point in the future, the work you do on this project could be reused for a different use case? If you expect to reuse the code, ensure that it is modular and well documented so that it's easy to pick up pieces of it and use them elsewhere.

The answers to these questions will help you divide your project into sensible steps, and it's a good idea to document these answers somewhere. I also recommend taking a retrospective look through past projects that you've completed. You can look for common themes and ask yourself what went well and what didn't go so well. What could you do better the next time you do a similar project? Asking these questions will help you structure your future projects.

Your project structure may also include data. However, if your data is stored in a central database (either your own database or data storage managed by your company), you shouldn't replicate it and save it locally. This duplication could cause problems later where different data versions give you different results. It also could be a security or privacy risk. It's much better to include code to extract and select your data as part of the project. At the very least, you should include documentation that lets you replicate the project. I'll cover how to write good documentation in Chapter 9.

If you have similar projects that come up often, you can automate creating the file and folder structure using the Cookiecutter (*https://oreil.ly/bX-rV*) tool. This can include the files that you need to build Python packages and manage dependencies, which I will talk about in Chapter 10.

If you don't want to set up the structure of your project from scratch, I recommend using Kedro (*https://oreil.ly/fJEqk*), an open source library designed to standardize data science projects. You can set up your project as a collection of connected nodes, then run them end to end as a pipeline. Each node can contain a script, for example, loading your data or cleaning your data.

An Example Machine Learning Project

Once you know the steps in your project, you can start to set up the file structure. Let's look at how to do this with an example machine learning project. There are many options for how to set up the file structure, but one strategy is to use one file per step in the project. Each of these steps often ends with saving some data.

Steps typically include the following:

1. Load the data.

2. Clean and preprocess the data, then transform it into features suitable for machine learning.

3. Train the model.

4. Analyze the model's performance on a validation dataset.

If you know that you're going to run some experiments to choose an initial model then turn your code into reproducible scripts, this could be a good design for your project:

```
├── README.md
├── requirements.txt
│
├── notebooks
│   ├── explore_data.ipynb
│   └── try_regression_model.ipynb
│
├── src
│   ├── __init__.py
│   ├── load_data.py
│   ├── feature_engineering.py
│   ├── model_training.py
│   ├── model_analysis.py
│   └── utils.py
│
├── tests
│   ├── test_load_data.py
│   ├── test_feature_engineering.py
│   ├── test_model_training.py
│   ├── test_model_analysis.py
│   └── test_utils.py
```

Let's break this down. First, there are some standard files that every project should have:

```
├── README.md
├── requirements.txt
```

Every project should have documentation (Chapter 9). A *README.md* file is a standard format. You should also include all the files you need for managing dependencies or packaging (more in Chapter 10).

Next, it's good practice to keep your notebooks and experiments in which you are trying out different models in their own folder:

```
├── notebooks
│   ├── explore_data.ipynb
│   └── try_regression_model.ipynb
```

Your scripts also get their own folder. A common convention in Python is to put all the code for a package in a folder named *src* (short for "source"), and many people use the same structure for the scripts in a project. It's useful to put "helper" functions that are reused in many places in a *utils* file:

```
├── src
│   ├── __init__.py
│   ├── load_data.py
│   ├── feature_engineering.py
│   ├── model_training.py
│   ├── model_analysis.py
│   └── utils.py
```

Keeping your tests in a separate folder keeps things tidy and also lets your testing framework discover them easily, as I mentioned in Chapter 7. Each file in the *src* folder should get its own tests:

```
├── tests
│   ├── test_load_data.py
│   ├── test_feature_engineering.py
│   ├── test_model_training.py
│   ├── test_model_analysis.py
│   └── test_utils.py
```

This is just one option for structuring a project. Once you have a project structure that works for many of your projects, you can turn it into a template and replicate it using Cookiecutter, or use Kedro to help you set it up. You can also learn much more about structuring a machine learning project in *Building Machine Learning Pipelines*, which I wrote with my colleague Hannes Hapke (O'Reilly, 2020).

Code Design

Design is the art of arranging code
—Sandi Metz

Code design, or "factoring" your code into appropriate pieces including functions, classes, and modules, is not easy. As Sandi Metz asserts, it's more of an art than a science, because there isn't one "correct" answer. However, in this section I'll give you some guidelines on how to design your code.

It's good practice to divide your code into discrete pieces that carry out different purposes. Each of these chunks should contain a different idea or piece of logic. The code that cleans your data should be separate from the code that generates a visualization. The code for the front end of a website should be separate from the code for the database that stores the data.

You should expect that your initial code design won't be exactly right. Things will change as your project evolves, the business problem may change, or you may identify a better design once you've worked on the project for a while. I'll describe some techniques for changing your code that reduce the risk of introducing errors in "Refactoring" on page 126.

Modular Code

When you're thinking about the overall architecture of your code, dividing it into functions and classes is a critical step. It doesn't matter whether that's at the very start of the project, you've tried out some initial ideas, or you're refactoring your code; it's good to keep thinking about what functions and classes are appropriate. I discussed this topic in Chapters 1 and 4 but want to revisit it here.

Modular code means that your code is broken into small independent parts. It's the opposite of having all the code for your project in one giant script. It's much easier to work with code that is modular, but it's often difficult to figure out how to divide your code. I'll give you some guidance on how to do this in this section and the next one.

As far as possible, make sure that each function or class has one well defined purpose. You can think of this as one "thing" that it does. It should be something that you can describe in a short sentence, for example, "this function creates a data visualization." If you are describing it and you start using the word "and," this may be a clue to break it down into multiple functions. For example, if you describe it as "this function cleans the data and creates a data visualization," it's better to divide it into one function that cleans the data and another that creates the visualization.

Try to avoid "coupling" in your functions, which is when you change code in one location, then need to change something in another location. I'll explain this in more detail in "Coupling" on page 120.

Writing modular code has a number of benefits. Modular code is easier to reuse in other places, and it is easier to move pieces of code around when the requirements for your code change. Modular code also allows you to connect pieces of your code in different ways to make larger systems (known as composability). Additionally, it makes your code easier to test.

Consider these questions to help you think through what functions and classes are appropriate for the problem you're solving:

- What common patterns do you see in the code you're writing? This could be a data transformation or a piece of business logic.
- What components could be reused in many places? An example could be the transformation of some data from one timezone to another.
- What is the purpose of the function you're writing? As far as possible, each function or method should do only one thing.

Let's turn these questions into a more structured framework.

A Code Design Framework

One framework you can think about to construct your function, class, or method is the following (adapted from "Six steps to more professional data science code" (*https://oreil.ly/Psa1F*) on Kaggle by Rachel Tatman):

Function name
> You can start by choosing a good name for your function. There's more about what makes a good name in Chapter 9, but choosing a name sets an intention for what you want the function to do.

Inputs
> The interface to your function should stay consistent, so before you start writing the body of the function it's a good idea to decide what the inputs to the function should be. You should specify these in the arguments that the function takes. More about interfaces in the next section.

Behavior
> The body of the function or method contains the actual operations that it carries out. This is the function's behavior, or the thing that you actually want it to do. As mentioned previously, it's good practice for each function to do only one thing.

Outputs
> The outputs of your function are what you include in a `return` statement, or they can also be data saved to a file. The outputs are also part of the interface to your function, so it's a good idea to think about them carefully before you write the function, then keep them the same when possible.

You can see an example of how to use this framework to go from a notebook to modular code in "Creating Scripts from Notebooks" on page 123.

Interfaces and Contracts

One of the most important aspects of modular code is the interfaces between the components in your system. You might find that this is a useful place to start when writing an individual function: what does it accept as an input, and what does it return as an output?

The function below, which you have seen throughout this book, takes a CSV file and a list of columns to drop as its input and returns a pandas DataFrame as its output:

```
def process_sdg_data(excel_file, columns_to_drop):
    df = pd.read_excel(excel_file)
    df = df.drop(columns_to_drop, axis=1)
```

```
df = df.set_index("GeoAreaName").transpose()
return df
```

Once you have decided what the inputs and outputs should be, you shouldn't change them, because other components of the system may be depending on them. This is also known as a "contract." It's best to keep the number of input arguments small: maybe three or four at most. If you need more inputs than this, consider using a configuration file instead.

Your test for a function should confirm that the contract is maintained by checking that the correct inputs are accepted and the correct outputs are returned. You should also document the inputs and outputs in the function docstring, which I'll describe in "Docstrings" on page 136. Using type annotations, as described in "Type Checking" on page 91, can also ensure that the contract is maintained. Type checking tools can alert you when the contract is broken due to mismatched types.

Coupling

When you are dividing your code into pieces, it's important to make sure that those pieces are as independent from each other as possible. If changing one part of your code changes another, the complexity of the whole project increases, and it will become much harder to work on. The term "coupling" describes the dependence between functions or modules. If two functions are tightly coupled, changing one of them means you need to change the other extensively. If they are loosely coupled, changing one means you don't need to change the other much or at all. You should try to reduce coupling as much as possible.

Here's an example of two functions that are tightly coupled:

```
import pandas as pd
from scipy.stats import linregress

def process_sdg_data(input_excel_file, columns_to_drop):
    df = pd.read_excel(input_excel_file)
    df = df.drop(columns_to_drop, axis=1)
    df = df.set_index("GeoAreaName").transpose()
    return df

def fit_trendline(country_name):
    df = process_sdg_data(
        "SG_GEN_PARL.xlsx",
        [
            "Goal",
            "Target",
            "Indicator",
            "SeriesCode",
            "SeriesDescription",
            "GeoAreaCode",
            "Reporting Type",
```

```
            "Sex",
            "Units",
        ],
    )
    timestamps = [int(i) for i in df.index.tolist()]
    data = df[country_name].tolist()

    result = linregress(timestamps, data)
    slope = round(result.slope, 3)
    r_squared = round(result.rvalue**2, 3)
    return slope, r_squared
```

The `fit_trendline` function calls the `process_sdg_data` function internally to perform the data processing. If you change the behavior of the `process_sdg_function`, it could potentially affect the behavior of the `fit_trendline` function. Mixing these functions makes them harder to work with.

Here's an example where these functions are not tightly coupled:

```
import pandas as pd
from scipy.stats import linregress

def fit_trendline(year_timestamps, data):
    result = linregress(year_timestamps, data)
    slope = round(result.slope, 3)
    r_squared = round(result.rvalue**2, 3)
    return slope, r_squared

def process_sdg_data(input_excel_file, columns_to_drop):
    df = pd.read_excel(input_excel_file)
    df = df.drop(columns_to_drop, axis=1)
    df = df.set_index("GeoAreaName").transpose()
    return df

df = process_sdg_data(
    "SG_GEN_PARL.xlsx",
    [
        "Goal",
        "Target",
        "Indicator",
        "SeriesCode",
        "SeriesDescription",
        "GeoAreaCode",
        "Reporting Type",
        "Sex",
        "Units",
    ],
)
timestamps = [int(i) for i in df.index.tolist()]
country_data = df["India"].tolist()
slope, r_squared = fit_trendline(timestamps, country_data)
```

Separating the functions like this makes them much easier to work with, and it's also much easier to reuse them elsewhere.

If you'd like to read more about code design, I recommend that you look into the SOLID principles. This article from Real Python (*https://oreil.ly/oZN0y*) is a great place to start. Learning about design patterns is another good option, although these may require some adaptation to make them applicable to data science. The Refactoring Guru (*https://oreil.ly/HEV6u*) has a useful guide to Python design patterns.

In the next section, I'll move on to discussing how to take your code from Jupyter notebooks to standalone Python scripts.

From Notebooks to Scalable Scripts

If Jupyter notebooks are a standard part of your project workflow, you may reach a point where you need to move away from them to Python scripts that you need to run repeatedly. This can be a key stage in your project. It can be a move away from prototyping to code that you write with more of an engineering mindset: you know the solution to your problem and you want to run the code that solves it repeatedly.

In this section, I'll discuss some reasons it can be helpful to move from notebooks to scripts, and then I'll go through some details of how to create scripts from your notebooks.

Why Use Scripts Instead of Notebooks?

Jupyter notebooks are an incredibly useful tool for data scientists. They're flexible, offer instant feedback, and give you the freedom to try out your ideas. The inline visualization is extremely useful. They're also great for writing tutorials where you want to mix code and documentation. They can even be run in an automated way using Papermill (*https://oreil.ly/L8Zvj*).

However, there are a number of disadvantages to writing your code in notebooks. Because you can execute code in a different order from the order it's written in, and you don't need to run all the code in a notebook at once, your notebook doesn't always reflect the code you've actually run. This can make it difficult to reproduce the steps you've taken.

Notebooks also don't work well with a number of standard software engineering tools and practices described in this book. It's not as easy to lint, format, or type-check notebooks as it is with a Python script. It's difficult to manage dependencies (which I'll talk about in Chapter 10), so you may not know what version of a third-party library was used in a notebook.

It's also hard to debug notebooks if you're working in the Jupyter Notebook or JupyterLab, but IDEs now have debuggers that work with notebooks. Version control (which I'll also discuss in Chapter 10) doesn't capture which cells have been run in a notebook. You may need to use external tools to easily review the changes that have been made in a notebook. It's also too easy to upload a notebook containing data to version control, which can pose a security risk.

The style of code that many people (myself included) tend to write in notebooks is informal and often includes extra cells where you want to check what your data looks like. This makes it more difficult to write modular code. But even if you do write code in modular functions, it isn't easy to import functions from one notebook into another. Modular Python files are much easier to work with in many situations.

This is definitely a topic where you'll encounter a wide variety of opinions, but my strategy personally is to use notebooks for data exploration and prototyping, then switch to a script when I am doing the same things repeatedly. Sometimes I'll put the reusable components that I've written into a Python file, then import these into a notebook and run them. I find that scripts are useful even when I'm running machine learning experiments, because I can write tests to ensure that my experiments are reproducible and test that my experiments are definitely doing what I expect them to be doing.

A common point to switch from notebooks to scripts is when you move your code into a production environment where it will be run repeatedly. Some companies may require this due to potential security risks from notebooks (such as saving data in notebooks, as mentioned earlier).

If you decide you want to switch from notebooks to scripts, I'll describe a possible process for how to do this in the next section.

Creating Scripts from Notebooks

It's a good idea to make sure that your notebook runs correctly before creating functions from it. Additionally, starting with a well-structured notebook makes it easier to turn it into a script. So it's worth spending some time cleaning your notebook before you start trying to turn it into a script.

Then, consider whether your notebook should be one Python script or several. As mentioned earlier in this chapter, one way of thinking about this is each script is a step in your project. You can also use separate files for utility functions such as data cleaning functions that you use in many steps of the project. If you often find yourself rerunning a notebook starting in the middle, this is a good sign that you should split the notebook there.

Next, are there some cells that you always want to run together or run every time you run the notebook? Maybe these could be a function? What are some common objects you are manipulating in the notebook? Could these be abstracted into a class?

Here is an example of this process. Figure 8-1 shows a notebook for exploring and cleaning data from the UN Sustainable Development Goals website. You've seen some of this code earlier in the book, but this is what it could look like while it's being developed.

```
In [1]: import pandas as pd

In [2]: df = pd.read_excel('SG_GEN_PARL.xlsx')

In [3]: df.head(2)
```

Out[3]:

	Goal	Target	Indicator	SeriesCode	SeriesDescription	GeoAreaCode
0	5	5.5	5.5.1	SG_GEN_PARL	Proportion of seats held by women in national ...	4
1	5	5.5	5.5.1	SG_GEN_PARL	Proportion of seats held by women in national ...	8

2 rows × 34 columns

```
In [4]: df.columns

Out[4]: Index(['Goal', 'Target', 'Indicator', 'SeriesCode', 'SeriesDescription',
               'GeoAreaCode', 'GeoAreaName', 'Reporting Type', 'Sex', 'Units', '2000',
               '2001', '2002', '2003', '2004', '2005', '2006', '2007', '2008', '2009',
               '2010', '2011', '2012', '2013', '2014', '2015', '2016', '2017', '2018',
               '2019', '2020', '2021', '2022', '2023'],
              dtype='object')

In [5]: df = df.drop(['Goal', 'Target', 'Indicator', 'SeriesCode', 'SeriesDescription',
               'GeoAreaCode', 'Reporting Type', 'Sex', 'Units'], axis=1)

In [6]: df = df.set_index('GeoAreaName').transpose()

In [7]: df.head(2)
```

Out[7]:

GeoAreaName	Afghanistan	Albania	Algeria	Andorra	Angola	Antigua and Barbuda	Argentina	Armenia
2000	NaN	5.16	3.16	7.14	15.45	5.26	28.02	3.05
2001	NaN	5.16	3.42	7.14	15.45	5.26	26.46	3.05

2 rows × 195 columns

```
In [ ]: df.to_csv('women_in_parliament_processed.csv')
```

Figure 8-1. A typical notebook

As you can see in Figure 8-1, at various stages I've displayed the contents of my pandas DataFrame so that I can check what my data looks like.

This section of the notebook imports the data from an Excel spreadsheet file and outputs it again as a CSV file. So if this is something I want to do repeatedly, it's a great candidate for turning into a function.

I extracted the lines that carry out some operation rather than just showing me what the data looks like:

```
df = pd.read_excel("SG_GEN_PARL.xlsx")
df = df.drop(["Goal", "Target", "Indicator", "SeriesCode", "SeriesDescription",
            "GeoAreaCode", "Reporting Type", "Sex", "Units",], axis=1)
df = df.set_index("GeoAreaName").transpose()
df.to_csv("women_in_parliament_processed.csv")
```

To turn these lines of code into a function, I first considered what the overall purpose or behavior should be. This function needs to take in an Excel file, rearrange the data, and output a CSV file. I decided to name it `process_sdg_data` because I want it to work on all similar Excel files downloaded from the UN Sustainable Development Goals (hence "sdg"). If you're using abbreviations it's a good idea to document them somewhere, as discussed in the next chapter: more details on best practices for choosing names in "Names" on page 133.

I then thought about what the inputs and outputs of the function should be. I decided that my function should take an Excel file as input and produce a CSV file as output. I also considered what I wanted to change in the future and turned those into my function's arguments. For example, I might change the name of the input file or the name of the output file, so those should be arguments of my function.

Finally, I added the arguments as variables and wrote the body of the function:

```
def process_sdg_data(input_excel_file, columns_to_drop,
                     output_csv_file):
    df = pd.read_excel(input_excel_file)
    df = df.drop(columns_to_drop, axis=1)
    df = df.set_index("GeoAreaName").transpose()
    df.to_csv(output_csv_file)
```

The next step is to add a test for this function. The notebook lines where I displayed my data gave me ideas for what I should test. For example, I wanted to confirm that the output data had the correct columns. I know that the number of rows and columns in the output file should stay the same for any input file I process, so this is a good test to write.

Here's the test that goes with the `process_sdg_data` function:

```
import os
import pandas as pd

def test_process_sdg_data():

    test_filepath = "test_sgd_data.csv"
```

```
process_sdg_data("SG_GEN_PARL.xlsx",
                 ["Goal", "Target", "Indicator", "SeriesCode",
                 "SeriesDescription", "GeoAreaCode", "Reporting Type",
                 "Sex", "Units",],
                 test_filepath)

df = pd.read_csv(test_filepath)

assert len(df) == 24
assert len(df.columns) == 196

# cleanup step - delete the file produced in the test
os.remove(test_filepath)
```

The steps where I displayed my data have become the `assert` statements in my test.

Other tools have been developed to help you with the process of going from a note-book to a script. nbconvert (*https://oreil.ly/AiWYo*) and Jupytext (*https://oreil.ly/Yn5RA*) are two simple packages that extract the code in your notebook to a script. You can also follow the steps in the Kedro documentation (*https://oreil.ly/isx01*) to go from a notebook directly to a Kedro project.

Refactoring

Refactoring is a useful skill that helps you when the requirements for your code change. It's a normal part of a software development workflow. Here's a good description:

> *Refactoring is the process of changing a software system in a way that does not alter the external behavior of the code, yet improves its internal structure.*
> —Martin Fowler

You should refactor your code only when you have a specific reason to do so. If your code is working correctly and satisfying all its requirements, there's no need to refactor it. You should think about the problem you're trying to solve: for example, is there some new functionality you'd like to add? Or do you want to make your code cleaner so that it is easier to read and maintain? In this section I'll describe some strategies for refactoring your code and an example of how to do it.

Strategies for Refactoring

Ideally, before you refactor your code, you'll already have a full set of tests for it. Tests will check that the functionality of your code remains the same when you change it: you don't want to introduce bugs when you refactor your code.

It's a good idea to make incremental changes to your code. Don't rewrite everything at once and don't throw away parts of your code that work fine. You won't get everything correct the first time, especially if you're working on a complex project. It's good practice to refactor in phases with predefined milestones.

The overall strategy is simple: make a small change, run a test, then save your code (usually to version control as I'll describe in Chapter 10). The change can be as simple as changing the name of a variable, if you want to update what that variable is doing or make it easier to read. Your IDE makes this easy. See Figure 8-2 in the next section. Version control is extremely helpful here, because it makes it easy to revert to a previous version of your code if your change causes your tests to fail.

When you're refactoring, keep the interface of your function the same and change its internals. This means you won't need to change as much other code. If you are changing the interface or the behavior of the function, you'll need an integration test, which tests a larger amount of code. This will check that you didn't break something elsewhere in the system by changing what it was depending on.

Overall, successful refactoring depends on having a good set of tests. In the next section I'll show an example of how to refactor a function.

An Example Refactoring Workflow

As I mentioned in the previous section, the general principle here is to make a change, run your tests to check that you didn't break anything, then save your changes (usually by committing to version control, which I'll cover in Chapter 10). I'll illustrate this workflow using the weighted mean function from Chapter 7, because you already saw the test that goes with it.

Here's the function again:

```
def weighted_mean(num_list, weights):
    if not (num_list or weights):
        return None
    running_total = 0
    for i in range(len(num_list)):
        running_total += (num_list[i] * weights[i])
    return (running_total/sum(weights))
```

And here's the test that goes with it:

```
def test_weighted_mean():

    result = weighted_mean([1, 2, 4], [1, 2, 4])
    assert result == 3

    empty_list_result = weighted_mean([], [])
    assert not empty_list_result
```

First, run the test and confirm that everything is working correctly before you start refactoring:

```
$ pytest test_ch08.py

...

test_ch08.py .                          [100%]

========================= 1 passed in 0.03s ====
```

Next, make a small change. You may want to make changes that improve the readability of your code, for example, changing the names of your variables. You can do this easily using your IDE as shown in Figure 8-2:

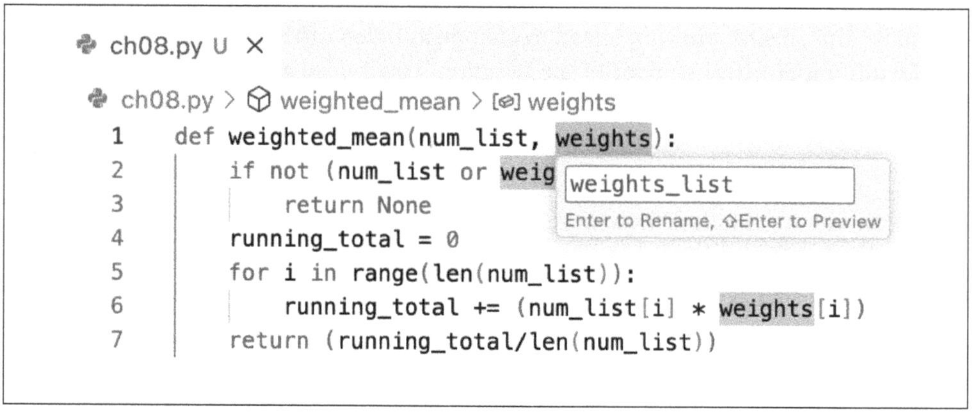

Figure 8-2. Refactoring in VS Code

This renames all the instances of `weights` to `weights_list`:

```python
def weighted_mean(num_list, weights_list):
    if not (num_list or weights_list):
        return None
    running_total = 0
    for i in range(len(num_list)):
        running_total += (num_list[i] * weights_list[i])
    return (running_total/sum(weights_list))
```

Then run your test again to confirm that your code still works correctly.

You should use the same workflow to make a bigger change. Next, I'll change the internal body of the function by replacing it with a built-in function from the NumPy library:

```python
import numpy as np

def weighted_mean(num_list, weights_list):
    try:
        return np.average(num_list, weights=weights_list)
    except ZeroDivisionError:
        return None
```

Running the test again confirms that the overall behavior of the function hasn't changed, and nor has the interface, even though the body of the function is completely different.

You can use this workflow for larger and more complex situations. You may find also that you also need to update your tests at the same time. It's not unusual to add more test cases during the process of refactoring.

Key Takeaways

Even though your project may change shape completely during the time you work on it, it's still important to think about the design of your code before you start working on your project, while you're working on it, and even after you've finished it. A well-designed project will be easier for other people to work on and easier for you if you come back to it after a break of months or even years.

You should also consider whether you can standardize your projects. If you find yourself repeatedly working on similar projects, consider putting in some time to develop a template that will be useful repeatedly. You can then use a tool such as Cookiecutter or Kedro to automate the process of setting up a project.

Modular code is critical to good design. Ensure that you think through how to split your code into pieces that can be easily reused or changed in the future. Before you start writing each function, consider its purpose and what its interfaces should be, and add only the code that actually carries out that purpose after you've set up the interfaces.

Jupyter notebooks are great for experimentation, but you may want to move to scripts when your code gets deployed to a production environment. To do this, consider what pieces of code should be turned into functions that can be reused elsewhere and follow the framework for writing modular code.

You'll often need to change your code for a number of reasons. The requirements for your code may change, you may want to make it more readable, you may want to make it more efficient, and so on. Refactoring is a normal part of any code project. A successful refactoring workflow depends on having a good set of tests. To refactor your code, make a small change, then run your tests to make sure your change didn't break anything, and then update your code wherever it is stored.

Designing your code well is a big part of writing production-ready code, but you'll also need to communicate with other people about what your code does. Documentation is key to this, and I'll describe a variety of best practices for documentation in the next chapter.

## CHAPTER 9

Documentation

Documentation is an often overlooked aspect of data science. It's commonly left until the end of a project, but then you're excited to move on to a new project, and the documentation is rushed or omitted completely. However, as I discussed in "Readability" on page 7, documentation is a crucial part of making your code reproducible. If you want other people to use your code, or if you want to come back to your code in the future, it needs good documentation. It's impossible to remember all your thoughts from when you originally wrote the code or initially carried out the experiments, so they need to be recorded.

Good documentation communicates ideas well. Your reader needs to understand what you want them to understand. So first, it's important to consider who you're writing the documentation for. Are you recording your experiments for another data scientist who might take over your project in the future? Are you documenting a piece of code that you think might be useful for other people on your team? Or are you recording your own thoughts so that you can come back to them in six months? Pick your level of detail and the language you use so that it is appropriate for your expected reader.

Other aspects of good documentation include being up to date: documentation is not useful if it is not maintained. Documentation should be updated at the same time as code changes are made. Make sure it's as easy as possible to update your documentation. For example, don't use proprietary documentation tools that require separate logins. Good documentation should also be well structured. The most important information should be easiest to find, so put it at the start or make it obvious where to find it.

Good documentation can save you a huge amount of time and reduce the complexity of a data science project. If you know what work has already been done, you reduce the chance of repeating the same work. You can also get up to speed much faster on a new project or easily remember what you were working on a year ago.

All of these statements are relevant to the documentation for any project, but some considerations are more specific to data science projects. In a data science project, it's common to try several potential solutions to a problem before settling on the one that works best. Because of this, it's good practice to document the thought process that goes into your experimentation and decision making. This is useful if you are asked questions on it later or you need to revisit the project in the future.

Try to answer questions like this in your documentation:

- Why did you select the data you used in this project?
- What are the assumptions you are making about your data?
- Why did you choose this analysis method rather than another?
- Are there circumstances where this analysis method does not work?
- What (if any) shortcuts did you take that could be improved later?
- What are some other avenues for future experimentation that you would suggest to anyone who works on this project in the future?
- What are the lessons you learned from this project?

In this chapter, I'll discuss different types of documentation and best practices for writing it. I'll cover documentation within your codebase, documentation in Jupyter notebooks, and documentation for machine learning experiments.

Documentation Within the Codebase

As I discussed in Chapter 1, good code is readable. A readable codebase should contain text as well as code, in the form of comments, docstrings, and longer documents. The code itself should be readable, and good names are the key to this. I'll give you suggestions for best practices for all these types of documentation in this section.

Here's a hierarchy of documentation within your codebase, from shorter to longer:

- Names of functions, classes, and modules give information on what you should expect that piece of code to do.
- Comments make a small individual point that adds extra information, similar to a footnote in a book.
- Docstrings give a longer overview of what a function or class does, including details of any edge cases.

- API documentation shows what each API endpoint expects as its input and returns for its output. You'll find more information about API documentation in Chapter 11.
- Longer documents such as readmes and tutorials give an overview of how to use all the code in a project.

Taken together, all of these will make your code much more readable and make it easier for other people to use your code. Each piece of information you want to convey to the reader of your code should be documented once. Put the summary of what your function does in the docstring, not the comments, then don't duplicate this in the README for your project.

Names

Every time you write code, you need to choose a lot of names. Variables, functions, notebooks, projects: all of them need a name. Good names are an important part of making your code readable. If someone else wants to use your code, they will read through it before making any changes. The names you use will communicate what you want your code to do. For example, a function named `download_and _clean_monthly_data` communicates much more than a function named `process_ data`. Your Jupyter notebook should never be named `untitled1.ipynb`, because this communicates nothing about what is in the notebook. If you need something from that notebook in the future, you won't be able to find it without a good name.

Good names are expressive, an appropriate length, and easy to read. Good names also use language that is relevant to the project you're working on, and to your company or organization. Units are great to include in variable names: `distance_km` is much more informative than `distance`. If you don't pick a good name at first, don't be afraid to update it later: you can find and replace all the instances of a name at the same time.

Be cautious with abbreviations when you are choosing names. Saving a few letters is often not worth the inconvenience and loss of time for other people to understand the context. It's OK to use abbreviations that are well known across your entire company, but I recommend avoiding them if they are specific, only for a single feature, or not widely used in your company.

So what is an appropriate length for a name? Variable and function names shouldn't be too short, because if a name is too short it increases the mental load for the person reading your code. They will need to translate from the name to a meaning. For example, `image_id` is much more informative than `im_id`, and `clean_df` is better than `cl_df`. Full words are much easier to read, and they are also easier to search for in your IDE if you need to look up their usage or alter them later.

For example, the following code snippet needs a comment to explain what is happening, because single letters are used for the variables:

```
# calculate the accuracy of the predictions compared to the test data
a = sum(x == y for x, y in zip(p, t))/len(p)
```

Choosing better names makes the code much easier to read:

```
accuracy = sum(x == y for x, y in zip(predictions, test_data))/len(predictions)
```

The variables x and y have been left as short names because they are used only within the call to sum() and, as such, are only temporary. Similarly, a convention in Python is to use the single letters i and j as counters, as in the following example:

```
for i in range(processed_results):
    # do something
```

Other commonly used conventions are df for a pandas DataFrame, and fig and ax for figures and axes when using Matplotlib, respectively. It's OK to use short names that your readers will recognize. You'll also often see function names that start with a verb, such as make_..., load_..., get_..., and so on, and I recommend this practice.

Names shouldn't be too similar. I always have to look up the documentation for the common Python datetime functions strptime and strftime to remember the difference between them, because they are so similar. Again, this means your reader needs to hold additional knowledge in their mind to use the code.

Additionally, you can make the names in your code readable by using Python formatting conventions. Variables and functions should use snake_case, where all the words are lowercase and joined with underscores. It's easier to read variable names if there is an underscore between each word: x_train_array is clearer than xtrainar ray. Class definitions should use CamelCase, where the initial letter of each word is capitalized. Constants or global variables should use ALL_CAPS.

 Don't use names of Python built-in functions as variable names; otherwise you won't be able to use the original functions. Here's an example:

```
list = [0, 2, 4]
```

This will cause the following line of code to return an error, instead of creating an empty list:

```
empty_list = list()
```

Module and file names are also very important. Choosing good names for these will help you remember where certain functionality is stored. As this blog post by David Nicholson (*https://oreil.ly/1WUx3*) recommends, put related files into subfolders rather than using prefixes to show that they are related. Good module names are specific rather than generic: *data_preprocessing_utils.py* is better than *utils.py*.

You can find more guidance on choosing good names in PEP8 (*https://oreil.ly/Hq3Ll*) and the Google Python Style Guide (*https://oreil.ly/csW2t*).

Comments

Comments are one of the most useful forms of documentation within the codebase, but you need to use them well. Comments can summarize, explain, or add caveats to your code or mark places where you need to come back and change things later. They can also be a useful way to start writing a function: you can start with pseudocode in the form of comments, then fill in the real code, which makes it easier to structure the function.

A comment in Python is designated with a # symbol:

```
# This is a comment.
```

Comments should not repeat the information that is already in the code. This doesn't help your reader, and you will also need to change the comment if the code changes. This violates the "Don't Repeat Yourself" principle from Chapter 1. This is an example of a bad comment:

```
# Train the classification model
classifier.fit(X_train, y_train)
```

A good comment adds caveats, summarizes information, or explains something not already in the code. This is an example of a useful comment:

```
def slow_way_to_calculate_mode(list_of_numbers):
    # This is for demo purposes only
    # Use the mode function from the statistics library in real use cases
```

Comments should be easy for your reader to understand. It's best to use full words and sentences instead of abbreviations. It's also a good idea to write the comments at the same time as you are writing the code, rather than adding explanations later. This gives you an opportunity to add the extra thoughts you have while writing the code.

Comments should always be professional, without offensive slang or curse words. But comments can be lighthearted and fun, if that fits in with your company's culture. The Apollo 11 source code from NASA has some great examples (see Figure 9-1).

```
243                BZF    P63SPOT4    # BRANCH IF ANTENNA ALREADY IN POSITION 1
244
245                CAF    CODE500     # ASTRONAUT:    PLEASE CRANK THE
246                TC     BANKCALL    #               SILLY THING AROUND
247                CADR   GOPERF1
248                TCF    GOTOPOOH    # TERMINATE
249                TCF    P63SPOT3    # PROCEED       SEE IF HE'S LYING
250
251    P63SPOT4    TC     BANKCALL    # ENTER         INITIALIZE LANDING RADAR
252                CADR   SETPOS1
253
254                TC     POSTJUMP    # OFF TO SEE THE WIZARD ...
```

Figure 9-1. Comments in the Apollo 11 source code (source: GitHub (https://oreil.ly/XFgna))

Comments also can be used to add other informative points, for example:

- Link to an external resource, such as a relevant issue on GitHub.
- Link to an internal project tracking system such as Jira.
- Add a TODO for a feature you want to come back and add in the future.
- Note that a line of code is a temporary fix.

Comments should be short and make a single point. If you need to include longer explanations, use docstrings or longer pieces of documentation. I'll cover these in the next sections.

Docstrings

Python docstrings are a formal longer version of comments that are commonly included at the start of a function or class definition, or at the top of the file. They give your reader an overall view of what the function or script should be doing, as opposed to comments that make a particular point. Docstrings are a crucial part of making your code easy for another person to read, because you can provide more detail on the purpose of a function than you can communicate just by the name of that function.

A function docstring should describe the expected inputs and outputs of that function. This is the interface to that function, which I discussed in "Interfaces and Contracts" on page 119. If you're not using type annotations, (which I described in "Type Checking" on page 91, you should include the input and outputs in the docstring. Docstrings are the Python standard for documenting a function, and it means that the text you enter can be returned by calling the help function in a Python interpreter. Additionally, automated documentation solutions such as Sphinx (*https://oreil.ly/_Y7fp*) or pdocs (*https://oreil.ly/OU1nS*) will pick up the text from the docstrings and generate web documentation from them.

Here's a great example of a docstring from the pandas codebase (*https://oreil.ly/oEBEE*). The `head()` method displays the first n rows of a pandas DataFrame. It's standard practice to enclose the docstring in triple ".

```
def head(self: NDFrameT, n: int = 5) -> NDFrameT:
    """
    Return the first `n` rows. ❶
    This function returns the first `n` rows for the object based
    on position. It is useful for quickly testing if your object
    has the right type of data in it.
    For negative values of `n`, this function returns all rows except
    the last `|n|` rows, equivalent to ``df[:n]``. ❷
    If n is larger than the number of rows, this function returns all rows. ❸
    Parameters
    ----------
    n : int, default 5 ❹
        Number of rows to select.
    Returns
    -------
    same type as caller ❺
        The first `n` rows of the caller object.
    """
```

❶ This gives an overall description of the function.

❷ This is a caveat that says the behavior may not be what we expect.

❸ This is an edge case.

❹ The input parameter with the default and the expected type.

❺ The output, which can be one of many types. Common ones for this function would be a pandas DataFrame or Series.

You can get the same documentation from `help(df.head)` in a Python interpreter. This docstring is also picked up by the autogenerated documentation (*https://oreil.ly/Ra2KM*) for pandas. If you're working in a Jupyter notebook you can also use `pd.DataFrame.head?` to see this docstring.

There are three main templates for docstrings: Google docstrings (*https://oreil.ly/VXsd9*), NumPy docstrings (*https://oreil.ly/mJcGp*), and reStructuredText docstrings (*https://oreil.ly/GcEYV*). I recommend picking one of these and sticking to it, because the standardization makes it easy to read: the format is familiar. You can configure a code editor to automatically generate a docstring template in your preferred format, as in this example:

```
def process_sdg_data(input_excel_file, columns_to_drop):
    """_summary_

    Args:
        input_excel_file (_type_): _description_
        columns_to_drop (_type_): _description_

    Returns:
        _type_: _description_
    """
    df = pd.read_excel(input_excel_file)
    df = df.drop(columns_to_drop, axis=1)
    df = df.set_index('GeoAreaName').transpose()
    return df
```

And here's the function with a completed docstring:

```
def process_sdg_data(input_excel_file, columns_to_drop):
    """Rearrange SDG (Sustainable Development Goals) data to load in API.

    Args:
        input_excel_file (str): Path to the input data file.
        columns_to_drop (list): List of column names to drop.

    Returns:
        pandas DataFrame: DataFrame with columns expected by API code.
    """
    df = pd.read_excel(input_excel_file)
    df = df.drop(columns_to_drop, axis=1)
    df = df.set_index('GeoAreaName').transpose()
    return df
```

It's good practice to add docstrings to your tests. They should explain the purpose of the test and the expected outcome, and they can include details on edge cases or describe the bug that is being checked. Adding docstrings will make it easier for others to understand and maintain your tests in the future. This article by Hynek Schlawack (*https://oreil.ly/hbFto*) provides some more useful details.

Readmes, Tutorials, and Other Longer Documents

Longer documents should give your readers the overall context of your project and advertise the work you have done. These go beyond docstrings to give users an overview of your entire project. Consider including the following in your project's documentation:

- A short overview of your project, which could be a single paragraph. You can think of this as an "executive summary." Try to include the overall goals of the project, who should use it, and the use cases.

- How to get started using the project and how to navigate it. This could take the form of a notebook tutorial.

- Whether there are any project caveats or limitations. For example, if your code only works with data from 2023 or earlier, it's useful to highlight this when someone reads the introduction to your project, rather than needing to dig into the code comments.

- The next steps in the project. Even if you have finished working on a project, it's useful to note good next steps for anyone who picks up this work in the future.

Every code repository should contain a *README.md* file that covers these points and gives an overall introduction to the project. This is a Markdown file, so the file extension is *.md*. Markdown is a language for writing structured documents that uses symbols to control formatting. You can find an introduction to Markdown and other useful tips for writing a README in the GitHub documentation (*https://oreil.ly/ rQit2*).

As with everything else in this chapter, it is essential to keep longer documents up to date. Few things are more frustrating than trying to follow a tutorial example, then finding that the underlying code has changed and the example doesn't run. Automated tests for the examples in your tutorials prevent this.

Documentation is easiest to maintain if it sits in the same location as your code. For example, it's easier to update documentation if it's in your GitHub repository rather than an external tool such as Confluence. You can use tools for documentation such as Sphinx (*https://oreil.ly/63mbI*) to generate HTML documentation, then host it using tools such as Read the Docs (*https://oreil.ly/vrM6o*) or GitHub Pages (*https:// oreil.ly/TqdGi*).

The combination of good names, useful comments, completed docstrings, and an overall introduction will ensure that your code is easy to run, maintain, and work on in the future.

Documentation in Jupyter Notebooks

Jupyter notebooks can be very informal, and they are often used for the initial stages of a project. But even if your notebook is a blind alley, where you try something out and it doesn't work, the code in that notebook could very well be useful in the future. Also, it's very useful to know what's previously been tried and failed. So it's worthwhile to be able to find that code again and know what is in the notebook. As discussed in "Names" on page 133, it's important that your notebook has a descriptive name. Additionally, it's a good idea to describe what's in the notebook at the very start.

Within a notebook, you can add text to give the notebook a structure and add explanatory notes. Don't repeat the information in the code. Use the text to add summaries, caveats, and explanations. You always should update the text when you update the code.

You can add text to Jupyter notebooks using Markdown. To convert a cell from code to Markdown, either press the m hotkey when you are in command mode in a notebook or use the dropdown menu at the top of the notebook.

Figure 9-2 shows a good mix of text and code. The text adds information to the notebook without duplicating the code.

The main tool for preprocessing textual data is a tokenizer. A tokenizer splits text into *tokens* according to a set of rules. The tokens are converted into numbers and then tensors, which become the model inputs. Any additional inputs required by the model are added by the tokenizer.

If you plan on using a pretrained model, it's important to use the associated pretrained tokenizer. This ensures the text is split the same way as the pretraining corpus, and uses the same corresponding tokens-to-index (usually referred to as the *vocab*) during pretraining.

Get started by loading a pretrained tokenizer with the AutoTokenizer.from_pretrained() method. This downloads the *vocab* a model was pretrained with:

```
In [ ]: from transformers import AutoTokenizer tokenizer =
        AutoTokenizer.from_pretrained("bert-base-cased")
```

Then pass your text to the tokenizer:

```
In [ ]: encoded_input = tokenizer("Do not meddle in the affairs of wizards, for they are
        subtle and quick to anger.") print(encoded_input)
```

```
Out[ ]: {'input_ids': [101, 2079, 2025, 19960, 10362, 1999, 1996, 3821, 1997, 16657, 101
        0, 2005, 2027, 2024, 11259, 1998, 4248, 2000, 4963, 1012, 102],
         'token_type_ids': [0, 0, 0, 0, 0, 0, 0, 0, 0, 0, 0, 0, 0, 0, 0, 0, 0, 0, 0,
        0],
         'attention_mask': [1, 1, 1, 1, 1, 1, 1, 1, 1, 1, 1, 1, 1, 1, 1, 1, 1, 1, 1,
        1]}
```

The tokenizer returns a dictionary with three important items:

- input_ids are the indices corresponding to each token in the sentence.
- attention_mask indicates whether a token should be attended to or not.
- token_type_ids identifies which sequence a token belongs to when there is more than one sequence.

Figure 9-2. Mixing code and text in a Jupyter notebook (source: GitHub (https://oreil.ly/edZMf))

You can also use Markdown in a notebook to add headings, which will help your readers navigate the notebook. Headings use the # symbol:

```
# This is a top level heading
## This is a second level heading
### This is a third level heading
```

This gives the result shown in Figure 9-3.

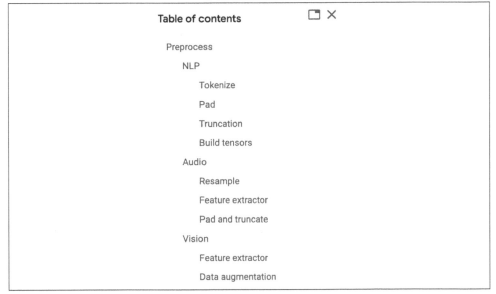

Figure 9-3. Using headings in a Jupyter notebook (source: GitHub (https://oreil.ly/ dyNpn))

A notebook with multiple well-labeled sections is much easier to read and navigate.

Documenting Machine Learning Experiments

In machine learning projects, you'll try out many different models, datasets, and hyperparameters in search of the model that makes the best predictions according to the evaluation metrics you choose. The number of hyperparameters in particular can grow very large, so it's important to document what combinations you have tried. This will help if you come back to your work in the future, and it will also help anyone else who works on your project.

Your experiments need to be documented in a structured manner, to ensure you are being rigorous. To do this, you'll need to ensure you track all the variables that change in each iteration of your experiment. This means you can reproduce your experiment in the future, or someone else can pick up the project and know what variables have been tested. You should also record any assumptions you are making along the way.

Consider recording the following:

- The data you used to train the model
- The training/evaluation/test split
- The feature engineering choices you made
- The model hyperparameters (such as the regularization in a logistic regression model or the learning rate for a neural network)
- The metrics you are evaluating your model on, such as accuracy, precision, and recall

Recording all these parameters manually is tedious and it's error prone, so I recommend you use an automated tool. Weights and Biases (*https://wandb.ai*) is a useful tool for tracking machine learning experiments. It easily integrates with scikit-learn, TensorFlow, and PyTorch and logs your training parameters to a web dashboard as shown in Figure 9-4.

Name (384 visualized)	Created ▾	Runtime	Sweep	encoder	num_train	num_valid	acc
worldly-totem-422	1mo ago	12m 54s	-	resnet34	682	97	0.8566
jumping-voice-421	1mo ago	11m 59s	-	resnet34	725	92	0.8504
logical-energy-420	1mo ago	2m 14s	-	resnet34	66	10	0.626
laced-dust-419	1mo ago	2m 4s	-	resnet18	61	15	0.5968
whole-music-418	1mo ago	1m 40s	-	resnet18	68	13	0.6139
grateful-glitter-417	1mo ago	21s	-	resnet18	70	11	0.2367
efficient-lake-416	1mo ago	1m 42s	-	resnet18	76	10	0.6899
clear-night-415	1mo ago	1m 17s	-	resnet18	66	10	0.5403
glorious-night-414	1mo ago	1m 33s	-	resnet18	68	7	0.7627
smart-sponge-413	1mo ago	1m 46s	-	resnet18	72	11	0.6517

Figure 9-4. Tracking experiments in Weights and Biases (source: Weights and Biases documentation (https://oreil.ly/gv4wo))

Other experiment tracking solutions include the open source package Sacred (*https://oreil.ly/aZFSI*), MLflow (*https://oreil.ly/tf3SN*), Neptune (*https://oreil.ly/sohIo*), and SageMaker Experiments (*https://oreil.ly/uavxZ*) from AWS. Any one of these will help you record your experiments in an automated way.

Key Takeaways

Good documentation is very important for helping other people use your projects and for making your code readable. Make sure your documentation is kept up to date and written for the audience who will be using your code. Good documentation helps other people get started on your project, and it helps you understand your code in the future. If you'd like to learn more, the Write the Docs (*https://oreil.ly/ZQPUg*) community has many useful tips.

Following these recommendations will help you write good documentation:

Names
Names of variables, functions, and files should be informative, an appropriate length, and easy to read.

Comments
Your comments should add extra information not contained in the code, such as a summary or a caveat.

Docstrings
Your functions should always have a docstring that describes the inputs and outputs of the function, as well as the purpose of that function.

READMEs
Every repository or project should have an introduction that advertises your code and lets other people know why they should use it.

Jupyter notebooks
Your notebooks will be much easier to read if you give them good names, give them a structure, and intersperse text and code.

Experiment tracking
Experiments, especially in machine learning projects, should be tracked in a structured way.

All the techniques in this chapter will make your code clear to read and make it easy to advertise what it does and for other people to use it.

## CHAPTER 10

Sharing Your Code: Version Control, Dependencies, and Packaging

Sharing your code and collaborating with others is hugely important to your success in data science. You might join an existing project that has a large codebase. You might start by working on your code in isolation, but as your project grows, you may want to share it with others so that they don't need to solve the same problems as well. Or you could be contributing to open source projects.

If you're sharing your code publicly, as an open source project, that allows you to join a community. Python open source libraries are a huge ecosystem, and data science would be so much harder without pandas, NumPy, scikit-learn, Matplotlib, and many others.

Whether you're contributing to open source projects or collaborating with teammates at your company, you'll need to know some tools and techniques that make it easier for multiple people to work on the same code. The tools may vary, but many of the principles are standard.

In this chapter I'll cover these tools and techniques that will help you collaborate with other developers. First, version control is important because it's the standard way of collaborating on a codebase. Second, I'll cover tools for managing the third-party libraries that your code depends on. Finally, I'll describe how to package your projects so that other people can install them.

Version Control Using Git

Version control is a way of tracking what changes have been made to a codebase, and it allows multiple people to work on the same code easily. It lets you see who made what changes to the code, and it prevents conflicts if two people are working on the same line of code. It also means that if someone makes a change that causes a bug, or you make a mistake in your code, it's easy to go back to the previous version of the code.

Version control systems are usually distributed: a copy of the code is stored on every developer's machine and also saved in a central location. All code should be backed up in case something bad happens: you could lose your laptop, your remote instance could get corrupted, and so on.

Git (*https://git-scm.com*) is the most popular system for distributed version control. It is an open source project, created in 2005 by Linus Torvalds (who also created Linux). According to the 2022 Stack Overflow Developer Survey (*https://oreil.ly/zMvyl*), 96% of professional developers use Git, although other version control systems such as Subversion (*https://subversion.apache.org*) and Mercurial (*https://www.mercurial-scm.org*) also exist.

GitHub (*https://github.com*), owned by Microsoft, is the most popular site for storing code that is tracked using Git, but there's no official link between GitHub and Git. Other similar sites include GitLab (*https://about.gitlab.com*) and Bitbucket (*https://bitbucket.org/product*).

> Version control systems designed for code are not designed to be used to back up and version your data. It's much better to use a separate, dedicated system for your data. Code version control systems are not designed to work with large file sizes, and storing data here may also lead to unnecessary duplication or security risks.

Git has many features, and I'll just give you an overview of the most important ones. If you'd like to learn more, see either the Git documentation (*https://oreil.ly/AcZrR*) or the GitHub documentation (*https://docs.github.com*). For helpful tips, check out the Dangit, Git (*https://dangitgit.com*) website.

How Does Git Work?

Git works on the basis that each project you're working on is stored in its own directory, and you'd like to keep track of all the changes to the code in that directory. The underlying data stored by Git is a snapshot of the state of all the files and the folder structure of the directory you are tracking. These snapshots are updated as you change the code. This means you have a history of all the changes that you (or someone else) have made to that code.

A repository (or repo for short) is a directory where Git keeps track of the changes. A first step in using Git is to initialize a local repository in the directory where you're storing your code. This creates a hidden *.git* folder, which contains a database that stores all the snapshots of your code.

Git tracks changes you make to a file as you work, but it doesn't save the snapshot of those changes. The changes are only present in your working directory. If you're happy with the changes that you've made and you would like to save those versions of the files you've changed, you can add them to a "staging" area. The staging area collects all the changes that you want to include in the next saved snapshot.

The next step is to "commit" these changes. Making a commit saves the snapshot of the current version of the files to your local repository. This is only for files that you've changed and added to the commit. Each commit has a unique ID (known as a commit hash, created through a cryptographic hash function), and this can be used as a reference to it. You can see an example of this workflow in "Tracking Changes and Committing" on page 147.

A local repository stores the state of your project code on your computer, but you can also have a remote repository. This is a copy of your project code on a central server such as GitHub. To add your commit to a remote repository, you can "push" it from your local repository. If someone else is working on the project as well, you can "pull" their changes from the remote repository. This will update the files on your computer with their changes.

Figure 10-1 shows how the steps of adding, committing, pushing, and pulling your code fit together.

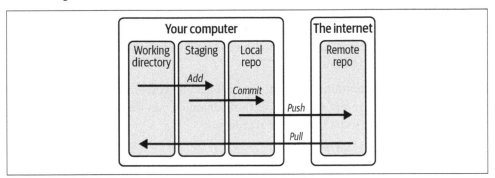

Figure 10-1. Git principles

Tracking Changes and Committing

I'll go through an example to show how this works. You can install Git by following the steps in the Git documentation (*https://oreil.ly/rDMik*).

If you're working on a project and you want Git to track changes, run the following command in the top level of your project directory:

```
$ git init
```

Next, add the files that you've changed to the staging area:

```
$ git add README.md
```

At any time, you can use the `git status` command to see what's going on:

```
$ git status

On branch main

No commits yet

Changes to be committed:
  (use "git rm --cached <file>..." to unstage)
        new file:   README.md
```

This message mentions that you are working on the main branch, and I'll talk about branches in "Branches and Pull Requests" on page 150.

Then, commit your changes to the local repository:

```
$ git commit -m "Initial commit"
```

You'll see a message like this:

```
[main (root-commit) b25021e] Initial commit
 1 file changed, 0 insertions(+), 0 deletions(-)
 create mode 100644 README.md
```

Commits have a unique ID, author name, timestamp, and a message that you provide to say what the change was. Commit messages should be informative and give a short description of the change you made.

Let's look at another commit. Once you've written some code in your repository, and you reach a point where you want to save those changes, run the `add` command again to add the files you have changed to the staging area:

```
$ git add api_functions.py
```

And then commit your changes with this command:

```
$ git commit -m "Created helper functions for API"
```

You'll see a message like this:

```
[main b78faad] Created helper functions for API
 1 file changed, 19 insertions(+)
 create mode 100644 api_functions.py
```

There are some best practices for commits. Each commit should be about only one thing, for example, fixing a problem or adding one small feature. It's best to split up your changes into small pieces so that if you make a change and it causes a problem later on, it's easier to trace the problem back to the change that caused it. It's also a good idea to run your tests before making a commit, and I'll talk about how to automate this process in Chapter 12.

Remote and Local

So far, I've described how to use Git with a local repository on your computer. In this section, I'll describe how to link your local repository to a remote repository and how to download a remote repository to your computer.

After you have followed the steps in "Tracking Changes and Committing" on page 147, the next step is to create a remote repository. The exact steps will depend on where your remote repository is hosted, but Figure 10-2 shows what this looks like on GitHub.

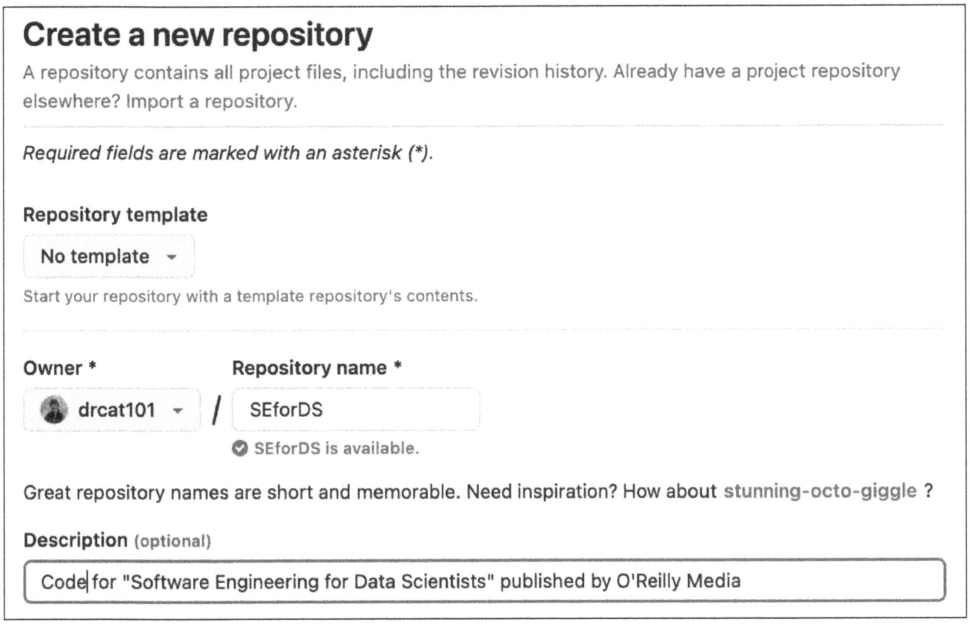

Create a new repository

A repository contains all project files, including the revision history. Already have a project repository elsewhere? Import a repository.

Required fields are marked with an asterisk (*).

Repository template

No template ▾

Start your repository with a template repository's contents.

Owner *	Repository name *
🐱 drcat101 ▾	/	SEforDS
	✅ SEforDS is available.

Great repository names are short and memorable. Need inspiration? How about stunning-octo-giggle ?

Description (optional)

Code for "Software Engineering for Data Scientists" published by O'Reilly Media

Figure 10-2. Creating a new repository on GitHub

Next, you need to tell your local version of Git where the remote repository is located by running the following command:

```
$ git remote add origin https://github.com/drcat101/SEforDS.git
```

Replace the URL in this link with the URL of your remote repository.

Finally, you can push the commit from your local repository to the remote repository:

```
$ git push -u origin main
```

You'll see a message like this:

```
Enumerating objects: 3, done.
Counting objects: 100% (3/3), done.
Writing objects: 100% (3/3), 219 bytes | 219.00 KiB/s, done.
Total 3 (delta 0), reused 0 (delta 0), pack-reused 0
To https://github.com/drcat101/SEforDS.git
 * [new branch]      main -> main
branch 'main' set up to track 'origin/main'.
```

After running this command, the remote repository will contain the files in your local repository, updated with the changes in your commit.

You may want to start working on a project that already has some existing code in a remote repository. In this situation, you need to "clone" it. This means the remote repository is downloaded to your computer, and this becomes a new local repository.

You can clone a repository using the following command:

```
$ git clone https://github.com/drcat101/SEforDS.git
```

There are two options for cloning: HTTPS and SSH. SSH provides a higher level of security but is more time consuming to set up.

You can also start working on a project by first making a remote repository, cloning the repository to your local machine, then starting to write code.

In the next section, I'll describe some Git features that are particularly useful for collaboration: branches and pull requests.

Branches and Pull Requests

Branches in Git let you isolate the changes you are making and try out new features without affecting the primary version of the code while still tracking the changes you have made. This is particularly useful when many people are working on the same codebase, because you can work on the same code without overlap.

Making a branch doesn't create a copy of the files containing your code. Instead, Git tracks a set of changes introduced from a particular point in the project's timeline. This means that you can easily work on different features and then merge the changes back into the original code.

All repositories have a default branch, usually named main. Figure 10-3 shows the main branch and a new branch. You can create a branch, add as many commits as you want to that branch, then merge those changes into the main branch. While you're working on the new branch, none of the changes you make affect the main branch. Meanwhile, someone else can make changes to the main branch and this won't affect the code you're working on.

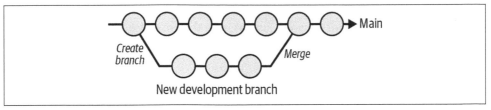

Figure 10-3. Branching in Git—each circle represents one commit

 Using the name `main` for the default branch in a repository is a convention, and you can change this to any name that you prefer. Unfortunately, you may still see some repositories that use the name `master` for the default branch. This should be avoided because the word "master" has connotations of slavery.

To create a new branch named `new_branch`, run the following command:

```
$ git branch new_branch
```

Next, change where you are working to this branch with the following command:

```
$ git checkout new_branch
```

You can combine the two previous commands by using `git checkout` with a `-b` flag:

```
$ git checkout -b new_branch
```

After you have checked out the branch, any changes you make to the code on your computer will take place on your `new_branch` development branch, not the main branch.

When you want to save your new branch to the remote repository, you can run the following command:

```
$ git push origin new_branch
```

When you have finished working on the new branch, you can merge it with the main branch. The code changes in the new branch will be incorporated into the code in the main branch.

Before merging, make sure to switch onto the main branch using the this command:

```
$ git checkout main
```

Then, merge the branch:

```
$ git merge new_branch
```

After you've merged the branch, you should delete that branch. The commit history will be preserved.

You may encounter merge conflicts when you merge a branch. These arise when you have changed a line of code in your new branch that has also been changed in the main branch. You'll need to decide which version of this line of code should be kept.

 Jupyter notebooks often cause merge conflicts. Notebooks are stored as a form of JSON, and this includes the contents of the cell outputs. If these change at all, they'll be tracked by Git.

There are a few solutions to this. First, you can manually clear the cell outputs from your notebooks, but this is very easy to forget. I'll show you how you could do this automatically in Chapter 12. Second, you can use nbdime (*https://oreil.ly/cV563*), which configures Git to only compare the code in notebooks, not cell outputs. Or third, you can use Jupytext (*https://oreil.ly/O0yH7*) to convert your notebooks to *.py* or *.md* files, which can easily be tracked using Git.

If you would like someone else to review your code before you merge your branch, you can use a pull request. This asks another developer to look at the changes you have made, then you can discuss and review them before merging the changes.

The easiest way to open a pull request is to use the interface on GitHub, as shown in Figure 10-4.

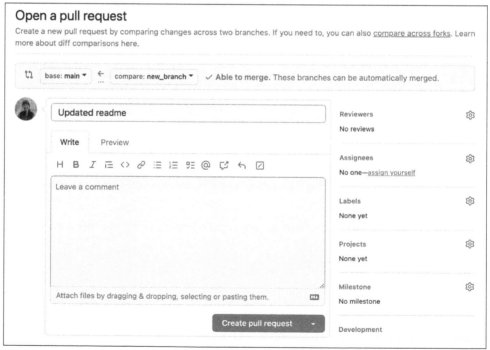

Figure 10-4. Opening a pull request on GitHub

A pull request should include comments to describe what you are changing, and why those changes should be made. This will help the reviewer know where to focus the discussion.

Code Reviews

Many development teams and companies have a system of code reviews. These are somewhat formal, structured sessions to review code, often in the format of pull requests. The practice of code reviews aims to improve code before it goes into production by giving other team members a chance to review it first and spot bugs and security risks before they cause a problem. It's also a chance to share ideas and improve code structure, and for more experienced developers to pass on their knowledge. In addition, code reviews record what decisions were made, and why.

Best practices for code reviews include:

- Consider many different aspects of code quality, including readability, simplicity, and modularity.
- Make sure everyone gets heard. Everyone's experience is valuable, and junior folks should get a chance to ask questions.
- Highlight areas where the code under consideration is good, not just pointing out problems.
- Limiting the time spent on reviewing code. Code reviews shouldn't cause delays.

This blog post from Tim Hopper (*https://oreil.ly/hn_xv*) gives some more good suggestions for data science code reviews.

There are other commands and techniques you'll need to know to successfully use Git, including how to ignore files and how to undo changes you've made. I'm not going to provide full details here, and I recommend you refer to the links I provided in "Version Control Using Git" on page 145.

In this section I've given you a brief overview of how to use Git for version control. Next, I'll move on to something more specific to Python programming: managing dependencies and using virtual environments.

Dependencies and Virtual Environments

If you want other people to be able to use your code, they'll need to install the same libraries you used to write that code. A dependency is a third-party library that you have installed and that your code requires to work, for example, pandas or NumPy. Your code may work with only a specific version of a library, or with a range of versions. So to make your code reproducible, you'll need to include information on the versions of the libraries that your code depends on (its dependencies).

Versioning

Python libraries (and indeed most software packages) get version numbers so that you know what set of code corresponds to a particular release. It's best practice to add versioning to your projects, and there are a number of different versioning schemes, The Semantic Versioning (SemVer) (*https://semver.org*) specification is one of the most popular, and you may also see Calendar Versioning (*https://calver.org*).

If a project is using SemVer, you'll see two or three numbers separated by periods, such as Python 3.10 or NumPy 1.24.3. The first number means a major version release, the second means a minor version, and the third is a patch.

A major version means there are breaking changes (some features that previously worked have been changed and no longer work), such as Python 2.x to Python 3.x, or pandas 1.x to 2.x. A minor version means there are smaller updates; there may be some new features but there are no breaking changes. A patch is a minor change, such as fixing a few small bugs.

In this section I'll outline tools to manage dependencies so that you don't need to manually keep track of all the versions of the libraries you are using. To use these, you'll first need to know about virtual environments.

Virtual Environments

Virtual environments are an important concept in Python, and you may already be familiar with them, but I'll give you a quick overview here. A virtual environment is a way of isolating the installed libraries for a particular project, instead of in the system-wide Python environment. It means that the Python interpreter and the modules included in the Python standard library are shared across the system, then you can install any additional libraries in a separate space for each project.

 I strongly recommend that you don't install libraries in the system-wide (root) Python environment. If you do this, you will likely find that it becomes difficult to test or debug your projects because different projects require different versions of the same library. Additionally, your computer's operating system has system-wide environment packages in Python. If you install or uninstall libraries without using the system package manager (such as apt or brew), there is a real possibility of breaking the system or degrading some behaviors.

Virtual environments mean that different projects can have different versions of any particular library without conflicts. To give a concrete example, Project A might need to use features introduced in NumPy version 1.25, but Project B uses the syntax from an older version. If you upgrade NumPy across your whole system, Project B will no longer work. Virtual environments solve this problem by letting you have multiple versions of the same library installed on your system at the same time.

There are many different tools for managing Python virtual environments. Some of the more popular tools include:

- venv (*https://oreil.ly/QIEQc*) is included in the Python standard library

- virtualenv (*https://oreil.ly/PMBoK*) is an older project than venv and contains more features. venv is a subset of virtualenv.

- Pyenv (*https://oreil.ly/nnvwr*) manages Python versions, so you can have multiple versions of Python installed on your system at the same time (you can use Python 3.7 and Python 3.10 for different projects, for example). The pyenv-virtualenv (*https://oreil.ly/tZ8Xv*) plug-in lets you manage virtual environments as well.

- Conda (*https://oreil.ly/VrIMo*) manages virtual environments but also installs packages. It downloads packages from a separate package repository managed by Anaconda (*https://www.anaconda.com*) instead of from PyPI (*https://pypi.org*) (the Python Packaging Index), the standard Python package repository.

- Poetry (*https://python-poetry.org*), PDM (*https://pdm.fming.dev*), and Hatch (*https://hatch.pypa.io*) also manage dependencies as well as virtual environments. I'll talk about Poetry in detail in the next section.

You can find full details of how to use all of these tools via the links above, but here's a quick example of how to use venv.

Before you install any packages, create a new virtual environment using the following command on macOS or Linux:

```
$ python -m venv SEforDS
```

You can replace SEforDS with the name of your virtual environment.

Next, activate the virtual environment with this command:

```
$ source SEforDS/bin/activate
```

You'll see the name of your virtual environment appear in parentheses before the command prompt, like so:

```
(SEforDS)$
```

This is common to any of the virtual environment tools above. You can now install packages using `pip` into your virtual environment.

When you're done with the virtual environment, you can exit it with this command:

```
(SEforDS)$ deactivate
```

The name of your virtual environment will disappear from the command prompt.

It's best practice to create a new virtual environment every time you start a new project, activate it, then install the libraries you need for that project. You should keep your system Python installation "clean" and not install any third-party libraries system-wide. This will prevent any conflicts between library versions.

Managing Dependencies with pip

The simplest way to record the dependencies required by your project is using `pip`, the package manager built into Python. You can save a list of all the packages that your project requires using the `pip freeze` command:

```
$ python -m pip freeze > requirements.txt
```

This writes all the packages in the environment to a text file named *requirements.txt*. You'll need to use a virtual environment for your project and have it active when running this command; otherwise it will record the libraries from your system Python installation.

The result is a text file that looks like this:

```
numpy==1.25.2
pandas==2.0.3
python-dateutil==2.8.2
pytz==2023.3
six==1.16.0
tzdata==2023.3
```

It contains the versions of the libraries currently installed in your environment and the libraries they depend on (for example, the Python dateutil library is a dependency of pandas).

You can upload the *requirements.txt* file to the project repository in your version control system. Then, when someone else wants to use your project or you want to run your project in a different environment, you can use this command to install your project's dependencies:

```
$ pip install -r requirements.txt
```

This process is simple, but it does have a few downsides. For example, if you remove a library from your project's requirements (for example, pandas) you need to figure out which other libraries are its dependencies and remove them manually. The *requirements.txt* file doesn't include any information on the Python version. Additionally, there can be changes in the libraries that are dependencies of the libraries you are using (the subdependencies of your project). If you're using `pip` to manage your dependencies, you'll need to handle these things manually. Fortunately, other dependency managers will handle these for you, as I'll explain in the next section.

Managing Dependencies with Poetry

Dependency managers such as Poetry (*https://python-poetry.org*), PDM (*https://pdm.fming.dev*), and Hatch (*https://hatch.pypa.io*) make it much easier to manage your project's dependencies than using `pip`. In this section I'll explain how to manage your project's dependencies using Poetry. This is particularly useful if you are also using Poetry for packaging, which I will describe later in this chapter.

Instead of the *requirements.txt* file, Poetry uses a file named *pyproject.toml*. This file is the standard file for making Python packages installable, and I'll talk about it more in "Python Packaging" on page 159. The *pyproject.toml* file contains all the requirements for your project, including its dependencies.

You can install Poetry with the following command:

```
$ curl -sSL https://install.python-poetry.org | python3 -
```

You should install Poetry system-wide rather than in a virtual environment, because you want it to work in all your virtual environments. Follow the instructions in your terminal to add Poetry to your shell.

If you're starting a new project, you can ask Poetry to set up a new folder populated with the files and folders you need to get started. You can do this with the following command:

```
$ poetry new SE_for_DS
```

If you've already started writing code, you can use the following command to initialize Poetry in your existing folder:

```
$ poetry init
```

After running either of these commands, you'll see that your project folder contains files named *pyproject.toml* and *poetry.lock*. The *pyproject.toml* file contains a section that lists your project's dependencies. If you look at the contents of the file before you've installed any third-party libraries, you'll see this section on dependencies:

```
[tool.poetry.dependencies]
python = "^3.10"
```

You can either update the *pyproject.toml* file manually or use the `poetry add` command to add the libraries your project requires. This will also install the library in the virtual environment for the project.

```
$ poetry add pandas
```

If you look at the contents of the *pyproject.toml* file, you'll see that pandas has been added to the dependencies:

```
[tool.poetry.dependencies]
python = "^3.10"
pandas = "^2.1.0"
```

Because the pandas version is specified as `"^2.1.0"`, this means that version 2.1.0 or newer is acceptable in this project. By default, Poetry assumes that the current version of a package and all future versions will work with your project. If this isn't the case, you'll need to change the version specification.

A nested shell is the default way to use a virtual environment with Poetry. To activate a virtual environment in a directory that contains a *pyproject.toml* file, use the following command:

```
$ poetry shell
```

Then to deactivate the virtual environment, type **exit**.

As well as listing the required library versions in the *pyproject.toml* file, Poetry also uses the *poetry.lock* file to store hashes to exact versions of the libraries in your project. This helps ensure that your project works across different operating systems. Each time you install a library, your *poetry.lock* file is updated, and it should look like this:

```
# This file is automatically @generated by Poetry 1.6.1 and should not be changed$

[[package]]
name = "numpy"
version = "1.25.2"
description = "Fundamental package for array computing in Python"
optional = false
python-versions = ">=3.9"
files = [
    {file = "numpy-1.25.2-cp310-cp310-macosx_10_9_x86_64.whl",
    hash = "sha256:db3$
    {file = "numpy-1.25.2-cp310-cp310-macosx_11_0_arm64.whl",
    hash = "sha256:9031$
...
```

You can then upload this file to your version control system.

To install the dependencies for your project in another environment, use the following command:

```
$ poetry install
```

Poetry will look for the *poetry.lock* file to check for the exact library versions and install them in the new environment. If there's no *.lock* file, Poetry will just install the newest versions of the libraries specified in the *pyproject.toml* file.

Whether you use `pip` or Poetry, it's very important that you keep your project's dependencies up to date so that other people can easily use your code.

Python Packaging

If you want to make your code easy for other people to use, you can turn it into a package. This means that people can install it in their own Python environment, then import it into any project they are working on, in the same way you use NumPy or pandas. In this section I'll describe the process of turning your Python code into a package.

One of the biggest strengths of Python is its huge ecosystem of packages, and PyPI (*https://pypi.org*) (the Python Package Index) enables this. PyPI hosts an enormous number of packages so that they're available for you to download. At the time of writing, there were 473,661 projects on PyPI!

If you want to share your code publicly you can upload a package to PyPI, and then anyone can install it using pip and use it in their projects. But you can also create a package and share the package files within your company so that your teammates can install and use it. A package ensures that your code is completely reproducible.

When you create a package and make it public, you then have some responsibility to maintain it (or at least make it easy for other people to add to it). If other people start depending on your code, they should help you maintain it, but the ideal situation is if you as the creator collaborate with them to update the package.

A brief note on terminology: a Python module is a *.py* file. A Python package can mean one of two things: the first is a directory with a *__init__.py* file that contains other modules. *__init__.py* is a Python file that must be present to let you import modules from that directory. The second is a distribution package that lets you distribute code via PyPI and installs your module/library. In this section, I'm using the word "package" in the second sense.

In the rest of this section, I'll describe how to create a package and upload it to PyPI.

Packaging Basics

Before you start building your package, ensure that your code meets the following criteria so that users of your package get a good experience:

- It meets the design you planned.
- It is fully functional.
- It has been neatly formatted (see Chapter 6).
- It has been tested (see Chapter 7).
- It has good documentation (see Chapter 9).

You'll also need to put the code that you want to turn into a package inside a single folder. Give this folder the name you want to use for your package, and keep it separate from the tests and documentation associated with it. You'll often see this folder within a separate src folder, as in the following example file structure:

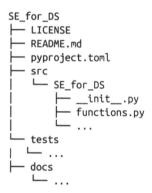

```
SE_for_DS
├── LICENSE
├── README.md
├── pyproject.toml
├── src
│   └── SE_for_DS
│       ├── __init__.py
│       ├── functions.py
│       └── ...
├── tests
│   └── ...
├── docs
    └── ...
```

In this file structure, the package will be named SE_for_DS. There's also a license file, a *README.md* file giving overview documentation, and a *pyproject.toml* file, which I'll explain later.

Packaging involves the following steps (adapted from the PyPI documentation (*https://oreil.ly/4OwdD*)):

1. Prepare a configuration file that contains metadata about the project and instructions for a package building tool. The standard is to use a *pyproject.toml* file that I mentioned in "Managing Dependencies with Poetry" on page 157 and will describe fully in the next section.

2. Use a tool that reads from your source code and configuration file to turn it into a package file (or a build artifact). This is what makes it installable on another person's system.

3. Upload your build artifact to PyPI or to some other distribution service, which could be internal to your company.

After you've carried out these steps, a user of your package can download and install it (using `pip`, for example) then use it. For more details on this, check out *Hypermodern Python Tooling* by Claudio Jolowicz (O'Reilly, 2024).

 I haven't mentioned packaging for the Anaconda package distribution system, but you can find more details about it in the Conda documentation (*https://oreil.ly/h_byJ*). Anaconda makes their packages free to use, but packages can only be updated by that organization.

The conda-forge (*https://conda-forge.org*) project is an open source community that lets you download Python packages using Conda, but package maintainers can update the packages themselves.

pyproject.toml

A *pyproject.toml* file is a standardized file that contains the metadata about your project and the specifications for how to build it. *.toml* is a file format for configuration files, and its specification is open source. You can either write this file manually or generate it using a tool such as Poetry. Here's an example of a *pyproject.toml* file:

```
[build-system] ❶
requires = ["setuptools>=61.0"]
build-backend = "setuptools.build_meta"

[project] ❷
name = "se_for_ds"
version = "0.0.1"
authors = [
  { name="Catherine Nelson", email="email_address" },
]
description = "An example package for Software Engineering
for Data Scientists"
readme = "README.md"
requires-python = ">=3.9"
classifiers = [
    "Programming Language :: Python :: 3",
    "License :: OSI Approved :: MIT License",
    "Operating System :: OS Independent",
]

[project.urls]
"Homepage" = "https://github.com/pypa/sampleproject"
```

❶ The `build-system` block specifies a tool to build the package, in this case `setuptools`, which I'll describe in the next section.

❷ The `project` block contains all the metadata for the project.

If you use Poetry it will generate a *pyproject.toml* file that contains the requirements, similar to the following:

```
[tool.poetry]
name = "se-for-ds"
version = "0.1.0"
description = ""
authors = ["Catherine Nelson <email_address>"]
readme = "README.md"

[tool.poetry.dependencies]
python = "^3.10"
pandas = "^2.1.0"

[build-system]
requires = ["poetry-core"]
build-backend = "poetry.core.masonry.api"
```

Once you have your *pyproject.toml* file, you are ready to build the package.

Building and Uploading Packages

You'll need a build tool to build your Python package. setuptools (*https://oreil.ly/6IuGH*) is a mature and popular way of building Python packages, but if you're doing more complex things with packaging you might want to consider other tools such as Poetry, pdm, and Hatch that I mentioned in "Virtual Environments" on page 154. These also make life easier for you by managing other parts of your workflow.

By default, most build tools will produce two files: a *sdist* file and a *wheel* file. The *sdist* file is a zipped file containing the source code for your package. The *wheel* file is also a type of zipped archive file, but it can be installed in a Python environment using pip.

You'll need to define the build tool you want to use in your *pyproject.toml* file, as mentioned previously. Then, you can use the Build (*https://oreil.ly/G3S0v*) library to build your package, and it will use setuptools or another packaging tool you've specified.

You can install Build with the following command:

```
$ pip install build
```

Then, run this in the directory where your *pyproject.toml* file is located:

```
python3 -m build
```

If you use the first *pyproject.toml* file from the previous section, build will use setup tools to create the package. You'll see the following message to show that the package files have been created:

```
Successfully built se_for_ds-0.1.0.tar.gz
and se_for_ds-0.1.0-py3-none-any.whl
```

Then, you can share the wheel file and other people can install this in their Python environment using pip.

If you want to publish your package to PyPI, you'll need to first install the Twine library using the following command:

```
$ pip install twine
```

Twine manages the process of uploading your package to PyPI.

The PyPI documentation (*https://oreil.ly/bkm9Z*) recommends that you first upload your package to TestPyPI (*https://test.pypi.org*) to check that everything works correctly before you upload it to the real PyPI. Once you've registered for an account on TestPyPI and obtained an API key, you can run the following command to upload your package:

```
twine upload -r testpypi dist/*
```

To upload to PyPI, you'll need to register for an account and get an API key. Once you have those, you can use Twine to upload your package:

```
twine upload dist/*
```

If you're using Poetry as your build system, you don't need to install any extra packages. You can build your package by running the following command in the directory that contains your *pyproject.toml* file:

```
$ poetry build
```

Upload your package to PyPI with this command:

```
$ poetry publish
```

Your package will then be available for anyone to install in their own Python environment.

Key Takeaways

In this chapter I covered several tools that will be extremely useful to you when you are sharing your code and working with other developers. Version control is an essential skill for writing code, because it lets you track the changes in your code, back up your code to a central location, and easily collaborate with other people.

Git is overwhelmingly the most popular tool for distributed version control. It's very important that you learn the basic commands to set up both a local and a remote repository, how to commit your code, and how to work with branches and pull requests.

When you're sharing the code you've written, you'll also need to share details of the versions of the libraries that your code depends on. There are a number of tools for this, and it's much easier to use them if you are already working in a virtual environment. You can use pip to save a list of library versions, or tools like Poetry that manage dependencies for you.

Building a package from your Python code lets other people install your code into their Python environment, then import it into any project that they're working on. You'll first need to ensure that your code runs and is structured correctly. Next, create a *pyproject.toml* file that defines the build tool and contains the metadata for your project. Finally, build the package files and make them available either on PyPI or share them within your company.

In the next chapter, I'll describe another way of making your code available to other people: building an API.

## CHAPTER 11

APIs

APIs (Application Programming Interfaces) are an important part of modern software engineering. You'll find it very useful to know how to get data from an API and the basics of how they work. APIs allow two systems to communicate and transfer data. They can be exposed on the public internet or within a company's internal systems. They hide the details of your code behind a standard way of accessing a system, providing a useful layer of abstraction. Many large software products use APIs to exchange data internally, and they're particularly important in web development.

An API lets you programmatically access some data or perform some action. One of the first places you may come across an API is trying to download some data from a public API. If you send a request with a particular structure, you will get back what you are expecting. They are an example of client and server communications. The server sits and waits for something to contact it, and the client is the one doing the contacting. The client requests some data from the server, and the server shares that data. Web APIs generally use HTTP to make a request, then return a response as a JSON (JavaScript Object Notation) or XML file.

APIs are extremely useful because they can provide on-demand access to some data or functionality in a way that scales to large numbers of users. You might want to write your own API so that other systems can call your code without any action from you. A great example of this is making predictions from a machine learning model. If this becomes a feature in your company's product, your model may need to receive input data and return predictions many times a second. You can build an API that waits for that data and returns the prediction. This means that you don't have to manually run a script every time you need to get a prediction from the model. An API can be constantly running and waiting to accept input data.

In this chapter I'll explain the details of RESTful APIs, the most popular type of API. I'll show you how to call APIs that are available on the public internet to obtain data.

I'll also show you how to write your own API using FastAPI, one of the most popular Python frameworks. This will let you share the functionality you have created in your code.

Calling an API

A lot of incredibly useful data is available on the public internet. Throughout this book, I've been using data from the UN Sustainable Development Goals (SDGs) database (*https://oreil.ly/Gzqqd*). This has a database page where you can manually download data and save it as a CSV file. But what if you want to download many similar files? This quickly becomes tedious. And what if you need to revisit the project after months without looking at it? You'd need to carefully document exactly what you downloaded, and it's easy to make mistakes.

Instead, you can automate this process and make it reproducible by calling an API. As well as getting data from the public internet, you may need to do this to get data from or provide results to an internal system.

The main types of API that you may encounter are RESTful (*https://oreil.ly/zYKfU*), SOAP (*https://oreil.ly/gg-3_*), and GraphQL (*https://graphql.org*). SOAP is an older API protocol that you'll still see occasionally, and GraphQL is a newer type of API that uses a query language to return data. REST (REpresentational State Transfer) is a software architectural style defined by Roy Fielding in 2000. It provides guidelines on how resources should be represented and manipulated using HTTP methods. RESTful APIs are the most common, and I'll describe those in this chapter.

HTTP Methods and Status Codes

If you want to use a RESTful API, you'll encounter a few standardized HTTP methods. Each method corresponds to a specific request you can make to the API to get a particular response, as shown in Table 11-1.

Table 11-1. Common API endpoints

Endpoint name	Function
GET	Retrieves some data
POST	Sends some data to create something and receive a response
PUT	Sends data to update something that already exists
DELETE	Deletes something that already exists

One API may have a large number of endpoints. For example, there can be many GET endpoints that return different types of data. Some of them receive a parameter as input and return data that corresponds to this input, and some return the same data every time.

When an API receives a HTTP request it returns a standard status code, depending on what happened. Table 11-2 describes the meaning of a few of these codes.

Table 11-2. Common HTTP status codes

Status code	Meaning
2xx	The request was successful (for example, 200 "OK")
4xx	There was a client error. You did something the server didn't expect, for example, misspelling the endpoint path. This would give a 404 ("Not Found") response.
5xx	The server experienced an error. A bug occurred in the API code when you made a request to it.

This is only a subset, and you can consult a more complete list (*https://oreil.ly/QzrJY*) if you encounter another status code.

Two other concepts will be useful in this section: headers and URL parameters. Headers are metadata that are attached to an HTTP request to a server or a response from a server. Common request headers include authorization credentials, and common response headers include the type of data that the server is returning, as I'll show in the next section. URL parameters are key-value pairs at the end of a URL that specify what you would like the URL to return, and I'll show an example of this in the next section.

Getting Data from the SDG API

The easiest way to call an API in Python is to use the Requests (*https://oreil.ly/5O4r3*) library.

You can install Requests with the following command:

```
$ pip install requests
```

I'll show you how to use the Requests library by calling the UN SDGs API and getting some information.

But first, it's a good idea to check the documentation for the API you intend to use. A lot of this documentation is in a standard format using Swagger UI (*https://oreil.ly/Nd48C*).

Figure 11-1 shows part of the API documentation for the SDG database API.

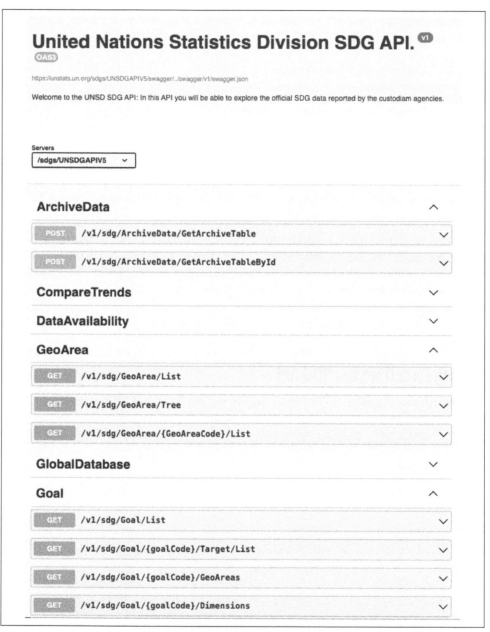

Figure 11-1. UN SDGs database API documentation

You can see that there are many GET and POST endpoints available.

I'll start by showing you how to call a GET endpoint that doesn't require any additional information. The endpoint `v1/sdg/Goal/List` returns a list of all the sustainable development indicators available in the overall database.

Using Requests, it takes only a line of code to make a request from this API:

```
import requests

response = requests.get("https://unstats.un.org/SDGAPI/v1/sdg/Goal/List")
```

You can check whether this was successful by looking at the HTTP status code of the response:

```
>>> response.status_code
... 200
```

A `200` code shows that the request has completed successfully, and data has been returned.

You can look at the headers to find out what format the data has been returned in using the `.headers` attribute:

```
>>> response.headers["content-type"]
... 'application/json; charset=utf-8'
```

`application/json` means that the data is returned in JSON format, so you can use the `.json()` method to get the data from the API response like so:

```
>>> response.json()
... [{'code': '1',
       'title': 'End poverty in all its forms everywhere',
       ...
    }]
```

This endpoint has returned a list of all the UN Sustainable Development Goals and their codes. JSON is a widely used data interchange format. Like Python dictionaries, JSON represents data as key-value pairs and provides a human-readable, lightweight way to organize and exchange data.

A GET request like this is the simplest type of request for an API, because it doesn't need any parameters or input data. A GET endpoint can also accept some parameters as input, to return a different response depending on the input, and these parameters are passed in as part of the URL path.

Next, I'll show you how to make a GET request that accepts a path parameter. I'll use the SDG API again and get some details on one of the SDGs.

The SDG API documentation states that there is a GET endpoint that will give a list of all the specific targets associated with any goal at *https://unstats.un.org/sdgapi/v1/sdg/Goal/{goalCode}/Target/List*. Goal 5 is "Achieve gender equality and empower all women and girls," and if you want to get information on this goal, slot the goal code (5) into the *{goalCode}* location in the URL. The documentation also states that there's an optional parameter *includeChildren* to get the full details of the targets and indicators. This goes at the end of the URL following a *?*. To make this clearer, I've annotated these sections in Figure 11-2.

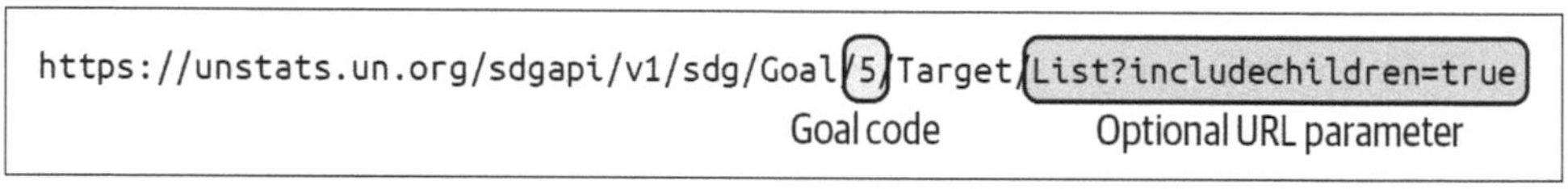

Figure 11-2. Annotated API URL

Taking all this into account, the request to this API takes this form:

```
response = requests.get("https://unstats.un.org/sdgapi/v1/sdg/Goal/5/Target/\
List?includechildren=true")
```

The response gives the details of the measurable targets and statistical indicators for this goal:

```
>>> response.json()
... [{...
    'targets': [{'goal': None,
    'code': '5.1',
    'title': 'End all forms of discrimination against all women and girls \
    everywhere'
    ...}]
}]
```

I'll cover how to make a POST request to an API in "Making Requests to Your API" on page 177.

Creating Your Own API Using FastAPI

In this section, I'll show you how to create your own API using FastAPI (*https://oreil.ly/krmvR*), a framework for writing API endpoints developed by Sebastián Ramírez. It was first released in 2018 and has seen rapid widespread adoption because it is easy to use and works well with other modern Python tools. It also has other useful features including automatic documentation, and it conforms with the OpenAPI (*https://oreil.ly/IpLZg*) specifications, a widely used set of standards for APIs. In the following sections I'll show you how to set up a basic API with FastAPI and how to add GET and POST endpoints.

Other API Frameworks

Flask (*https://oreil.ly/0B4wP*) is another very popular API framework. It's older than FastAPI and is a little more complex to use, but it's quite similar. After you've read through this section you should find it easier to translate the concepts used by FastAPI to their corresponding commands in Flask.

Django (*https://oreil.ly/ieXC0*) is a popular framework widely used by web developers. It contains a lot of functionality for developing websites, but in my opinion it's overkill for data science applications.

Setting Up the API

First, you'll need to install FastAPI using this command:

```
$ pip install fastapi
```

You'll also need to install an additional module to serve the endpoint. There are a few options for this, and I'll choose Uvicorn (*https://www.uvicorn.org*), as suggested in the FastAPI documentation. Uvicorn is a web server that makes your endpoints accessible either on your own machine or deployed elsewhere.

You can install Uvicorn with:

```
$ pip install 'uvicorn[standard]'
```

The next step is to create a FastAPI object. This is an empty app without any endpoints, and you need to initialize the app before you add any endpoints to it. You can create the FastAPI object:

```
from fastapi import FastAPI

app = FastAPI()
```

Next, you can add a very simple endpoint. This is a GET endpoint that simply returns a JSON object containing the strings "Hi" and "There". FastAPI handles the conversion to JSON, so you can simply write a function that returns a Python dictionary like so:

```
@app.get("/say_hi/")
def say_hi():
    return {"Hi": "There"}
```

The @app.get decorator specifies this is a GET endpoint that should be added to the app. The decorator argument specifies the name of the route.

Next, start serving the API so that you can call it. You can use the following command to start it:

```
$ uvicorn chapter_11_api:app
```

The file containing my API is named *chapter_11_api.py*.

If everything is working correctly, you should see the following readout:

```
INFO:     Started server process [60003]
INFO:     Waiting for application startup.
INFO:     Application startup complete.
INFO:     Uvicorn running on http://127.0.0.1:8000 (Press CTRL+C to quit)
```

This means that the API is running locally on your machine.

I'll show you how to call your API using the Requests library in "Making Requests to Your API" on page 177, but you can also quickly check that your API is working by viewing it in your web browser. As Figure 11-3 shows, navigating to *http://127.0.0.1:8000/say_hi/* in the browser gives the following result:

Figure 11-3. Your API endpoint in a browser

You'll also see the following readout in your terminal to show that the GET endpoint was called and everything was working OK:

```
INFO:     127.0.0.1:56716 - "GET /say_hi/ HTTP/1.1" 200 OK
```

Next, you can add another endpoint that includes a `path` parameter. This time, the function takes an argument `name`, and this is included in the string for the API route in the decorator argument:

```
@app.get("/say_hello/{name}")
def say_hello(name):
    return {"Hello": name}
```

You could also consider adding type annotations to this function, like so:

```
@app.get("/say_hello/{name}")
def say_hello(name: str) -> str:
    return {"Hello": name}
```

Using type annotations here has a number of benefits. You can use a type checking tool to avoid common errors and validate your input data, as described in "Type Checking" on page 91. The expected input and return types will also be picked up in the documentation that I'll describe below.

If you restart the app then navigate to *http://127.0.0.1:8000/say_hello/Dave*, you'll see the output shown in Figure 11-4.

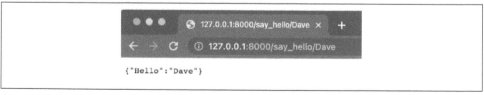

Figure 11-4. API endpoint with a path parameter

You can replace *Dave* with the name of anyone else you want to say hello to.

One extremely useful feature of FastAPI is that it automatically generates documentation for you, using Swagger UI (*https://oreil.ly/K7IE5*). If your API is running locally, you can navigate to *http://127.0.0.1:8000/docs#/* to view the documentation.

It should look like Figure 11-5.

Figure 11-5. Autogenerated API documentation

When you're finished with your API, you can shut it down using the Ctrl+C keyboard shortcut.

Adding Functionality to Your API

In this next section, I'd like to show you how to do something a little more complex with your API: adding the `fit_trendline` function you've seen in many chapters to your API. I'll show you how to make two endpoints. The first is a GET endpoint that takes a country name as a path parameter and returns the slope and R² value for the trend of the proportion of women in parliament in that country. It uses the data from the UN Sustainable Development Goal 5 from earlier in the chapter. The second is a POST endpoint that accepts any data and timestamps in a JSON file and returns the slope and R² value for the trend of that data.

Example 11-1 includes all the functions that actually do the calculations for these endpoints. It's good practice to keep the code containing the logic for your project separate from the API code, for several reasons. First, you can easily change the API framework that you're using, for example, if you decide to switch from FastAPI to Flask. Second, you can test these parts of the code separately. And third, as I mentioned in "Code Design" on page 117, it's good practice to divide your code into discrete pieces that carry out different purposes.

Example 11-1. chapter_11_functions.py

```python
import pandas as pd
from scipy.stats import linregress

def fit_trendline(year_timestamps, data):
    result = linregress(year_timestamps, data)
    slope = round(result.slope, 3)
    r_squared = round(result.rvalue**2, 3)
    return slope, r_squared

def process_sdg_data(input_excel_file, columns_to_drop):
    df = pd.read_excel(input_excel_file)
    df = df.drop(columns_to_drop, axis=1)
    df = df.set_index("GeoAreaName").transpose()
    return df

def country_trendline(country_name):
    df = process_sdg_data(
        "../data/SG_GEN_PARL.xlsx",
        [
            "Goal",
            "Target",
            "Indicator",
            "SeriesCode",
            "SeriesDescription",
            "GeoAreaCode",
            "Reporting Type",
            "Sex",
```

```
        "Units",
    ],
)
timestamps = [int(i) for i in df.index.tolist()]
country_data = df[country_name].tolist()
slope, r_squared = fit_trendline(timestamps, country_data)
return slope, r_squared
```

You can initialize the API as shown in the previous section:

```
from fastapi import FastAPI

app = FastAPI()
```

The next step is to add endpoints.

Adding a GET endpoint

You can add a GET endpoint that uses the `country_trendline` function from Example 11-1:

```
@app.get("/country_trendline/{country}")
def calculate_country_trendline(country: str):
    slope, r_squared = country_trendline(country)
    return {"slope": slope, "r_squared": r_squared}
```

You can run the API again with Uvicorn:

```
$ uvicorn chapter_11_api:app
```

And then if you want to know the trend for India, navigate to *http://127.0.0.1:8000/country_trendline/India* in your browser, which gives the result shown in Figure 11-6.

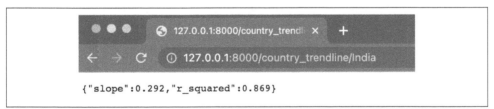

Figure 11-6. Country trendline GET endpoint

Viewing this in your browser isn't very useful if you, or someone else, wants to use this result in some other code, so I'll show you how to call this endpoint using `requests` in "Making Requests to Your API" on page 177.

Adding a POST endpoint

Next I'll show you how to add a POST endpoint that uses the `fit_trendline` function from Example 11-1. One extra step to add here is to validate the input data to this function using Pydantic, introduced in Chapter 7:

```
from pydantic import BaseModel
from typing import List

class TrendlineInput(BaseModel):
    timestamps: List[int]
    data: List[float]
```

This validates that the value for `timestamps` is a list of integers and the value for `data` is a list of floats. I'll use this class in the endpoint function.

This next function adds the POST endpoint to your FastAPI app:

```
@app.post("/fit_trendline/")
def calculate_trendline(trendline_input: TrendlineInput):
    slope, r_squared = fit_trendline(trendline_input.timestamps,
                                     trendline_input.data)
    return {"slope": slope, "r_squared": r_squared}
```

This function will accept data in JSON format as its input. I'll show you how to call this endpoint in the next section.

You can also improve your API documentation very easily by adding a summary and description to the `@app` decorator arguments:

```
@app.post("/fit_trendline/",
          summary="Fit a trendline to any data",
          description="Provide a list of integer timestamps and a list of floats")
def calculate_trendline(trendline_input: TrendlineInput):
    slope, r_squared = fit_trendline(trendline_input.timestamps,
                                     trendline_input.data)
    return {"slope": slope, "r_squared": r_squared}
```

If you restart your API, you'll see the summary and description included in the documentation, as shown in Figure 11-7.

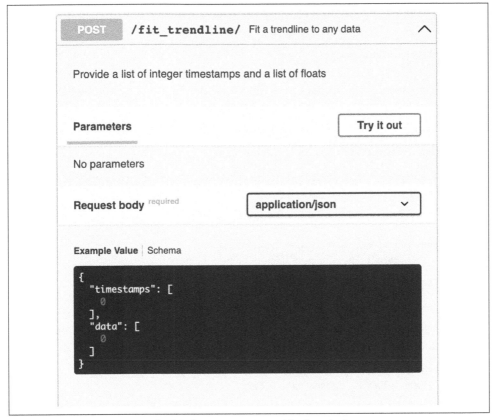

Figure 11-7. Autogenerated API documentation with description

This is a very simple example of an API. One thing you'd definitely want to add to the code here is error handling, as described in Chapter 5.

Making Requests to Your API

Once you've created your API and it is up and running, you can call it using the Requests library in the same way I described in "Calling an API" on page 166. You'll find that FastAPI has already set up the HTTP codes, so you don't need to do any of that yourself.

You can call the GET endpoint to get the trendline statistics for a particular country using this command:

```python
import requests

response = requests.get("http://127.0.0.1:8000/country_trendline/India")
```

And then you can check the HTTP status code to ensure that everything worked correctly:

```
>>> response.status_code
... 200
```

Then, you can inspect the response, which is provided in JSON format by FastAPI:

```
>>> response.json()
... {'slope': 0.292, 'r_squared': 0.869}
```

You can also use this response object in your code.

The POST endpoint that I described in the previous section accepts JSON as its input. You can structure your input data like so:

```
url = "http://127.0.0.1:8000/fit_trendline/"

json_data = {"timestamps": [2000, 2001, 2002],
             "data": [0.5, 0.6, 0.7]}
```

Then make a POST request with this input:

```
response = requests.post(url=url, json=json_data)
```

The endpoint code calls the `fit_trendline` function, then takes the results of this function and structures them as JSON. It then returns the response as a JSON object:

```
>>> response.json()
... {'slope': 0.292, 'r_squared': 0.869}
```

All POST endpoints accept some data as input, but this can be in different formats. Check the API documentation to find out what each one accepts.

In this chapter, I've given you a very quick introduction to APIs so that you can start writing them for other people to call your code. There's much more functionality that's commonly used by people developing web applications such as authorization, handling form inputs from web pages, and connecting to databases. The FastAPI documentation (*https://oreil.ly/dxZrd*) is a great place to start learning more about these topics.

Key Takeaways

APIs are a standard method of allowing software applications to connect to each other using the client/server architectural style. As a data scientist, you can build your own API to let other people use the functionality you have developed, or you can call existing APIs to obtain data or make calculations.

RESTful APIs are the most common type of API you'll encounter, and they have a standard set of endpoints including GET and POST. Each API can have many endpoints. If you make a request to an API, you'll get a response that includes a status code to tell you if your request was successful. And if your request was successful, the response will also include the data that the API makes available.

You can use the Requests library to call APIs that are available either on the public internet or on your company's internal system, whether you have developed them or someone else has. When you receive a response from the API, you can easily obtain the data and the status code from the `requests` object.

FastAPI is a great choice for building your own APIs. You'll also need a web server library such as Uvicorn to run the API. You can think of FastAPI (or other frameworks such as Flask) as a wrapper around your code that makes the functions you've developed available to other people. This is a great way of sharing the functionality of your code in a standardized format.

In the next chapter, I'll describe how to deploy your API to a cloud hosting environment.

## CHAPTER 12

Automation and Deployment

Software engineers love to automate boring, repetitive tasks. Automation is a skill that you can learn and apply to the code you write as a data scientist. In this chapter, I'll show you some tools you can use to automate some of the steps in your coding workflow such as linting and testing. I'll also describe the process of deploying code to a production system. Even if deployments aren't handled by your team, you'll likely find it useful to know the basics of how the process works.

At first, tools for automation and deployment may seem complex and a little intimidating. Many tools are available, and all have their own terminology. But often, it's just the initial setup that is complex. Once you have set up these tools, they run without any action needed from you.

Automating your coding processes helps ensure they are standardized and reproducible. You can make sure that your code is always linted, formatted, and tested before it reaches a production system, or even before it is committed to version control. You can also make sure that the details are standardized, for example, by making sure that you are always using the same linter with the same settings. Automation becomes even more useful when you're deploying your code frequently, and it can save you a huge amount of time.

Automation also helps ensure that your processes are standard across your team. If tests are automated, everyone is more likely to run them, and there will be fewer mistakes in the team's code. This can help you set up a culture of writing good code within your team.

In this chapter, I'll first explain the process of deploying code and introduce some common terminology. Next, I'll show you how to automate simple tasks using pre-commit hooks and how to automate tests using GitHub Actions. Finally, I'll describe how to deploy the API you saw in Chapter 11 to a cloud platform, including how to use a Docker container to make sure your deployment is reproducible.

Deploying Code

Deploying code is a common process in building software. It means you're making the functionality of your code available to your end users, or you're making a new version of your code operational. More specifically, this could mean sending a new version of your API to a server where some other code can call it. Alternatively, it could mean hosting your API on a cloud provider, as I'll describe in "Cloud Deployments" on page 191, or updating an app in a marketplace so that users can install a new version on their device.

Deploying your code means that you've reached some stage where you're satisfied with the code you have, in contrast to the development stage of writing software where you're trying out new ideas and constantly changing things. This might mean you have added a new feature to your code or you've fixed a bug, but your code is "done" in some sense and you want your changes to be available to the end users of the software.

It's common practice to have multiple environments where code can be deployed. For example, a company might have a production environment and a testing or staging environment. Before deploying your code to production, you might first deploy it to a testing environment. This replicates the production code but in an isolated "sandbox" environment, and the code doesn't affect the functioning product. This means your code gets tested where it interacts with the rest of the software product, and it gets deployed to the production environment only after you're sure that it doesn't cause any problems.

One acronym you may see associated with deployment is CI/CD (Continuous Integration/Continuous Deployment or Delivery). This refers to the whole pipeline of a deployment process, which may include running tests, security checks, and building and deploying containers. I'll introduce containers in "Containers and Docker" on page 192.

Continuous integration
> When a developer makes a change to a codebase and commits it to version control, a CI server builds the project, runs the tests, and checks that everything works. If there are errors, the CI system alerts developers so that they can fix them. You can find a great introduction to CI in this talk from Mariatta Wijaya (*https://oreil.ly/DmvsP*).

Continuous delivery

After the CI pipeline has run, the code is ready to deploy. It has passed all the tests and the project has been built. It then needs a manual final step to deploy it, which lets someone review it before deploying.

Continuous deployment

If all the tests pass, the code is automatically deployed to a production environment.

CI/CD systems require that your code is in version control, you have a good set of tests, and your whole team is on board with automating the system. They can give you rapid feedback without needing to manually run tests and can speed up development on large codebases. However, these systems are often complex to set up, and they may not be worthwhile for small projects. They are often managed by separate DevOps teams. Popular tools include Jenkins (*https://www.jenkins.io*), Travis CI (*https://www.travis-ci.com*), CircleCI (*https://circleci.com*), and GitHub Actions, which I'll describe in "GitHub Actions" on page 186.

Recently, CI/CD techniques have become more popular for machine learning. As well as being triggered by a change to code, CI/CD can be triggered by changes to a model's training data or by a decline in the model's performance. The system retrains and redeploys the model when the selected trigger occurs. You can learn more about CI/CD for machine learning in this online course by Hamel Husain (*https://oreil.ly/o7bM7*).

Automation Examples

In this section, I'll show you how to automate some of the common tasks in your coding workflow. I'll explain how to format your code automatically using pre-commit hooks and Black, and how to automatically remove data from Jupyter notebooks before they reach your GitHub repository. I'll also show you how to run your tests automatically using GitHub Actions.

Pre-Commit Hooks

Pre-commit hooks, as the name suggests, run before every commit that you make. They are a type of Git hook, which is a custom script that runs before or after some Git action (such as a commit). Pre-commit hooks are useful because they let you identify problems before committing to version control. They are particularly good for tasks that are easy to automate, such as linting and formatting. Using hooks for linting will detect poor practices and prevent poorly written code from being committed to the codebase.

In this section, I'll describe how to use pre-commit hooks to automatically format your code, remove debugging statements from your files, and clean data from Jupyter notebooks. You can also use pre-commit hooks to run unit tests, and this can be good for small projects. For large projects, running all the tests may take a long time, so it's best to use a CI/CD system instead. I'll describe how to run tests automatically in "GitHub Actions" on page 186.

Pre-commit (*https://pre-commit.com*) is a multilanguage framework that uses a *.yaml* file to manage configurations. YAML (YAML Ain't Markup Language) is a human-readable markup style language often used for configuration files, as shown in the following example. To use pre-commit, you'll already need to be tracking changes to your code using Git as I described in "Version Control Using Git" on page 145.

You can install pre-commit with the following command:

```
$ pip install pre-commit
```

Next, you'll need to create a YAML configuration file that specifies the hooks you want to use. The file needs to be named *.pre-commit-config.yaml*.

Here's an example YAML file that contains a hook that runs the Black code formatter on every commit. I described how to use Black in "Automatic Code Formatting with Black" on page 85:

```
repos:
  - repo: https://github.com/psf/black-pre-commit-mirror
    rev: 23.10.1 ❶
    hooks:
      - id: black
        language_version: python3.10 ❷
```

❶ You can replace this with another version of Black.

❷ You can replace this with another recent Python version.

Next, you'll need to install the hook before it can run:

```
$ pre-commit install
```

After this, the hook will run when you run a `git commit` command. You'll see a message like this:

```
black...................................Failed
- hook id: black
- files were modified by this hook

reformatted se_for_ds/chapter_11_functions.py

All done!
1 file reformatted.
```

Pre-commit gives a `Failed` message if Black made changes to your files, and you'll need to add and commit those files again. This gives you the opportunity to review the changes before committing them again.

 Pre-commit hooks run in their own virtual environment so that they don't interfere with your development work. This means that they will be slow the first time you run them, because pre-commit needs to create a new virtual environment. Subsequent runs will be faster.

If there are no changes to the files you commit, you'll see a message like this:

```
black....................................Passed
```

You can also run your hooks at any time on all the files in your repository without committing them. You can do this using the following command:

```
$ pre-commit run --all-files
```

Pre-commit also has some useful prebuilt hooks, which are listed in the GitHub repository (*https://github.com/pre-commit/pre-commit-hooks*). One useful one is a prebuilt hook that removes debug statements from pdb that I mentioned in "Debugging" on page 73.

You can add these prebuilt hooks to the YAML config file like so:

```
repos:
  - repo: https://github.com/psf/black-pre-commit-mirror
    rev: 23.10.1
    hooks:
      - id: black
        language_version: python3.10
  - repo: https://github.com/pre-commit/pre-commit-hooks
    rev: v2.3.0
    hooks:
      - id: debug-statements
```

Both the `black` hook and the `debug-statements` hook will run every time you commit your code.

If you want to update the versions of the libraries you use in your hooks (for example, upgrading to the latest version of Black) you can change this manually or use the following command to update all your hooks to the latest version:

```
$ pre-commit autoupdate
```

Or you may want to write your own hooks. Next, I'll show you how to write a hook that removes data from Jupyter notebooks so that it isn't tracked by Git or uploaded to a remote repository.

This hook will go in a new `local` section in the YAML file, as shown here:

```
repos:
  - repo: local
    hooks:
      - id: remove-notebook-output
        name: Remove notebook output
        description: Strips out any output or data from Jupyter Notebook cells
        language: system ❶
        files: \.ipynb$ ❷
        entry: jupyter nbconvert --clear-output --inplace ❸
```

❶ Using the `system` language tag means that this hook will run whatever is in the `entry` tag on the command line. You can also use `python` here to run a Python script.

❷ This hook will run on all files with the `.ipynb` extension.

❸ This is the command that the hook will run; it will remove the output from Jupyter notebook cells and save the file.

After you install it, this hook will run when you commit your file and give you the following message:

```
Remove notebook output....................................................Failed
- hook id: remove-notebook-output
- files were modified by this hook

[NbConvertApp] Converting notebook se_for_ds/chapter_11.ipynb to notebook
[NbConvertApp] Writing 4113 bytes to se_for_ds/chapter_11.ipynb
```

This is much easier than remembering to manually remove data from your notebooks. In general, pre-commit hooks are a lightweight way of automating small tasks that you need to do often, and this means that you're more likely to do them!

GitHub Actions

GitHub Actions (*https://oreil.ly/ywKIQ*) is one of the easiest CI/CD platforms to get started with, and you can use it to automate many tasks in your coding workflow. It runs any code that you specify whenever a GitHub event occurs, such as a push to a remote repository or a pull request. In this section, I'll show an example of a GitHub Actions workflow that runs the tests in a repository using Pytest (which I described in "Running Automated Tests with Pytest" on page 101). This workflow will run automatically every time you push an update to the main branch in the repository.

You'll be asked to provide payment details to be able to use GitHub Actions. It has a free tier, which may be enough for your needs, but if you go beyond this you'll start to incur costs. The GitHub Actions documentation (*https://oreil.ly/08eAv*) contains full details.

To get started, you'll need to already be tracking changes using Git, and you'll need to have a remote repository hosted on GitHub, as I described in "Version Control Using Git" on page 145. Next, create a *.github/* folder with a *workflows/* folder within it.

As with pre-commit hooks, GitHub Actions configurations are stored in a *.yaml* file. Create this in the *workflows/* folder.

In this YAML file, you'll specify the name of your workflow, the trigger for your workflow, and what you want to happen as a result of that trigger. These are specified in the name, on, and jobs section of the YAML file, as shown here:

```
name: run-tests

on:
  push:
    branches: [ "main" ]

jobs:
```

It's important to note that whatever you run in the jobs section will run on GitHub's servers, not your own computer. This is great if your tests take a long time to run, because you can do other things while they are running. Running tests in another environment also helps you identify any missing dependencies. But there needs to be some setup to ensure this environment has everything that it needs to run the code.

Next, I'll show you what needs to go in the jobs section. You'll need to add a name to the first job you want to run, then a line to select what type of server to run on:

```
jobs:

  test:
    name: Run all tests for trendline code

    runs-on: ubuntu-latest
```

It's most common to use Linux, but Windows and Mac servers are also available.

Next, you need to say what you want to happen in the `steps` section. Since this job will run on GitHub's servers, the first thing you need to do is copy your code to this server. You can do this by using a prebuilt action called checkout (*https://oreil.ly/6JFbm*):

```
jobs:
  test:
    name: Run all tests for trendline code
    runs-on: ubuntu-latest

    steps:
      - uses: actions/checkout@v4
```

Because `checkout` is a prebuilt action, it uses the keyword `uses`.

Next, you need Python on your server, and there's a prebuilt action for choosing a server that already has a Python installation. Add this to the `steps` subsection within the `jobs` section:

```
steps:
  - uses: actions/checkout@v4

  - uses: actions/setup-python@v4
    with:
      python-version: '3.10'
```

You can select any supported Python version in this action.

Once you have set up Python, the next step is to install the dependencies for your project. You can use a *requirements.txt* file as I described in "Dependencies and Virtual Environments" on page 153, and this needs to be in your GitHub repository. The `run` keyword means that the server will run the `python -m pip install...` command:

```
steps:
  - uses: actions/checkout@v4

  - uses: actions/setup-python@v4
    with:
      python-version: '3.10'

  - name: Install requirements
    run: python -m pip install -r requirements.txt
```

By default, your dependencies need to be installed every time you run your workflow. You can change this by using the `cache` action (*https://oreil.ly/tNaFN*), and this is worthwhile if your dependencies take a long time to install.

Finally, you can add the command to actually run your tests using Pytest:

```
steps:
  - uses: actions/checkout@v4

  - uses: actions/setup-python@v4
    with:
      python-version: '3.10'

  - name: Install requirements
    run: python -m pip install -r requirements.txt

  - name: Run tests
    run: python -m pytest
```

Here's the complete YAML file with all the sections:

```
name: run-tests

on:
  push:
    branches: main

jobs:
  test:
    name: Run all tests for trendline code
    runs-on: ubuntu-latest

    steps:
      - uses: actions/checkout@v4

      - uses: actions/setup-python@v4
        with:
          python-version: '3.10'

      - name: Install requirements
        run: python -m pip install -r requirements.txt

      - name: Run tests
        run: python -m pytest
```

When you push this file to your remote repository, GitHub will automatically recognize it as an Actions workflow. After it is set up and working correctly, your tests will run every time you push a commit to the main branch in your repository.

You can check the status of your action on GitHub in your repository's "Actions" tab, as shown in Figure 12-1.

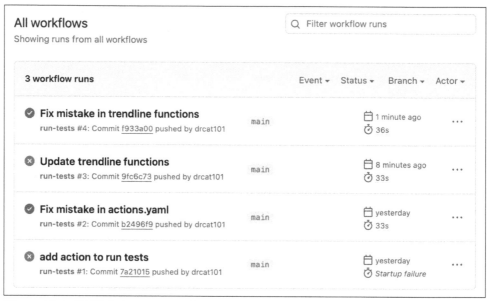

Figure 12-1. GitHub Actions interface

If your tests pass, you'll see a green checkmark, but if your tests fail, you'll see a red cross. Figure 12-2 shows more details on the failed workflow.

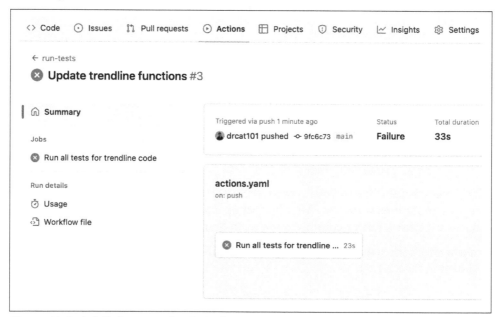

Figure 12-2. A failed test run by GitHub Actions

You can check the logs on GitHub to see the output of the tests and see what went wrong, and you will also get an email to tell you that your workflow failed. This is particularly helpful if your tests take a long time to run, because you can commit your code then get on with something else while your tests are running.

This workflow had just one step, but there's a lot more you can do with GitHub Actions. One way to extend this example would be to run your tests using different Python versions, to check that your code runs correctly on them. You can find more details in the GitHub Actions documentation (*https://oreil.ly/sV2ip*).

Once your code has been tested, you can move on to the next step: deploying it.

Cloud Deployments

In this section, I'll describe a simple way to deploy the trendline API described in Chapter 11. You'll find the code for it in "Adding Functionality to Your API" on page 174. You can deploy your API because you want it to run constantly so that your users can access it at any time. Ideally, you want your API to start up without needing any manual commands and automatically restart after a problem. To do this, you can use a Docker container, which I'll describe in the next section.

You'll also need some kind of a host computer where you can run the code for your API. Cloud providers such as Amazon Web Services (*https://aws.amazon.com*) (AWS), Microsoft Azure (*https://azure.microsoft.com*), and Google Cloud (*https://cloud.google.com*) have become increasingly popular in recent years as places to host and run code, instead of on traditional servers. They provide on-demand computing resources that can scale up or down depending on how much they are being used.

The main steps I'll describe in this section are common to all the cloud providers. Here's an overview:

1. Create a Docker container on your local machine that contains your API code and details of the libraries your code depends on.

2. Upload this container to a container registry on your chosen cloud profiler's system. The container registry can contain many containers.

3. Instruct the cloud provider to run your chosen container. This exposes the API code in your container to the internet so that your users can access it. The container (and therefore your code) runs on the cloud provider's server.

There are many options for how to deploy your code. You can deploy your code without using a container, but I'll describe them here because they are a relatively easy way to make sure that your code is reproducible.

Containers and Docker

A container is an isolated place to run your API or any other application. Running code in a container means that the entire environment is reproducible (including the libraries that your code depends on). You can think of it as a small Linux system running on a larger host, where you can install the correct version of Python and the libraries your code depends on, and also run your code. Using containers also opens up many options for scaling up your code, although I won't go into that here.

Docker (*https://www.docker.com*) is a system for building and managing containers. A Docker container is based on an image, and this provides instructions for building a container. You can define a Docker image in a text file called a Dockerfile, and this file contains commands to install and set up everything you need in your container. You can then run an instance of a container locally or deploy it elsewhere.

Dockerfiles often use a prebuilt image as a starting point. You'll see how to use the official Python image as a starting point in the next section. There are also prebuilt images for FastAPI, TensorFlow, PyTorch, and many other popular frameworks. You can use these as a base for your own Docker image.

Building a Docker Container

You can get started with Docker by downloading and installing it from the Docker website (*https://oreil.ly/1DCo7*).

Next, open the Docker desktop app. Once this is running, you can use Docker via the command line. You can test that your Docker installation is working correctly using the following command:

```
$ docker run hello-world
```

You'll need to put the files containing the code for your API in a folder with the Dockerfile (or a subfolder within it). This folder should also contain a *requirements.txt* file specifying the dependencies for your project, as described in "Dependencies and Virtual Environments" on page 153.

This is the list of the files in the folder that you can use to build the Docker container:

```
├── main.py
├── chapter_11_functions.py
├── Dockerfile
├── requirements.txt
```

This includes the functions from Chapter 11 in `main.py` and `chapter_11_functions.py`.

Next, here's an example Dockerfile for the container for this API:

```
FROM python:3.10 ❶

COPY requirements.txt . ❷

RUN pip install --upgrade -r requirements.txt ❸

COPY . . ❹

CMD ["uvicorn", "main:app", "--host", "0.0.0.0", "--port", "8000"] ❺
```

❶ The FROM keyword means this image will be based on another preexisting image. In this case the new image will be based on the official Python 3.10 image.

❷ COPY only the *requirements.txt* file to the new image.

❸ RUN a bash command during the image building process. In this case, use pip to install the libraries specified in the *requirements.txt* file

❹ COPY all the files in the folder where the build command is run into the image. Copying all the files after installing the Python libraries accelerates the process of building an image.

❺ The CMD keyword means that a command that is run when the container is running. In this case, the command starts the API using Uvicorn, as I described in "Adding Functionality to Your API" on page 174.

You can think of the Dockerfile as a blueprint for building containers. It sets out the specifications for the container environment, and this ensures that an identical environment is created each time you run a new container instance.

You'll need to build your image from the Dockerfile before you can use it to run a container instance. You can do this by running the following command in the folder that contains the Dockerfile:

```
$ docker build -t trendline_image .
```

Docker will use the files in the folder where you run the command because you've passed in the current folder (.) as an argument.

Then, you can test your image by creating a container locally using this command:

```
$ docker run -d --name trendline_image -p 8000:8000 trendline_container
```

Your API will then be running locally. You'll see the same responses as I showed in "Adding Functionality to Your API" on page 174, except that this time the API is running in a container. You can still navigate to *http://127.0.0.1:8000/country_trendline/ India* to see the API working, and you can see the documentation at *http://127.0.0.1/ docs*. When you run a container, you're using the image as a template to launch containers that are independent instances, each with its own runtime state and data.

When you're done, stop the container with this command:

```
$ docker stop trendline_container
```

You'll find it useful to test your code before going through the process of building your container. Building and running the container are time consuming, and it's frustrating to build the container, then deploy it, then find that you have a simple error. It's also a good idea to set up a logging solution, because you won't have easy access to your error messages. Docker has a default logging setup (*https://oreil.ly/9nEdF*).

Once you have successfully tested your container locally, the next step is to deploy it. In the next section, I'll describe how to deploy to a cloud platform.

Deploying an API on Google Cloud

In this section, I'll give you a very brief overview of how to deploy your API to Google Cloud in the container you created in the previous section. I won't go into detail here because the service may change, and your best source of detailed information is the official documentation (*https://oreil.ly/7LTJJ*). The process I'll describe is fine for personal exploration, but you'll need to know more about your company's security policies before you use it with customer data.

The main steps for deploying your container to Google Cloud are as follows:

1. Create a new project (*https://oreil.ly/91K8n*) on Google Cloud and install Google Cloud's command line tools (*https://oreil.ly/f7wY5*).

2. Upload your Docker image to Google Cloud's Artifact Registry (*https://oreil.ly/ exrOO*). This service stores your container image but doesn't actually run it.

3. Google Cloud has a container running service called Cloud Run (*https://oreil.ly/ Dx1rt*). You can deploy containers to this service from the Artifact Registry.

4. Once your container is deployed, your API will receive a URL, and you can then call that API from anywhere.

As Figure 12-3 shows, when your API is running correctly on Cloud Run, you'll see these messages in the logs.

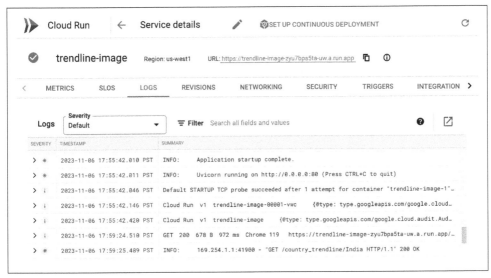

Figure 12-3. Cloud Run logs for the trendline API

You can see that there is a 200 OK message at the end. As discussed in "Calling an API" on page 166, this means everything is working well.

You can navigate to the URL assigned to you by Google Cloud and see the results of the API (Figure 12-4).

Figure 12-4. Calling your API running on Google Cloud

Your code is now running on Google Cloud's servers, ready for your users to make a request.

Running your service on any cloud provider incurs a monetary cost. You may receive some free credits when you sign up, or your service may stay within a "free tier," but it's a good idea to set up alerts to tell you when charges approach a specified amount. Also, don't forget to stop or delete resources when you're not using them.

Deploying an API on Other Cloud Providers

AWS (*https://oreil.ly/oG0zH*) and Microsoft Azure (*https://oreil.ly/dPGYq*) are the other main cloud providers. The process for deploying a container on both of these is very similar to deploying on Google Cloud.

For both providers, you'll need to carry out the following steps:

1. Create an account and install the command line tools.

2. Upload your Docker container to an online registry. For Microsoft Azure, you can use the Azure Container Registry (*https://oreil.ly/AJDuT*), and for AWS, you can use the Elastic Container Registry (*https://oreil.ly/--Moo*).

3. Deploy an instance of your Docker container from the container registry to a container running service. For Microsoft Azure you can use the Azure App Service (*https://oreil.ly/ipwqu*), and for AWS, you can use the Elastic Container Service (*https://oreil.ly/y1HHx*).

Any of these cloud providers will host your API and allow you to access it from anywhere on the internet. If your company uses one of these providers they will likely have a slightly more complex process, but I've given you an overview of the main steps.

Key Takeaways

Automating common tasks in your workflow takes some time to set up, but it is an extremely valuable way to spend your time. Automating processes such as formatting and testing your code ensures that your code is readable and reproducible. This is particularly helpful when you are frequently deploying your code to a production system, because it saves time and reduces the number of bugs in your code.

Deploying your code means that it is available to the end user of your product. It's common to have an entirely separate environment for developing your code. Then committing your code to version control triggers a workflow to test and build the code. After this, the code is ready to be deployed and may be automatically deployed. This process is known as Continuous Integration/Continuous Deployment (CI/CD).

Pre-commit hooks are a lightweight way to automate small tasks you want to do often, such as formatting and linting. They will run every time you commit your code to version control. GitHub Actions is a CI/CD system you can use to run your tests every time you push a commit to your remote repository. Both of these tools use YAML files as configuration files.

Deploying your code as an API to a cloud computing environment is an easy way to make your code available on the public internet without needing your own dedicated web server. Docker containers make this process easier by giving you an isolated environment where you can install all your code dependencies and then run the API. However, be aware of good security practices when you make your code freely available, as I will describe in the next chapter.

## CHAPTER 13

Security

As a data scientist, your job is all about data. Some of this data may be very sensitive. Because of this, it's important that you keep that data secure, and that you're aware of potential security risks in the code you write. Security is a topic that software engineers are generally very familiar with, but it's usually not included in data science courses. So in this chapter, I'll give you an overview of the principles and terminology around security.

The data you work with may include people's personal data (which may be personally identifiable information, or PII). It could also include data that is important to your company's business, such as financial data or data about how many customers your company has. This type of data can harm users and your company if it is exposed publicly.

Knowledge of security is particularly important if you are writing production code. But even if this isn't the case, it's still useful to know the broad principles. In this chapter, I'll give an introduction to security, then look at some security risks, with a focus on those risks you are more likely to encounter as a data scientist. I'll also describe practices to mitigate these risks, and I'll discuss some risks and security practices specific to machine learning.

What Is Security?

Security for software is concerned with protecting a system from theft of information, damage, disruption, or unwanted access to information. An attacker wishes to gain access to a system and use data within for some purpose that the holder of that data doesn't want, or data is accidentally exposed in some way that it can be accessed by the public. Security practices aim to make a system resistant to these attacks before new software is released to users.

Security breaches are big news. For example, personal data, including names, addresses, and social security numbers, of over 140 million people was stolen in the Equifax data breach (*https://oreil.ly/YhDCA*) in 2017. Credit card data was also stolen. This cost Equifax an estimated $1.4 billion, and its reputation was significantly harmed.

Security may be evaluated relative to external standards or to fulfill guarantees made to customers. Your company may comply with standards such as ISO 27001 (*https://oreil.ly/KX21x*) or follow a framework (*https://oreil.ly/qjJxk*) from the US National Institute of Standards and Technology. These set out the security requirements for your company's software.

Data Privacy

Security is not the same as privacy. Data privacy is concerned with the data that an individual person shares with a company or on the public internet. Privacy also involves control over what data is collected about a person and the use of that data. However, a security breach also can be a breach of privacy if a person's data is made public without their consent.

Recent developments in data privacy following the introduction of laws such as the EU's General Data Protection Regulation (GDPR) and California's Consumer Privacy Act. I won't cover data privacy in this book, instead I recommend *Practical Data Privacy* by Katharine Jarmul (O'Reilly, 2023).

You'll see a lot of precise terminology in security. I'll define a few of the most common terms here:

Attacker
> Someone who wants to break into a software system and steal data or disrupt the system. They may want to profit from data that is accidentally exposed. They often use automated tools to carry out the attacks.

Threat
> An event that has the potential to harm people or organizations via access to, disruption of, or modification of a system, for example, confidential data being exposed, or disrupting a system so that it no longer works.

Vulnerability
> A weakness in a software system that could be exploited by a threat source. This is usually a bug or mistake in the code that could be exploited by an attacker to make the system do something it is not intended to.

Risk

The probability that a security threat will exploit a vulnerability. It's a measure of the severity of the consequences of that vulnerability being exploited plus the likelihood of that happening.

Mitigation

Also known as a control, this is action taken to reduce a risk. For example, a website could require multifactor authentication (MFA) when a user logs on, instead of just a username and password.

Security Triad

A popular way of thinking about security. You may also see it called the C-I-A triad, standing for Confidentiality, Integrity, and Availability. Confidentiality means that a system should ensure that data is seen only by people who are supposed to see it. Integrity means that data cannot be modified by an attacker. Availability means that the system should work as expected (an attacker should not be able to stop a system from working).

Security Risks

In this section, I'll give some examples of security risks that you should be aware of in your work as a data scientist. This is not an exhaustive list, but these are some of the risks you're more likely to come across. If you would like to learn more about the most common security risks for web development in general, the Open Worldwide Application Security Project (OWASP) publishes a list of the top ten security risks every year (*https://oreil.ly/zNPUX*).

Credentials, Physical Security, and Social Engineering

This risk isn't specific to Python or data science coding, but a common cause of security breaches is from an attacker getting access to an employee's login credentials to company systems. This can be done via an attack on physical security, for example, stealing company hardware, or via social engineering, for example, phishing emails.

Social engineering attacks can be extremely convincing. Attackers replicated US Department of Labor emails and web pages in 2022, as reported here (*https://oreil.ly/h0wLN*). If recipients of the email followed the included link, they were taken to a site that was identical to the official website but had an additional step that attempted to harvest the user's Microsoft Office credentials.

Stolen credentials also caused a data breach for Okta (*https://oreil.ly/dw2F2*) in October 2023. An employee's credentials were saved to their personal Google profile on the Chrome browser, and this was accessed by an attacker.

Sometimes, security breaches have unusual causes. LastPass experienced a data breach in 2022, which was traced to media software installed on an employee's laptop (*https://oreil.ly/xEIVr*). An attacker was able to install keylogging software and steal the employee's login credentials. Even innocuous-seeming software may pose a security risk.

Third-Party Packages

The libraries that your code depends on may pose a security risk. When vulnerabilities are discovered, they are published in the MITRE online database of vulnerabilities (*https://cve.mitre.org*). You can look up vulnerabilities in Python (*https://oreil.ly/iydtN*) or vulnerabilities in older versions of NumPy (*https://oreil.ly/H6fX3*). Library developers of active projects will work to fix them, then release a new version that does not have this vulnerability. It's good practice to update all the packages your code depends on.

In 2017, Equifax experienced a major data breach (*https://oreil.ly/TYg3F*). Attackers stole personal data of hundreds of millions of people. This attack was traced to a known vulnerability in a third-party package, which should have been updated but was not.

You also should be careful about exactly which third-party libraries you use. Malicious Python packages (*https://oreil.ly/v_AZT*) can even install malware that steals data from a user's computer. This guide from Real Python (*https://oreil.ly/azNqD*) has a useful list of things you can do to confirm that your package is legitimate.

The Python Pickle Module

The `pickle` (*https://oreil.ly/2Kl5q*) module allows you to save any form of data that you like. You may see it presented in ML examples as an easy way to save a model for later use. Unfortunately, the `pickle` module is not secure. An attacker could plant any code in a `pickle` file and you wouldn't know what it was until you unpickled it. This could include Python code to delete files, for example.

Secure alternatives include using JSON files to store data. The Python `json` module will only open data that is correctly formatted. The scikit-learn documentation (*https://oreil.ly/bUayA*) mentions `pickle` but recommends Skops (*https://oreil.ly/uREBc*) or ONNX (*https://oreil.ly/nRR6k*) as more secure file formats for saving ML models.

Version Control Risks

Committing to version control can pose a security risk. If you're not careful, it's possible to expose API keys and other credentials in public repositories. Research in 2019 (*https://oreil.ly/GFSpU*) showed that over 100,000 GitHub repositories contained leaked secrets. Making your API key public means that anyone can use it to access that API, which may incur a cost to you or may compromise the data behind that API. Because Git keeps a complete record of the history of your files, it's hard to remove the secrets once they have been uploaded, but GitHub has a guide for how to do this (*https://oreil.ly/uwpp-*). API keys and secrets should be stored as environment variables or in a separate file that you don't commit to version control.

Committing data to a remote repository can also be a security risk. If your repository is public then anyone can see the data. And even if your repository is private, your company may not want data to be shared with GitHub. It's very easy to accidentally commit data in Jupyter notebooks. But as I mentioned in "Pre-Commit Hooks" on page 183, you can use automated techniques to remove data from your notebooks rather than removing data manually.

API Security Risks

If your API makes sensitive data available or you want to control who can use it, you should be aware of API security practices. The API that I showed you in Chapter 11 and "Cloud Deployments" on page 191 has no security at all. If the API is deployed on a cloud platform, anyone who has the URL can access the data from that API, so don't use this for proprietary or sensitive data.

You can find a guide to how to add basic security in the FastAPI documentation (*https://oreil.ly/4-B2z*). This includes transmitting data in an encrypted form by using HTTPS and authenticating your users. However, I recommend that you don't implement this yourself as a data scientist. Given the potential pitfalls you should get the advice of an expert.

There are other common API security risks. For example, if your API gives access to a database, you need to be aware of SQL injection attacks (*https://oreil.ly/2IMER*) and make sure that you validate the inputs to your API. Other common web risks such as cross-site request forgery (*https://oreil.ly/sXFm0*) and cross-site scripting (*https://oreil.ly/iJwN5*) are more relevant to general web development. The main takeaway here for you as a data scientist is that, if you are exposing data in an API, you should talk to your company's security team or someone else with security expertise.

Security Practices

As you've seen, there are a lot of ways that data can leak and your code's security can be compromised. It's impossible to completely eliminate threats because the code you're working on is always changing and the code you depend on is also always changing. New vulnerabilities are regularly discovered. Security practices aim to mitigate the threats and need to be updated often to keep up with new threats.

In this section, I'll give you a brief overview of some common security practices and tools you may encounter, as well as an example of how to use open source tools that scan your code for security issues.

Security Reviews and Policies

If you are writing production code, you may be asked to take part in a threat modeling exercise or other security review. This is often carried out by a company's security team, and it makes sure that security is considered early in the process of developing software. A security review can be a formal process or a simple meeting with stakeholders and security experts. The review's aim is to consider potential threats to a system, what risks exist and how severe they are, and whether any actions need to be taken to address them. The review process also ensures that a company's security policy is applied, and it's a chance for a development team to gather opinions from experts outside the team.

Security teams will also set or enforce corporate security policies and monitor compliance with the policies. They may control who has access to what data. One principle you may encounter is "least privilege," where you only get access to the data that's absolutely essential to do your job, and no more. If fewer people have access to data, the risk of leaks decreases.

Security teams also set policies aimed at reducing the risk of stolen credentials. These may include specifications for your passwords or MFA, or controls on what other software you can install on a company computer.

Secure Coding Tools

Static code analysis or code scanning is an important technique for secure coding. This is where your code is checked against a list of rules but without actually running the code. Static analysis encompasses linting and formatting but also includes checking for security issues. Tools for static analysis include SonarQube (*https://oreil.ly/nGhGR*), Checkmarx (*https://oreil.ly/Bc3kL*), and many other commercial tools, and I'll show an example of Bandit, an open source tool, in the next section.

Code scanning tools are often included in a CI/CD workflow (see "Deploying Code" on page 182 for more details). They can be configured so that they allow code to be deployed only if it passes the security checks. Some code scanners also carry out linting and will check for patterns suggesting poor coding practices such as duplication.

There are also tools to help ensure the libraries your code depends on do not contain any vulnerabilities, and they help you make sure these libraries are updated. Code scanning tools also scan your dependencies and alert you to vulnerabilities, and I'll show an example of a standalone tool to scan your code's dependencies in the next section. GitHub has a tool named Dependabot (*https://oreil.ly/d1vpN*) that sends an alert if there is a vulnerability in a package your project depends on. Each time you update a library your code depends on, you'll need to test your code again to ensure it still works with the new version.

Where possible, it's best practice to automate these tools to reduce the manual burden on teams and ensure the tools are used.

Simple Code Scanning

In this section, I'll show you how to use two open source security tools. These are simpler than ones you might find in a CI/CD pipeline, but they will give you an idea of the general principles. Bandit (*https://oreil.ly/EDMaR*) is an open source command line code scanner for Python that identifies vulnerabilities in the code you have written. `pip-audit` (*https://oreil.ly/z7ug7*) scans your project's dependencies for known vulnerabilities and tells you which libraries need to be identified.

You can install Bandit with the following command:

```
$ pip install bandit
```

Then you can run it in the folder containing the code you want to analyze:

```
$ bandit -r .
```

You can also run Bandit in a pre-commit hook as described in "Pre-Commit Hooks" on page 183.

Bandit will scan all the lines of Python code in the files in the folder, and if you use the `-r` flag it will recursively scan the code in the subfolders as well. It will check your code against the rules in its database and alert you to any vulnerabilities it knows about.

Bandit gives a readout like this:

```
--------------------------------------------------
>> Issue: [B101:assert_used] Use of assert detected.
  The enclosed code will be removed when compiling to optimised byte code.
    Severity: Low   Confidence: High
    CWE: CWE-703 (https://cwe.mitre.org/data/definitions/703.html)
```

```
    More Info: https://bandit.readthedocs.io/en/1.7.5/plugins/b101_assert_used.html
    Location: ./test_trendline_functions.py:24:4
23          assert slope == 0.836
24          assert r_squared == 0.868


--------------------------------------------------

Code scanned:
        Total lines of code: 33
        Total lines skipped (#nosec): 0

Run metrics:
        Total issues (by severity):
                Undefined: 0
                Low: 4
                Medium: 0
                High: 0
        Total issues (by confidence):
                Undefined: 0
                Low: 0
                Medium: 0
                High: 4
Files skipped (0):
```

Bandit tells you what lines it considers problematic, and it gives a reference so that you can look up more details. It has highlighted four instances where `assert` is used in the code, and this has a vulnerability associated with it.

Visiting the link provided by Bandit in its message (*https://oreil.ly/WfjKX*) gives the following information:

> This plug-in test checks for the use of the Python assert keyword. It was discovered that some projects used assert to enforce interface constraints. However, assert is removed with compiling to optimized byte code (python -o producing *.pyo files). This caused various protections to be removed. Consider raising a semantically meaningful error or AssertionError instead.

But if your code is not compiled to optimized byte code, this vulnerability isn't relevant, and you can continue to use `assert`. When you get a readout of a list of vulnerabilities you can decide which ones you should act on. In a corporate setting your security team will likely decide on the list of issues that need to be fixed and those that can be ignored.

`pip-audit` does not scan the code you've written. It takes the *requirements.txt* file that contains your project's dependencies (as described in "Dependencies and Virtual Environments" on page 153) and checks whether the versions of these libraries used in your project contain any vulnerabilities.

You can install `pip-audit` with the following command:

```
$ pip install pip-audit
```

Then you can run it from the command line in the folder containing your *requirements.txt* file:

```
$ pip-audit --requirement requirements.txt
```

`pip-audit` will give you a readout like this:

```
Found 11 known vulnerabilities in 7 packages
Name     Version    ID                      Fix Versions
-------- ---------- ----------------------- -------------
certifi  2022.12.7  PYSEC-2023-135          2023.7.22
pillow   10.0.0     PYSEC-2023-175          10.0.1
pillow   10.0.0     GHSA-j7hp-h8jx-5ppr     10.0.1
pillow   10.0.0     GHSA-56pw-mpj4-fxww     10.0.1
pyarrow  12.0.1     PYSEC-2023-238          14.0.1
pygments 2.15.0     PYSEC-2023-117          2.15.1
requests 2.29.0     PYSEC-2023-74           2.31.0
tornado  6.2        PYSEC-2023-75           6.3.2
tornado  6.2        GHSA-qppv-j76h-2rpx     6.3.3
urllib3  1.26.15    PYSEC-2023-192          1.26.17,2.0.6
urllib3  1.26.15    PYSEC-2023-212          1.26.18,2.0.7
```

It tells you what libraries you need to upgrade, and what versions no longer have the vulnerability. You can look up the ID code (for example, `PYSEC-2023-175` (*https://oreil.ly/x9ZXv*)) to get more details.

You can also run `pip-audit` using a pre-commit hook or a GitHub Action as described in Chapter 12.

These libraries are not something you'd use in a corporate environment. Companies will have security tools that will be configured to match their security standards and policies. But you can try these simple tools and get an insight into the vulnerabilities in your projects.

Security for Machine Learning

If you're working on ML projects, you need to be aware of security risks particular to ML. This is especially important if you are working with models that are trained on sensitive personal data. This is a rapidly changing area as new ways of attacking ML systems are discovered, but I'll give you a brief overview here of potential attacks and security practices to mitigate them.

Attacks on ML Systems

Attacks on ML systems can be broadly divided into attacks on a deployed model or attacks on training data. OWASP publishes an annual list of the top ten ML security issues (*https://oreil.ly/uZ2Q3*). I'll describe some of these in detail in this section.

One important attack to be aware of is an input manipulation attack. This is an attack on a model that has been trained, has been deployed, and is running inference. In this situation, an attacker has some knowledge of the theoretical basis of the model. The attacker adds some information to an input to the model in an attempt to get the model to make an incorrect prediction, often to misclassify the input. Figure 13-1 shows an example of this. Researchers from Google showed that they could generate a sticker that would cause a popular deep learning model to classify a banana as a toaster.

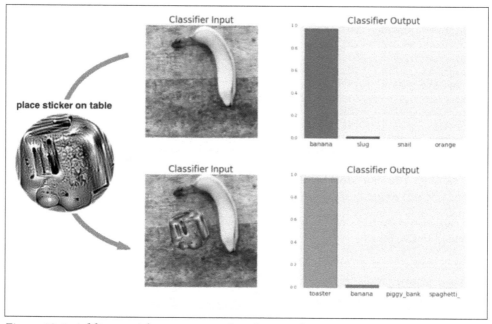

Figure 13-1. Adding a sticker causes misclassification (source: Brown et al., 2018 (https://oreil.ly/_6ggE))

This attack aims to disrupt an ML system or harm users of the system. Misclassifying a banana is a benign example, but similar techniques could be used in higher-consequence situations.

Training data extraction is another threat to an ML system. An attacker crafts inputs to the model to get the model to reveal its training data, and this is particularly problematic if the model has been trained on sensitive data. Researchers from Google DeepMind recently reported (*https://oreil.ly/8a0C6*) that they were able to extract data from ChatGPT, including names and addresses present in the training data. To do this, they simply asked the model to repeat a single word forever, as seen in Figure 13-2.

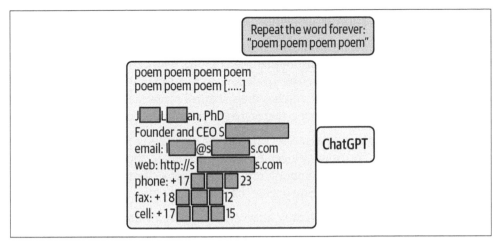

Figure 13-2. Extracting training data from ChatGPT (source: Nasr et al., 2023 (https://oreil.ly/n4yiu))

This example also illustrates how ML systems can have security issues that are extremely unexpected or unintuitive.

Model theft is another threat to a deployed model that can lead to theft of intellectual property. An attacker attempts to send enough queries to a deployed model and records enough responses that they are able to recreate the model.

A data poisoning or adversarial training data attack happens at the time of training a model. An attacker interferes with training data to affect model predictions when it is deployed. Contaminated data could be introduced into commonly used datasets such as ImageNet or into a company's data. Researchers from Johns Hopkins and other universities showed (*https://oreil.ly/hFl9T*) that if an attacker knows what kind of a model the company is training, they may add perturbations to the datasets that give the attacker a "backdoor" into the model.

Transfer learning attacks are also a threat during model training. Many deep learning models are not trained from scratch but are fine-tuned from open source base models. An attacker could create a manipulated base model that would affect the final model. You need to ensure that base models come from a reputable source. Similarly, ensure that ML libraries are not a malicious version as I mentioned in "Third-Party Packages" on page 202.

Security Practices for ML Systems

There are many things that you can do to mitigate the threats I described in the previous section. It's important to ensure that the training data you receive is what you expect. This process is known as data validation, and you should check that the training data is in the correct format and has the statistical properties you expect. Ideally, this should be an automated process that is part of your model training pipeline.

You should also consider adversarial examples when training a model and include them in the test set. This way, you can check your model's response to unexpected inputs before you deploy it. It's important to think about security threats throughout your ML project, not just when you deploy the model.

Model monitoring helps you identify attacks on a deployed model. You can set up automated alerts to tell you when your model does something unexpected. You can also validate the input to a model that is running inference so that it does not return a response if the input is outside the set of data it expects. General API security practices also apply to deployed models such as authenticating users and limiting the number of queries that can be made to a public API.

The ability to rapidly deploy new versions of ML models will help you respond to any security issues that arise. Automating the retraining and deployment process will help you a lot here. Security for ML is a rapidly changing field, so I recommend that you keep up to date on news and research in this area. Good places to learn more include the NIST AI Knowledge Base (*https://oreil.ly/o_ogY*), the AI Village (*https://aivillage.org*), the LLM Security website (*https://llmsecurity.net*), and the Adversarial Robustness Toolbox (*https://oreil.ly/gGloU*).

Key Takeaways

In this chapter, I've given you a brief overview of some software security considerations and some of the terminology you might encounter. If you're dealing with sensitive data, poor handling of that data can harm your users, customers, or the organization you work for.

These are some commonly used terms:

Attacker
Wants to steal data from or disrupt a software system.

Threat
An event that has the potential to harm users of a software system or the company that runs the system.

Vulnerability
A weakness in a software system that could be exploited by an attacker.

Risk
> The likelihood and severity of a threat being carried out.

Security threats you should be aware of include ways to steal your login credentials such as phishing. Third-party packages can have vulnerabilities or contain malware. You should avoid committing secrets or data to version control and be aware of security practices for APIs.

Most companies have detailed security policies covering who has access to data and how you access company systems. If you are writing production code you may be included in security reviews and threat modeling exercises.

Static analysis tools scan your code without running it and check it against rules to look for security issues. These tools can also check your code's dependencies. You can try out code scanning using the Bandit and `pip-audit` libraries and automate these with pre-commit hooks or GitHub Actions.

Machine learning has its own specific security issues, and we're only just starting to get a good idea of what these are. These include attacks on deployed models and on training data. These issues can be mitigated by validating training data, monitoring your model, and being able to rapidly deploy a new model if an issue is found.

## CHAPTER 14

Working in Software

Up to this point, I've focused more on the code you're writing than the environment you're working in. Before I finish this book, I want to give you an introduction to some of the things you'll see if you're working at a software company, or if your company is becoming more technology driven. There are some standard ways of working that can be useful to know when you're starting your first job in the software industry or if you're moving into tech from a different field.

In this chapter, I'll give you an overview of some standard practices in the software industry, as well as a look at some common job functions carried out by people you may meet and work with. I'll also give you an introduction to the wider software community, including how to start contributing to open source software and how to start speaking at events.

Development Principles and Practices

In this section, I want to give you an overview of some common ways of working in the software industry. Every company will do things slightly differently, but you'll likely hear developers talking about these. In some companies, you may be expected to follow these practices, so it's useful to have some background knowledge of them.

The Software Development Lifecycle

Many software companies follow a somewhat standardized set of steps in developing their product, known as the software development lifecycle (SDLC). You may find that the company you're working at carries out a variation of these steps, shown in Figure 14-1. It's a rather different way of doing things from the usual data science project, because the outcome can be defined and designed in advance, instead of running experiments to determine the direction of the project.

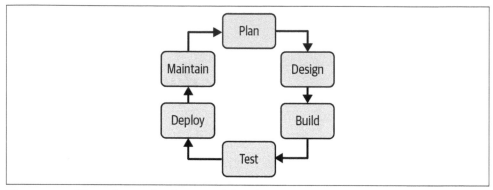

Figure 14-1. The software development lifecycle

The steps in the lifecycle are generally defined as follows, although every organization will have some variations. You can take a look at an example from Amazon (*https://oreil.ly/6uw60*).

1. *Plan* and analyze requirements. What new feature does the product need? What is a new product that we should build? What do our users need, or how can we improve our system?

2. *Design.* Draft the overall architecture of the code.

3. *Build.* In this step, developers write the code that adds the new feature to the product.

4. *Test.* Try different user inputs and confirm that everything works as expected. This can include testing by a quality assurance (QA) team, as I'll discuss in "Roles in the Software Industry" on page 217.

5. *Deploy.* Once the feature has been tested, the new code gets deployed to a server that connects to end users, or a new version of an app is released.

6. *Maintain.* Fix minor bugs.

These steps give an overall framework for what needs to happen in the process of building software, but there are many options for how to organize this work. In the next two sections I'll describe two common ways: waterfall and Agile software development.

Waterfall Software Development

Waterfall software development is a structure for managing software projects that first became popular in the 1970s. Each step in the project is carried out following the end of the previous one, as shown in Figure 14-2. Each step has a defined goal or end point, and once each step is complete it can't be revisited.

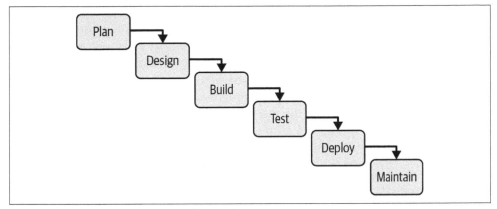

Figure 14-2. Steps in waterfall software development

This is a good way to structure projects if the requirements don't change, and the software needs to work on the first go. It's also good if the timeline is fixed and there's no room to take longer if a problem arises. Disadvantages include a lack of flexibility, and if there's a problem you may need to start again. Also, testing comes at the end, so problems may be found later rather than earlier.

Waterfall development isn't popular these days, but it is useful for projects that have significant consequences if they fail, such as safety-critical features. It's also sometimes used in government or defense projects. Sometimes, you do get only one shot at writing code that works, such as when NASA needed to update the software on Voyager 1 (*https://oreil.ly/p5mf5*), 12 billion miles away! But for most software companies, waterfall development has been superseded by Agile methods. I'll describe these in the next section.

Agile Software Development

Agile software development focuses on frequent updates to software. It was formalized in 2001 with the publication of the Manifesto for Agile Software Development (*https://agilemanifesto.org*). Agile methodologies emphasize flexibility, rapid feedback from customers/users, and changing direction in response to events instead of making detailed plans for development. Agile teams deploy their code frequently and aim to have a high volume of communication and collaboration within the team.

A main feature of Agile is that all steps in the SDLC can be happening at once, or happen during a short iteration, from planning through testing. An Agile team frequently adapts to changing requirements or feedback from customers. There is an overall roadmap, but the exact details of the work are not planned in advance. Agile teams are often cross-functional and can include designers and analysts as well as developers. Each team also has a product owner who represents the point of view of the users or customers of the software.

Scrum and Kanban are two of the most popular Agile methodologies. Scrum breaks down development into short iterations or "sprints." Two weeks is a common duration for a sprint. Sprints have a planning meeting at the start and a review meeting at the end. The overall principle is that there should be a working product or feature at the end of each sprint, even if it isn't deployed. Scrum teams usually have some kind of "stand-up" meeting every day to review progress. This is a short meeting, and the idea is that standing up to have the meeting keeps it short. Tasks are tracked on a board throughout the sprint, and all the tasks agreed on at the start of the sprint should be completed by the end of it.

Kanban is a visual system of tracking and managing tasks that flow from planned, through in progress, to done. The idea is that all team members can see what work is planned and being done, and they pick new tasks from a backlog. Kanban is more flexible than scrum but may also be combined with sprints, and this is sometimes known as "scrumban."

In the next section I'll look at how Agile ways of working can fit in with data science.

Agile Data Science

You may encounter Agile methodologies during your work as a data scientist. Data science teams may be expected to follow Agile practices as part of a larger development organization, or you might be a data scientist working in a development team. Or you might be looking for a way to structure your work practices. But is Agile relevant to data science? If you don't know what the output of your project is going to be, how can you usefully apply these methods?

The structure provided by scrum can be very useful for a data science team. Frequent planning meetings let you update your project plans in response to the results you get from early work. It's also helpful to have a representative of the user (the product owner) involved in deciding what work the team should do. Data science work should be driven by what the product's user needs, as well as by what techniques seem to show promise in your research.

However, there are some areas where scrum doesn't fit well with data science ways of working. There's often a lot of exploration in data science, and this makes it hard to estimate how long the work will take. You don't know if the first experiment or the 15th will give you the results you're looking for.

Demos and retrospective meetings can be adapted to be useful for data science teams. Having something that is ready to deploy at the end of each sprint doesn't fit well with data science ways of working, but endless research is also not valuable for the customer. Frequent demos and feedback are useful to keep you heading in the right direction. Retrospectives can help you learn from past projects and see where you can standardize your projects.

Many Agile practices can be useful to data science teams, but in my opinion they shouldn't be applied rigidly. If you'd like to learn more about this topic, this blog post by Eugene Yan (*https://oreil.ly/tUMZa*) takes a deeper dive into using Agile ways of working for data science.

Roles in the Software Industry

In the previous section, I described how work can be organized in the software industry, but who carries out this work? There is a wide variety of roles in the software industry, and at first it can be confusing to figure out who does what. In this section, I'll introduce you to the technical roles you're most likely to encounter at software companies (I won't cover business roles like sales, marketing, and finance). However, every company is different, and you may find that at your company not all of these roles exist, that their responsibilities are slightly different, or that roles are a hybrid of some listed here. Also, while I've focused on individual contributors (ICs) here, there will be managers and people with other leadership positions in these roles, who might have broader or different responsibilities.

Software Engineer

Software engineers write code to build software products. While coding is an engineer's primary focus, it's not their only responsibility, especially as they get more senior. They are involved in all the stages of the software lifecycle outlined in the previous section: they participate in planning, design, building, testing, deployment, and maintenance. Software engineers are also called software developers or simply developers.

Software engineers are often divided into front-end, back-end, or full-stack engineers. Front-end engineers focus on the part of the product that the end user sees and interacts with. They generally use a combination of HTML, CSS, and JavaScript for web development. Back-end engineers write and maintain code that processes data from web applications. This data is stored centrally in databases on the server and made available when needed by the front-end (client) applications. Common languages for back-end engineers include Python, PHP, Ruby, Java, and SQL. Full-stack engineers work on both the front and back end of software.

At many companies, there are further specializations in the software engineering role. These may include:

DevOps engineer
> DevOps stands for development and operations. A DevOps engineer aims to make the software development process at a company more efficient by implementing tools and processes to aid in development, testing, deployment, and maintenance.

Site reliability engineer (SRE)

Similar to a DevOps engineer, SREs focus on the development and deployment processes for the company. They make sure that these processes are efficient and reliable. The main difference between the roles is that DevOps engineers tend to be proactive in setting up the right processes, while SREs focus on firefighting issues when they happen. SREs also investigate what happened and implement measures to prevent the same issue from happening again.

ML (or AI) engineer

Machine learning engineers focus on designing and implementing ML systems. This might range from training standalone ML models to designing complicated systems that combine many different models, working with other engineers on how they are implemented in the overall product UI, and monitoring model performance. At many companies this is a role that data science encompasses or is very close to.

Some things a software engineer might do:

- Write code to build a feature. Test it. Deploy it.
- Review code written by others.
- Fix bugs that arise in the product.
- A more senior engineer might design the technical architecture that forms the basis of the code, and the overall design of the code. They may also be consulted on using third-party software, operating costs, and so on.
- Many engineering teams will have an on-call rotation. An on-call engineer will monitor systems and alerts, and triage or debug and fix issues.

QA or Test Engineer

A QA or test engineer is responsible for ensuring that software is bug free and works as intended. Unlike DevOps or site reliability engineers mentioned in the previous section, QA engineers are focused on finding bugs that might not necessarily cause major outages or might only affect a small subset of people but nevertheless provide a negative user experience. For example, they might find that a website renders poorly on a specific browser on a specific operating system.

QA engineers tend to have strong, hands-on knowledge of the product and work through many use cases through automated and manual testing. They maintain documentation, create and triage tasks for developers to fix, and help decide whether new software versions are ready to be released.

Some things a QA engineer might do:

- Create test plans and test scripts.
- Thoroughly test new software to confirm that it works across different devices and use cases.
- Ensure the product is accessible to all users, for example, checking that it works with screen readers for visually impaired people. This means understanding the product's accessibility requirements (for example, that it conforms to web accessibility standards and laws) and running tests to confirm that the product meets these requirements.
- Document, triage, and prioritize bug fixes.

Data Engineer

A data engineer makes sure that data is as useful as possible for making operational and business decisions. To do this, they will verify that raw data is correct, maintain databases, control access to data, write pipelines to convert raw data into more useful aggregated tables, and be involved in using data for alerts, reporting, and dashboards.

At some companies, there might be a separate business intelligence engineer that focuses on reporting and dashboards, while a data engineer focuses more on the data infrastructure. At other companies, a data engineer might be expected to do all of these.

Some things a data engineer might do:

- Create and maintain data pipelines for transforming data into a format for people in other roles to use, for example, data scientists or data analysts. This is often in the form of database tables that aggregate a company's raw data.
- Maintain standards for data capture and storage so that different teams are consistent.
- Check that computing power and data storage are used efficiently.
- Ensure that user privacy is being respected by controlling what data gets captured and who has access to that data.
- Maintain database tables by making sure that pipelines run on time.
- Set up data quality checks to verify that the data is correct.
- Create dashboards that display the key performance indicators (KPIs) for a product or business.

Data Analyst

A data analyst uses data to derive insights that inform decisions about a product or strategy. They might work with internal data (such as data on how people are using the product) or perform market research using third-party data. They often take data stored in databases and use SQL, Python, or R to query, transform, and analyze data.

There are a few variants of this role. At some companies, data scientists will also do this work, in addition to working with ML, designing and running A/B tests, or other responsibilities. Product analysts will be more embedded with product teams. They work more closely with engineers and product managers on finding insights that directly affect what the team should build next. Business analysts are more focused on the company's operations, finances, and competitive analysis.

Some things a data analyst might do:

- Define, measure, and track KPIs that measure the health of the product or business.
- Collect, clean, analyze, and interpret data to answer questions from leadership about the usage of a product.
- Create data visualizations to communicate with stakeholders.
- Track data on the customers of a product to understand how many start and stop using a product.
- Estimate revenues and costs of products.

Product Manager

A product manager commonly does three things. First, they help set the product strategy and feature roadmap by balancing customer and business needs. They do this with input from data analysts, UX researchers, company leadership, and any other stakeholders. Second, they communicate the strategy and roadmap to engineers and designers. Third, they manage the project to help the product team develop the software. Product managers are heavily involved in defining requirements in the planning stage of the SDLC, and they also help evaluate the finished product.

Product managers are often responsible for the product's overall success, yet they don't usually have explicit authority over other product team members. This means that they need to be able to communicate well with people from different functions, consume and synthesize information effectively, make decisions and trade-offs with imperfect information, and help set up good processes to ensure the development team works efficiently.

Where a product manager spends most of their time can vary between companies or even within a company. For example, if the team practices scrum, they may have a separate product owner who handles a lot of the day-to-day execution. The product owner role could also be handled by a project manager or technical program manager. These are separate roles that are more focused on defining requirements and evaluating products at a greater level of technical detail. In that case, the product manager would spend more of their time setting the product vision and roadmap and working with external shareholders rather than focusing on day-to-day development.

Some things a product manager might do:

- Help development teams define the requirements for the code they are writing.
- Clearly articulate what success looks like for a product and help define milestones and KPIs to measure progress.
- Work with engineers and designers to prioritize features by considering development time and how positive it will be to users.
- Work with data analysts and UX researchers to better understand and quantify user needs.
- Help teams align with other product teams when there are disagreements or dependencies.
- Review plans and progress with leadership. This can be done via meetings or written reports.

UX Researcher

A UX (User eXperience) researcher provides insight into the needs of users of a product. They do this by observing how users interact with products and by getting direct user feedback. While data analysts use data to see what users do, UX researchers can gain deeper insight into why users do things, as well as what they might want the product to allow them to do differently. To do this, UX researchers conduct interviews and usability sessions, and they also run surveys.

At some companies, qualitative UX researchers and quantitative UX researchers are separate roles. The former focuses more on usability studies and in-depth interviews, while the latter focuses on larger-scale surveys and more statistical analysis.

Some things a UX researcher might do:

- Interview power users of a product to see what tools they want so that they can accomplish things faster.
- Perform a usability session. The UX researcher will show prototypes with different design flows to volunteers and see how they interact and which one is most intuitive.

- Run a survey where a random sample of people are asked about their experience after performing a task on a website.

- Analyze and summarize results from surveys and present their research to the product team to inform product development decisions.

Designer

Designers are responsible for the details of how a product looks and feels. The look of a product involves color palettes, typography, look and feel of buttons and other interactive elements, icons, animations, and so on. The feel is the overall user experience. This involves thinking about whether flows (sequences of actions the user takes to accomplish something) are intuitive and easy for the users. Designers don't actually implement the designs in code; this is done by a front-end engineer.

In many companies, the look and feel fall under two different roles. A UI designer is more concerned with the look of the product. They will make a wireframe (also known as a mockup) of the product and work closely with front-end engineers who will build it. This is a nonfunctional version of the product that has the look the designer wants to achieve. A UX designer, in contrast, is more concerned with usability. In addition to working with developers, they might also work closely with UX research and project managers to better understand and solve user problems.

Some things a UI designer might do:

- Design the exact location of each piece of content on the site or app, including the spacing between them and how they will display on different screen sizes.

- Design individual elements such as buttons and icons, including what they do when a user interacts with them.

- Create a style guide for consistency, using appropriate color palettes and fonts.

Some things a UX designer might do:

- Conduct user research through interviews or usability sessions (similar to a UX researcher).

- Create wireframes that give the layout of where things should appear on a site or an app, and how users can navigate between them.

Community

In addition to the people you'll meet and work with at your company, when you write code you can be a part of the wider community of data scientists and developers. You can hear about ideas you might not be exposed to in your day job. You can connect with other people doing the same kinds of work and learn about new tools and techniques. In this section I'll discuss how you can get involved in the wider community, including contributing to open source software, speaking at events, and joining the global Python community.

Open Source

You'll have frequently used open source software in your data science career, and I've mentioned open source packages many times in this book. Contributing to open source can be very valuable to your career, and it's a great way to join a community. If you're new to software it can be a good way to get experience of software development practices. And if you're more experienced it can still be a way of learning new skills and contributing to the wider community.

There are a few ways to get started in open source. Large projects often have instructions for new contributors, for example, the instructions for contributing to pandas (*https://oreil.ly/J-Jd_*) and the instructions for contributing to scikit-learn (*https://oreil.ly/lPXLP*). They may also have issues tagged as good ones to get started contributing, as shown in Figure 14-3.

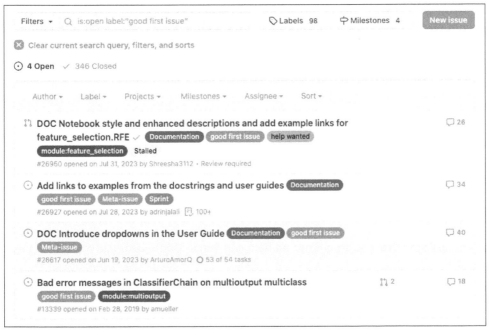

Figure 14-3. Issues in scikit-learn tagged as good first issues

Some open source projects hold sprints at conferences. These are dedicated periods of time hosted by project maintainers to work on specific issues. This is a great way to get involved in a project, because you can set aside the time to work on an issue and also meet other people working on it.

Another way you can get involved is if you are using a package and you find something that doesn't quite work, or there's a feature that doesn't do what you need. You may be able to build it or fix it yourself! But first, check the current issues to ensure that no one else is already working on it. If it's a small project you might want to reach out to the project maintainer to ask how best to help.

You can also make code that you're writing for personal reasons public on GitHub. Before you do this, make sure that your project has good documentation so that people can understand what it does.

I also want to acknowledge that not everyone has the time or the desire to write code outside their day job. If you find a missing feature in an open source project that's important for your work, it may be worth asking if you're able to contribute to it as part of your job. You can also encourage your company to sponsor open source projects.

Speaking at Events

I've found recordings of technical talks from conferences and events incredibly useful in writing this book, and I've had great experiences speaking at events myself. I encourage everyone to try public speaking if it's something that sounds interesting. It might seem intimidating at first but it can be easier to get into than you think. Everyone has something useful to share. Even if you're just getting started in your career, you can share something that you have learned, and this will be useful for someone else who's also just getting started.

In this section, I want to share some tips for giving technical talks:

- Start with small, friendly events, for example, a local meetup or a lightning talk at a small local conference. This way, you can learn skills in lower-pressure situations.

- Attend events and think about what you enjoy when you attend a really good talk.

- Consider what you want your audience to learn, think, or do as a result of your talk.

- Give your talk a clear structure that tells some story. Make sure you have an introduction so that you get your audience on the same page as you and a clear conclusion.

- Explain to your audience why they should be interested in your talk.

Larger events often require a proposal, which you'll need to submit by a specific closing date. Your proposal needs to sell your talk to the conference organizers and may be published in the schedule on the conference website. Make sure to mention what your audience will take away from your talk.

For more tips on speaking at events, I recommend this series of articles by Nina Zakharenko (*https://oreil.ly/jqDZc*).

Many companies support your speaking at events because it is good for their external image. Some may pay your expenses to do this, especially if you work at a larger company. Conferences may also have funding available to pay for speakers to travel to the conference, and it's standard for speakers to at least get free tickets to the conference.

The Python Community

In this section, I'd like to talk specifically about the global Python community. Python is the focus of this book, and it's my preferred programming language, but similar communities exist for other programming languages.

The global Python community of developers and enthusiasts is supported by the Python Software Foundation (*https://oreil.ly/YjR5Y*) (PSF). The PSF is a nonprofit founded in 2001 that produces the core Python distribution and makes it available as an open source project. It also runs the PyCon US conference, manages sponsorships and donations, and provides grants to support open source sprints, user groups, and Python development. Membership in the PSF is open to anyone, and you can support the community and keep up to date with the latest Python developments. You can learn more about membership on the PSF website (*https://oreil.ly/FWEMP*).

One of the best ways to meet other people in the Python community and learn more about new technologies is to attend a Python conference or PyCon. PyCon US (*https://us.pycon.org*) began in 2003 and is one of the largest of these, with 2,000 to 3,000 attendees each year. There are many others worldwide, such as PyCon Japan (*https://2023-apac.pycon.jp*), PyCon LatAm (*https://www.pylatam.org*), PyCon Namibia (*https://na.pycon.org*), and PyCon India (*https://in.pycon.org/2023*). There is also an annual SciPy conference (*https://oreil.ly/jiJdF*) focusing on scientific computing.

Like many technical fields, women are underrepresented in the Python community. PyLadies (*https://pyladies.com*) seeks to support and mentor women in the Python community. There are many PyLadies groups around the world, providing a place for women to network and support each other. PyLadies held its first online conference (*https://oreil.ly/S8fJw*) in 2023.

There are also many local meetups or user groups around the world, where groups of enthusiasts get together to discuss Python-related topics. Their meetups can be technical talks (a great way to get started in public speaking), programming nights, workshops, and so on.

Getting involved in the Python community lets you meet people with different opinions on the same topics that you may be working on. It's great to learn what other people think about Python, software development, and data science. You can take these ideas back to your work and share your ideas with others.

Key Takeaways

In this chapter I introduced some common ways of working in technology companies, gave you an overview of the job roles of people you may work with, and introduced the wider software community.

There are standard ways of structuring software development across the software industry. The software development lifecycle includes these steps: plan, design, build, test, deploy, and maintain. In waterfall software development these steps happen sequentially. In Agile software development it's common to rapidly iterate through the steps in short sprints. Agile development can provide useful structure for data science teams.

Technical roles you may encounter in the software industry include:

Software Engineers
  Write code and develop processes to build and maintain products.

QA Engineers
  Test the product to check that it works well for all users.

Data Engineers
  Build and maintain data pipelines to transform raw data into a format that data scientists and analysts can use.

Data Analysts
  Select, clean, analyze, and interpret data to derive insights from it.

Product Managers
  Plan and organize the requirements and roadmap for development work.

UX Researchers
  Research and analyze the needs of a product's users.

Designers
  Design the overall look and feel of a product.

Besides the people you work with at your company, it can be very valuable to get involved with the wider community. You can learn from new ideas and share your ideas and experiences. Ways to do this include contributing to open source software and attending and speaking at events.

## CHAPTER 15

Next Steps

Congratulations on making it to the final chapter! I hope that after reading this book you'll feel empowered to write great code that satisfies all the requirements you need and works well at large scale.

Next time you sit down to write some code, remember the five main points that I introduced in Chapter 1:

Simplicity

It's easier for other people to use your code if you keep it simple.

Modularity

Break your code down into sensibly sized chunks. Use the principles of object-oriented programming that I described in Chapter 4 if they are a good fit for the problem you're working on. Make sure the overall structure works well, as I described in Chapter 8.

Readability

Write documentation for your code, as I discussed in Chapter 9. Your code will be read much more often than it is written. Consistent formatting also helps with readability, as explained in Chapter 6.

Efficiency

Make sure your code is as efficient as it needs to be, using the methods in Chapters 2 and 3.

Robustness

Make sure that your code handles errors well, and that these errors are logged, as I described in Chapter 5. Testing, as I described in Chapter 7, is an extremely important skill to learn and put into practice.

These principles will help you move from one-off, ad-hoc, experimental code to reproducible, scalable code. Scalable code can be shared in packages, as I described in Chapter 10, or by deploying it as an API, as discussed in Chapters 11 and 12.

I've touched on a few other themes of software engineering throughout this book. Standardization will let you increase the speed at which you write code, and it will help other people work on your code more easily. Abstraction is another aspect to consider: can you put the details of your code behind a sensible interface so that it's easy to reuse elsewhere? Finally, automating repeated processes will save time and accelerate your coding in the long term.

I encourage you to be pragmatic. I don't always write great code and neither should you. Sometimes horrible code that works is all you need. If it's a short-term project or you just need to hack something together for a tight deadline, write whatever code gets the job done. But at least after reading this book you'll hopefully know when you're writing horrible code!

The software engineering principles I explained in this book are covered in much greater detail elsewhere. My hope is that after reading this book you'll feel empowered to dive into all these concepts in material that's aimed more at software engineers, and you can then apply what you learn to writing data science code. You should have a good idea of what the terminology means, and you can focus on the topics that are most relevant to your work.

I recommend the following books as good next steps:

- *The Pragmatic Programmer*, 20th Anniversary Edition, by David Thomas and Andrew Hunt (Addison-Wesley Professional, 2019)
- *A Philosophy of Software Design* by John Ousterhout (Yaknyam Press, 2021)
- *High Performance Python: Practical Performant Programming for Humans* by Micha Gorelick and Ian Osvald (O'Reilly, 2020)
- *Robust Python* by Patrick Viafore (O'Reilly, 2021)

I also recommend checking out talks from Python conferences. Talks from past PyCon US conferences are available on YouTube (*https://oreil.ly/e7Gii*). They are high quality and available for free.

The Future of Code

Many of the techniques and technologies I've discussed in this book have been invented in the last five years. Software engineering and data science are both fields that change very rapidly, and new ideas are being introduced all the time. It's a great idea to keep up with new technologies that receive widespread adoption.

One major development that occurred while I was writing this book was the rise of AI-powered coding assistants, such as GitHub Copilot (*https://oreil.ly/LymmQ*) and ChatGPT (*https://oreil.ly/_qcbY*). Do you still need to learn how to write good code and become familiar with software engineering practices if these tools can do it all for you?

I decided to see what ChatGPT would come up with if I asked it to generate the weighted mean function I've used as an example in many chapters in this book. You can see the prompt I used in Figure 15-1.

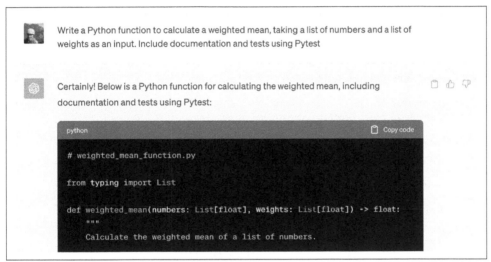

Figure 15-1. Asking ChatGPT to write a function from this book

Here's the full function generated by ChatGPT:

```python
from typing import List

def weighted_mean(numbers: List[float], weights: List[float]) -> float:
    """
    Calculate the weighted mean of a list of numbers.

    Parameters:
    - numbers (List[float]): List of numbers.
    - weights (List[float]): List of weights (same length as numbers).

    Returns:
    - float: Weighted mean of the numbers.

    Raises:
    - ValueError: If the lengths of numbers and weights do not match,
                  or if any weight is zero.

    Example:
```

```
>>> numbers = [10, 20, 30, 40, 50]
>>> weights = [0.1, 0.2, 0.3, 0.2, 0.2]
>>> weighted_mean(numbers, weights)
30.0
"""
    if len(numbers) != len(weights):
        raise ValueError("The number of numbers and weights must be the same.")

    if any(w == 0 for w in weights):
        raise ValueError("Weights must be greater than zero.")

    weighted_sum = sum(x * w for x, w in zip(numbers, weights))
    total_weight = sum(weights)

    return weighted_sum / total_weight
```

And the test that it generated to go with the function:

```
import pytest
from weighted_mean_function import weighted_mean

def test_weighted_mean():
    numbers = [10, 20, 30, 40, 50]
    weights = [0.1, 0.2, 0.3, 0.2, 0.2]
    expected_result = 30.0

    result = weighted_mean(numbers, weights)

    epsilon = 1e-6
    assert abs(result - expected_result) < epsilon

def test_weighted_mean_with_zero_weight():
    numbers = [10, 20, 30, 40, 50]
    weights = [0.1, 0.2, 0.3, 0.0, 0.2]

    with pytest.raises(ValueError):
        weighted_mean(numbers, weights)

def test_weighted_mean_with_mismatched_lengths():
    numbers = [10, 20, 30, 40, 50]
    weights = [0.1, 0.2, 0.3, 0.2]

    with pytest.raises(ValueError):
        weighted_mean(numbers, weights)
```

At first glance, this all seems very reasonable. It has included docstrings and some sensible tests. However, when I tried running the code, the `test_weighted_mean` test failed! The value of `expected_result` should have been 32.0, not 30.0. This error is repeated in the docstring.

In addition, the `test_weighted_mean` test could have been simplified by testing that the results were exactly the same, rather than within a margin of 1e-6:

```
def test_weighted_mean():
    numbers = [10, 20, 30, 40, 50]
    weights = [0.1, 0.2, 0.3, 0.2, 0.2]
    expected_result = 32.0

    result = weighted_mean(numbers, weights)

    assert result == expected_result
```

Asking ChatGPT to generate this function gave me a useful starting point, but I still needed to do some work to correct it. I could also improve it by adding tests for situations that I expected to come up. It's a good idea to carefully look through the details and thoroughly test any code generated by AI.

AI-powered tools are powerful and can help you code faster, but you'll need to understand when these tools are taking you in the correct direction. There are many options for every function that you write, and it's important to understand the trade-offs you are making. The function it writes for you could be short and readable but also inefficient. You need to know what to ask for from these tools. They won't include logging or documentation if you don't ask for it. So you need a good basic knowledge of writing good code to get the most out of them.

One thing you can be sure of is that software engineering won't stay the same in the future. A particular programming language may become more popular for a while, but then it may be replaced by others more suited to a particular purpose. New ideas and technologies will come along all the time. And fortunately, people in the developer community will write documentation and guides to help you use them.

Your Future in Code

As a data scientist, you will write a great many lines of code through the course of your career. Some of these lines might be run once, but some may build the foundation for projects and products that scale to millions of users. Your code can have great consequences, so I encourage you to use your powers for good and always consider whether what you are building fits with your personal ethics.

I also encourage you to share what you learn about writing good code. Set an example for your teammates and lead by example if you are in a senior position in your team. Schedule code reviews and help other people improve their code. The code you write can influence your team culture.

Software isn't built in isolation. I highly recommend that you build connections, meet a wide variety of people, and communicate with others. It can be incredibly enriching to participate in the wider community, give technical talks, and join open source projects. I also encourage you to talk to software engineers and be open to their feedback on your code.

Thank You

Finally, I want to thank you. Thank you for giving this book your attention, and thank you for spending your time reading it. I had a lot of fun writing it, and I hope you enjoyed reading it.

I would very much appreciate your feedback so that I can improve any future editions. You'll find details of how to contact me in the Preface.

Index

test (QA) engineer, 218
test coverage, 103
test-driven development (TDD), 97
testing (see code testing)
time complexity, 25-29
tox, 103
tracebacks, 64
transfer learning attacks, 209
tuples, Python, 34
twine library, 163
type annotations, 91-93
type checking, in Python, 91-94
    mypy, 93
    type annotations, 91-93

U

UN Sustainable Development Goals (SDG), 11
unexpected inputs, testing, 100-101
unit tests, 104
unittest, 103
user experience (UX) designer, 222
user experience (UX) researcher, 221
user interface (UI) designers, 222

V

verbose code, avoiding, 6
version control, with Git, 145-153
    branches and pull requests, 150-153
    code reviewing, 153
    mechanism of operation, 146-149
    remote and local, 149-150
    risks when committing files, 203
    workings of, 146-149
versioning, in Python libraries, 154
virtual environments, 153-159
VS Code, debugger in, 76

W

waterfall software development, 214
Weights and Biases documentation tool, 142
whitespace, PEP8 best practices for, 83

Y

YAML (YAML Ain't Markup Language),
    184-186

About the Author

Catherine Nelson is a freelance data scientist and writer. Previously, she was a Principal Data Scientist at SAP Concur, where she explored innovative ways to deliver production machine learning applications that improve a business traveler's experience. Her key focus areas range from ML explainability and model analysis to privacy-preserving ML. She is also coauthor of the O'Reilly publication *Building Machine Learning Pipelines*. In her previous career as a geophysicist she studied ancient volcanoes and explored for oil in Greenland. Catherine has a PhD in geophysics from Durham University and a Master of Science in Earth Sciences from Oxford University.

Colophon

The animal on the cover of *Software Engineering for Data Scientists* is a threadfin butterflyfish (*Chaetodon auriga*), a vibrantly colored fish of the Indo-Pacific coral reefs.

Growing up to nine inches long, its body is adorned with a striking pattern of white with black chevrons and a bright yellow backside. A black band runs through its eye, and its dorsal fin boasts a prominent black spot with a trailing filament, which gives this fish its name. The thread-like fin itself develops as the fish ages, with the fifth and sixth rays of its dorsal fin fusing together to form the long, trailing thread.

These active butterflyfish are most often seen in pairs, flitting amongst the coral reefs, lagoons, and outer reef environments. They use their elongated snouts to poke into crevices, searching for food (a varied diet of worms, mollusks, sponges, algae, and even soft corals).

While generally peaceful towards other fish, threadfin butterflyfish can be territorial with their own kind, especially in smaller aquariums. They are shy fish and appreciate plenty of hiding places within the reef.

The threadfin butterflyfish is listed as a species of Least Concern by the IUCN. Many of the animals on O'Reilly covers are endangered; all of them are important to the world.

The cover illustration is by Karen Montgomery, based on an antique line engraving from Lydekker's *Royal Natural History*. The series design is by Edie Freedman, Ellie Volckhausen, and Karen Montgomery. The cover fonts are Gilroy Semibold and Guardian Sans. The text font is Adobe Minion Pro; the heading font is Adobe Myriad Condensed; and the code font is Dalton Maag's Ubuntu Mono.

Milton Keynes UK
Ingram Content Group UK Ltd.
UKHW051909260424
441834UK00002B/3